Money to Byrne
?

David Byrne

Copyright © 2012 David A Byrne

All rights reserved.

ISBN:9781674316543

DEDICATION

To my dear Mum and Dad, my sisters, and to my wonderful children, all of whom suffered along with me during this ordeal.

About the author

David Byrne was born in Devon in 1964, the son of Irish Immigrants and the youngest of four children. After an accident at sea while in the Merchant Navy his father retrained as a welder and, when David was just three months old, the family moved to Essex.

On leaving school in the early 1980s, David embarked on his career in the City of London. He rose quickly through the ranks of several major institutions, holding managerial and directorship positions. He has consulted to trading houses across the globe and has spent sustained periods of time in Chicago and Asia. He has also been keynote speaker at international finance events and has appeared on television for numerous financial channels.

In 2012 David took on the role of Chief Executive Officer for an international financial institution; a decision that would take him on a terrifying journey and ultimately change his life forever.

David lives in London and, although still involved in the financial markets, now writes full time. His eagerly anticipated second book, a crime thriller, is well underway.

ACKNOWLEDGMENTS

Thanks for the support of my family who coped so well during such a stressful situation. My elderly parents were extremely strong, and my children never gave up hope throughout my time in China which kept my spirits high and hopes alive.

To my landlord and all the guys and girls at the bar for keeping my room like a shrine until I returned and for performing many tasks from scanning my mail to sending money through Western Union.

To my other friends who called China every day without fail and who gave me much support, advice and guidance regarding my defence, without which I may still be thousands of miles away.

A special thanks to those that have supported the book allowing me to complete this harrowing account.

To Jason Wang, the police captain in Anshan who took me under his wing and made me feel part of his family. For providing a coat and inviting me into his circle of friends. The final thank you is to the officers of the Anshan department of Public protection who treated me with courtesy, ensured my safety and completed a thorough investigation resulting in my release.

My thoughts remain with the victims, and I thank Chao Ma for reaching out.

NO thanks to the police in Shanghai.

ABSOLUTELY NO thanks to the British Consulate.

These events are true to the best of the authors recollection. Some names have been changed for their own protection and privacy, although many of you will know whom I'm referring to!

Money to Byrne

Prologue ... May 2014

It was the beginning of May and I was sitting in my apartment off Leman Street near Tower Bridge in London making plans for a night out with my children for my birthday. Although it was on the top floor of quite a smart new block and had been described by the letting agent as a "penthouse", it was in fact a compact two-bedroom residence. The rent was two thousand pounds a month which I shared with my flat mate, Renaat. He would arrive in London on a Tuesday and head back to Antwerp in Belgium on a Friday to see his wife and children. Like me he was in the investment business and managed money for a modest fund based in London. It was an ideal arrangement which left the apartment empty at weekends, allowing my children to stay over.

From November 2012, for eleven months I was employed as the CEO by a new company called *Euro Forex Investment Ltd (EFIL)*. It was the UK subsidiary of a private Asian business whose official name was *Euro Fx*. Being quite a mouthful to say, the name, *"Euro Forex Investments Limited"* was often shortened to *"Euro Fx"* by the Asian executives, both verbally and on literature. It was this seemingly innocuous, but deliberate, abbreviation that was to have dire consequences later.

Things hadn't felt right. Information flow had been lacking or inaccurate and I wasn't getting any answers. I had thought and hoped that maybe I had read the signs wrong, that the operation was bona fide. Eventually however, my concerns outweighed the risk of continuing in that prestigious position and in October 2013 I made the decision to tender my resignation. I did this with some reluctance as my CEO position was the career advancement I had been looking for, and the all-expenses paid travel to exotic locations was thrilling. And now, since leaving *EFIL* I had gone back to what I knew best; trading and consultancy. At home I had installed a multi-screen set up comparable with anything you would see in the dealing room of a major bank or investment house. There were four monitors linked by a quad card on the hard drive which was loaded with charts of the major foreign exchange data. This was exclusively for trading and was protected by the best firewalls. Separately, I had a laptop for handling emails and other correspondence, and an iPad for Skype, facetime or for browsing the web.

It was a Monday so Renaat had not yet arrived and I was staring at the monitors, watching the currency markets doing their price dance across the screens in the form of coloured lines; green for up, red for down. Although I was watching the markets, my mind was really trying to decide if we should go bowling or have a small party for my upcoming 51st birthday. There was a ping from my iPad sitting on the circular dining table alerting me that I had mail. I swivelled my chair and clicked on the inbox. There was one fresh entry titled:

"Euro FX Victim"

I opened the email which said simply, "Have you read your

mail?"

I scanned the other messages and could find nothing that the question could have been referring to, and just then the phone rang. My father was 86 at the time and, although in good health, he was quite a worrier. He told me that Chinese people had been knocking on his neighbours' doors asking if I lived at number 19. He was very agitated and upset so I told him not to worry, that I would get ready and head over to see him straight away. I replaced the receiver and, grabbing a fresh towel from the airing cupboard, stepped in the direction of the bathroom. It was then that I noticed a large brown envelope half pushed under my door. This in itself was strange as we had multiple security entry points in the building, and dedicated mailboxes in the reception. Prior to the first checkpoint was a diligent concierge who would never have been coerced into allowing unauthorized entry to the building. I picked up the envelope and read the address label.

"DAVID BYRNE, APT 106, CEO EURO FX"

I tore it open to reveal five A4 pieces of paper. The first was a series of photographs of the very apartment I was standing in, taken from every conceivable angle, including zoomed-in pictures of me sitting on my balcony. The second page was a similar layout of photographs but this time of my parents' house out in Essex. The third page was a cleverly constructed picture of my face obscured by Chinese prison bars, with the word "Criminal" in red ink printed diagonally across the picture. The final two pages were the heartrending descriptions of the plight being suffered by some of the victims that had been scammed out of billions of dollars. To this day it is not known exactly how much was stolen. Some reports mention $600 million while others claim the amount to be as high as $4 billion, but with the perpetrators still at large it is unlikely the true figure will ever be known.

As I looked at and read the pages again, I had no idea of what lay in store, but it marked the beginning of a journey that would span the continents with devastating consequences. This story tells of those events and how, during a harrowing year in China, I began a quest to clear my name and help the investors track down their stolen investment.

Chapter 1.   The early years

I grew up in South Ockendon, Essex; not such a bad place. It only had a population of a few thousand, most of whom were families that had relocated from the East End after the Second World War and there were a number of people that went on to great things and achieved notable success. Some forged careers in the City or became captains of industry, several others emigrated to far-flung corners of the world. Ockendon was certainly not an area like "Knightsbridge" or "Chelsea", where a trust fund paid for your education and your director's nameplate was already printed, awaiting your arrival at a private bank or stockbroker on your 23rd birthday. But it was no ghetto, with street gangs being one of the few career paths and it seemed to foster a spirit of entrepreneurship and a "can do" attitude among its youth.

One person that I became friends with at secondary school was Matthew Price. He was a very no-nonsense, kind and generous beast of a boy and he was the reason that I embarked on a career in the financial markets. Indeed, the series of events that would influence my decision to enter the world of trading and finance began during a mathematics exam in our final year. My family were from a blue-collar background, but maths was by far my strongest subject and I loved going to the lessons given by Mr Vaughan. He was a very strict Welshman with a glass eye that intensified his stare and he was a brilliant teacher. This was borne out by the fact that I aced my 'O' level a year early and was now doing a compressed course in advanced maths and statistics. However, because of the lack of funding and staff, I was required to re-sit the mock exams even though my papers would not be marked. I was expected to respect the exam room rules and conditions for the sake of those sitting the test for real.

One morning, I was relaxing in the school yard waiting for the bell that would signal the start of the exam when Matt approached me.

'Dave, have you got a minute?' he asked.

'Sure Matt, what's up?'

'Look', he said, then stalled as if he needed to say something important but didn't know how to start. 'If I don't pass these mock exams I'm not coming back to school, I'm just going to get a job.'

I gave it a moment, then asked. 'Is that it, or is there something else?'

As we began heading towards the school gymnasium that had been converted to a mega classroom for the purpose of hosting the examination he continued.

'Well, I've already been applying for jobs in the City and have been offered a position as a messenger. I think I'm going to take it, regardless of the results.'

I said that I didn't think this was a good idea as I felt he was smart enough to get good marks and a better job as a result. We reached the examination room where we were permitted to sit at any vacant desks which were arranged in pods of two, so Matt and I sat opposite each other. Because of the school's limited resources two people had to share one calculator. When one person had finished a question a supervisor would clear the answer screen and pass it to the other student. It was forbidden to pass the contraption directly for obvious reasons. Unbeknown to me however, Matt had figured out that there was a retrieve button on the calculator that would bring up the previous calculation on the screen, which is why he had generously suggested that I make first use of the device.

The weeks passed and then it was mock results day. I had got one hundred percent and hoped that Matt had done the same. I hadn't seen him all day but as I was heading home towards the school gates there he was. He had an unmistakable "I'm pissed off and want to kill someone" look on his face. I glanced behind over my left shoulder and then my right, wondering who he was looking at. There was a small group of girls deep in conversation and some lads having a little kick about with a football, but no one else. This could only mean one thing; his glare was for my benefit and mine alone.

'Why did you do it Dave? Thought it would be funny or something?' he spat.

'What are you talking about?' I asked, genuinely confused.

'What I'm talking about is I got zero in my maths mock and I got bollocked for cheating!'

I didn't understand at all.

'How can you be done for cheating and get a zero score. Did they just give you a zero score because you cheated? And by the way, what has any of this got to do with me?'

'Nope, I got every fucking question wrong … or should I say, *we* got every question wrong', he said.

He admitted to me how he had retrieved my answers every time we swapped the calculator and then written them down before the calculator was passed back to me. I couldn't see what had gone wrong for him with his plan until it suddenly dawned on me what must have happened. The first question on the exam paper was so easy that I just wrote it down and I didn't start using the calculator until question two. Unfortunately, Matt had inserted the answer for question two into the box for answer one, answer three for question two, and so on, out of sync for the whole paper! This explained both the zero score and the cheating reprimand; they must have thought he was trying to read my exam paper upside down from across the desks.

He did leave school pretty much straight away as he'd said he would and became a messenger and office gofer for the commodity traders at *EDF Mann* at Sugar Quay in the City. He took his no-fear, no-nonsense attitude with him and was soon embraced as a solid kid by his peers. In 1983 a new financial market was opening in London, *The London International Financial Futures Exchange* (*LIFFE*). It was a frenetic environment and no place for the easily intimidated. Even the various staged arenas where the different products were traded were called "pits" and felt more like a place where gladiators would exchange blows rather than financial products worth millions. *EDF Mann* decided that Matt would be ideal for this environment. He would stand his ground and ensure nobody messed with *Mann Group*. He was actually a very clever guy but just hated school. That exam episode had also taught him that effort and hard work was the way forward, not cheating. He subsequently excelled at his company and by 1984 Matt was earning four times my salary with his Christmas bonus alone that year worth thousands. I was very happy and proud of him but intensely envious at the same time. I decided that this is where I also wanted to be and started to steer my ship relentlessly in that direction until I eventually succeeded in getting my first position in the City.

Chapter 2.   How my City career began

It was the summer of 1980 and I was on my way, by *British Rail*, to my first day's work in one of the great financial cities of the world, London. I was just sixteen and, coming from a working-class family, that's what you did straight from regular education; you found a job. My father had been a merchant seaman, born in Dublin, who left Customs House docks at the tender age of fourteen and never went back. He would always say, "Get yourself a trade and an apprenticeship and you will never be out of work". However, my endeavours at school in metalwork and woodwork, as they were called then, produced recognisable if less than impressive results, and technical drawing had the immediate effect of a strong medication prescribed for insomnia. I could barely stay awake, slumped in a daze with my eyes held wide open by imaginary matchsticks. I could tell that my dad wasn't enamoured by the prospect of his son heading off to an office wearing a suit and tie, but at the same time I think proud that I was not prepared to settle for the Tuesday dole queue and evenings in the park with cans of *Woodpecker* cider.

I was nervous, worrying how I would adapt to a work environment comprised primarily of public school-educated, middle to upper class associates, mockingly assessing my capabilities of getting their lunch or coffee orders correct. Savile Row suits and the occasional bowler hat were still commonplace in London at that time which added to my feelings of class alienation and trepidation. But the 1980s had many surprises and changes in store for the working ants busily milling about the streets and alleys of the Square Mile.

That first year was one of enlightenment. Every day was an adventure, even the journey to and from work was a regular source of entertainment. The trains back then had manual doors and commuters, desperate to get home after a long gruelling day, would regularly risk life and limb to board the crammed carriages. On one occasion a young man launched his rucksack onto a departing train and, as the wheels turned faster and the bulk of the ageing, creaking rolling stock gathered momentum, he swung his beloved guitar into the carriage. However, he'd left it a bit late and as the train picked up speed, he realised with abject horror that he wouldn't be able to get on as well, that his luggage would be making that particular journey without him.

Over the coming months I gradually settled in and my colleagues established their suitable clubs of association according to interests, intellect and social background, only mixing together at mandatory social events such as Christmas parties. My small group of drinking buddies was also from a working-class background and we were all on a similar wage. For me at that time this amounted to about £2,200 per annum before tax and was supplemented by luncheon vouchers. There was a big drinking culture in London back then and this seemed particularly prevalent in the insurance industry where buying a sandwich at lunchtime was less important than having a pint with your friends. Unfortunately, pubs did not take luncheon vouchers in exchange for beer, and beer over food was our preference.

There was a very industrious Indian employee named Ali, an astute and observant young man who became aware of our frustration, especially when seeing our gloomy faces in the days approaching pay day, when our spirits were low, and cash was in short supply. There was a relaxation area on the lower floor to our office that contained a table tennis facility, a dartboard and a *Subbuteo* football table. One afternoon, I was alone in this basement area flicking the miniature players, wasting away the boring minutes of my lunch hour unable to spend them having a laugh in the pub. There was an almost imperceptible tap on the door. This was a free space open to all employees so I was confused why someone would request permission to enter. I stepped to the door and gently swung it open.

'Hello Mr kind David sir.' It was Ali. 'I have a discussion we would both enjoy that would make you most famous with your friends and solve many problems for all concerned.'

A few seconds passed before suitable words formed in my head and transferred to my mouth.

'I'm not sure what you do in the company Ali. I'm sure it's well above my pay grade, but you must be aware that I am a simple accounts junior. How can I solve any problems for anyone?' Ali's face was now bursting with eagerness to make his life-changing revelation.

'I am a devout Muslim and do not drink alcohol. But I do enjoy my egg sandwiches! You, however, do not like egg sandwiches I am thinking', he said.

The religious education we received at school in the Seventies consisted of stories from *The Bible* and looking back I can't believe how ignorant we were of other cultures when stepping out into the world.

Now I was thrown completely off kilter. Instead of asking him what he was talking about, I tilted my head and must have looked like an inquisitive puppy desperately trying to grasp its owner's instructions. Ali attempted a dramatic pause, a skill he had not yet perfected.

'My father owns many retail outlets and could possibly relieve you of this troublesome useless sandwich paper and replace it with real cash in order to facilitate your lunchtime activities.'

I was further confused by the negative left to right movement of his head that accompanied every affirmative answer he was hoping for or delivering. This familiar head movement, recognisable as a "no" in the western world, I found out actually meant "yes" in Indian culture. I was curious but getting a little irritated at the same time.

'What is it you want to say, Ali? In plain English please', I said, continuing to line up a penalty shot with the miniature Bobby Moore and faking disinterest. Some inborn instinct, which I didn't know I possessed, told me this was the correct way to handle the impending negotiation.

'My father would be willing to buy your luncheon vouchers at thirty pence for every fifty pence voucher providing you with much desired beer money.'

I asked if his father would also purchase the vouchers of my two drinking buddies, and later that afternoon, our quorum gathered in our meeting room, the gent's toilets on the second floor; me, Stephen Allen and Danny Murphy. I told them of the proposition that had been put to me and the shortest meeting in history was concluded. The course of action decided, we rifled through our desk drawers, pooling our luncheon vouchers which we then placed in a brown envelope. A sticky label was placed on the envelope clearly inscribed with Ali's name, the total amount of Luncheon vouchers -£50, and the amount of Queens tender expected - £30 pounds. The next day Ali came through on his part of the bargain and we arranged our night out.

Money to Byrne?

It was a Friday, London was buzzing, and the average price of a pint was thirty-five pence. After getting to a suitable stage of merriment, Danny suggested we head to the West End. I decided to bail on them as I had the furthest journey home and it was in the other direction, east. Steve also decided to call it a night, so Danny and another guy, Andy Rich, went on their way. They had struck a friendship due to their mutual interest of travelling the world to watch soccer matches. They were only on temporary contracts and were prepared for termination of their employment if they appeared to be hungover. I wanted a career as opposed to a job, so often found it prudent to avoid their antics. Loaded with cash they were ready to discover this alternative London, away from the chalk-striped suits and false guffaws of sycophantic employees, laughing with gusto at the unfunny jokes and anecdotes relentlessly pouring from their boring bosses' mouths.

The next day Danny recounted the night's events. Apparently, after spending all of their money they awoke that morning in a surgically white room. The previous night's bass music still seemed to be pounding in their heads, as if a rock band had reassembled its equipment inside their skulls and refused to end the gig. Danny said he looked across to the adjacent bed to see Andy staring at him. His eyes looked like they had been replaced by battered kiwi fruits randomly injected with traces of red food dye, but they still managed to convey a clear message; where the hell are we and how did we get here? Danny heard swishing and scrubbing noises coming from what turned out to be a kitchen area. He forced himself to his reluctant feet to investigate the source of the sound. There in front of him were two very attractive girls in nurses' uniforms. One of them, a blonde, made an expertly sultry glide towards Danny and draped her arms around his neck.

Money to Byrne?

She said, 'Morning Dan, did you really mean all those wonderful things you said to me last night?'

He couldn't remember a damn thing of course, including their names but said, "Of course I did, hon. You are even more beautiful this morning.' Her face turned from sultry to disgust and her arms released themselves from his person and assumed an indignant, dangerous pose.

'Don't lie you stupid, drunken prat! You were with Paula and my name's Nicola, by the way ... Hon!'

It was then Paula's turn to speak. 'Oh Dan, you were so great last night.'

He felt the beginnings of a "yeah I'm the man" smirk trying to etch itself onto his features. Until Paula spoke again.

'You were great when you tripped and smashed the coffee table, you were great when you managed to completely empty the contents of your bladder everywhere in the bathroom except where it was supposed to go, and you were great at throwing up in the kitchen before passing out on my bed. Now get the f out and come back in ten years when your balls have dropped, and you know what they're for.'

Dan told me that his exit from the nurse's accommodation in *King George's* hospital was swift and his hangover was further exacerbated by Andy's refusal to stop laughing at his verbal crucifixion back at the flat.

Over the next few months we would have the regular nights out and, even though my constitution became more resilient to the effects of alcohol, I still avoided the heavier evenings such as their soirees to the nurses' quarters at *King George's*.

Even with the supplementary income from the luncheon voucher arrangement the days leading up to payday saw us back to ham and egg sandwiches at the desk. Then came a déjà vu moment as I was, once again, honing my skills in the recreation area with my miniature soccer stars. There was a tap-tap-tap on the door.

'Come in, Ali. What can I do for you today?' His face and demeanour seemed to indicate there'd been a death in the family. Either that or he'd been fired.

'Mr David, I had a most unfortunate communication from my father. His pile of luncheon vouchers is growing but cash sales in his shop are slowing so he wishes to terminate our agreement. We had a long talk and I have convinced him to continue but he requires a small adjustment to the arrangement.'

'What kind of adjustment?' I asked Ali, knowing the direction but not the actual financial difference.

'He is only able to pay you twenty pence for every fifty pence voucher. He did not even want to do this but I told him you are a clever man and Allah has great things planned for you at this company. I told him with the utmost authority that our business relationship should be maintained for future more lucrative ventures with you and your colleagues.'

I didn't know who Allah was but guessed that this higher authority would not be seen on any directors' lists or company memoranda. I was also chuffed that at least someone, albeit just a colleague, had noticed my efforts at work. Once again, the instincts I did not know I possessed kicked in. We were being played!

The quorum assembled in the makeshift meeting room and I delivered the news and my plan to the members. We refused the new offer from Ali's father and, over the next two months, we maintained the appearance that it had had no effect on our lifestyle. We would ration our expenditure on alcohol, which was a good thing, and spend several lunch hours eating ham and egg sandwiches in one of the numerous little parks and green areas dotted around the city. At the same time Ali would spend his lunch hours eating egg sandwiches at his desk minus the ham (Muslims not eating pork of any kind was another thing omitted from my education back at *Culverhouse Comprehensive*), while we would return to the office each afternoon faking the merriment made possible previously by the additional cash in our pockets. After about two months of this our patience paid off.

One morning I found that Ali had left a note on my desk to meet him in "the place where the tiny men play games" at twelve-thirty. I wasn't sure at first where he meant - euphemistic thoughts of Christmas party shenanigans sprang to mind – before I realised, he meant the recreation area.

'Very good news Mr David! My father is prepared to increase his payment to twenty-five pence per fifty pence voucher instead of twenty. This is excellent news, no?' he said.

'No', I said without any malice. We had won the stand-off and I knew I had him.

I said bluntly, 'We have found another buyer. He pays us thirty-eight pence per fifty pence voucher.' Of course, this wasn't true but it was all part of the plan. 'I'll be honest with you, Ali. Our new guy does pay us thirty-eight pence, but some months he is unreliable and does not help us. If your father can match this price, we will give our business exclusively to him.' The surprise and confusion on Ali's face was absolute.

'But that will only leave my family four pence profit from each of the vouchers!' His look of surprise turned to shock, and his face went perceptively paler. His jaw snapped shut like a highly tensioned mouse trap triggered by an unfortunate rodent. He had opened his book to me and now it was my turn to be the false friend and offer a solution.

I tried to look concerned and deep in thought, pretending to calculate the pros and cons of a solution to the mutual benefit of both parties. This act was well rehearsed in my mind since the plan had been formed immediately after he tried to have on over on us weeks before.

'Look, Ali. If your father promises to maintain our original agreement at thirty pence, we will exclusively use him and everyone will be happy.'

He immediately agreed, confirming my suspicion that this had been his own little side-line. Even if his father had the method of conversion, it was Ali's decision and his alone. No telephone consultation was needed before he agreed to the deal. We were not harming anyone with this arrangement. It was a win-win situation as Ali's family were obviously making a profit and we were receiving cash, and it made no difference whatsoever to our employers.

It was this seemingly unimportant little episode that made me really understand how the City worked, indeed how the financial centres around the world operated. People have a commodity to sell either because a price is being offered above their purchase price, or because they need to sell something to realise capital to make a different purchase. In our case it was selling vouchers to buy beer. Ali's father, being a shop retailer, had a facility to cash in the vouchers at a higher price than he was paying us. Ali, in this case, was the broker, the guy in the middle who matches buyers to sellers taking a small slice of the action along the way. I quickly understood that it was this same process for all commodities be it gold, copper, bonds or currency. I had the necessary skills to succeed in this arena and I have luncheon vouchers to thank for this crucial insight.

Chapter 3.   A bit of my history

By the age of thirty, the dreams I'd had when I left school, for the most part had been achieved. Although some accomplishments had been allowed to slip away again, the decisions I had made over the years had generally been the correct ones and had kept my career advancement on an upward trajectory. I was fully aware of the ups and downs that come your way but anything catastrophic seemed like something that only happened to other people.

Back in the middle of the 1980s I had managed to move on from the insurance industry and had secured a position as a stock settlements clerk with the *Swiss Bank Corporation*. It was a move in the right direction towards trading and having a renowned Swiss bank name on your CV could do no harm at all. Working at such an institution was very much as one would expect. There was very little personality, a fixation on efficiency, and a snobbery that said "you have now entered the secret world of Swiss banking".

The dealers carried an arrogant air and the private client managers that dealt directly with the super-rich clients, even more so. I soon realised there was no way an average working-class kid would be allowed into this elite club. I had learnt a lot more about the markets, was grateful for the experience and, with my greatly enhanced CV, I was on the lookout again.

My break came when an institution called *The Continental Illinois National Bank and Trust company of Chicago* filed for chapter eleven, after running into difficulties. They were bailed out by the *Federal Reserve* but had lost many of their key staff and virtually all of their dealers. The talented staff had been poached by other banks and the less talented were happy to take voluntary redundancy. I was twenty-one but managed to secure a fairly senior position as head of international custody. It was still in settlements, but I knew there would be opportunities to gain more experience as many departmental responsibilities overlapped due to the depleted staffing levels.

After about a year, the company was starting to rebuild, and a memo was circulated stating that they would be looking to establish a presence on the futures market, *LIFFE*. This is where my school friend, Matt, worked and it was where I wanted to be. I applied for the position and succeeded in becoming a junior trainee in this crazy, but still very new trading floor. I knew I had a good chance of securing the job as it was only offered to permanent staff, and the majority of employees were temporary after the mass exodus following the bank's financial crisis.

There was one episode during my first year at *Continental Bank* that taught me no industry is devoid of corruption and it can be lurking in the most unlikely of places. It was clear that one of the busiest people in the whole company was a sweet little lady called Edith that worked in HR. She would timidly pigeon-step through the building every morning, delivering a shy hello to everyone. She would then proceed to her private off-limits sanctuary, with her antique tea set and horn-rimmed glasses, to begin payment and processing for the huge army of temporary staff. Everyone's shock was absolute when the police came in one day and removed her from her cubby hole in handcuffs. It turned out that more than fifty of the temporary employees did not exist and their salaries were being sent to various accounts owned by her. I grew up in an age where news channels covered stories of banks being robbed by gun-wielding criminals wearing masks, so this "white-collar" crime by such a demure perpetrator had been a complete eye-opening revelation to me.

Down on the trading floor, *Continental Bank*, was not a big player, so I decided to move on. Within two years I was the floor manager of *Fimat Futures*, twenty-three years old earning fifty thousand pounds a year plus substantial bonuses, an expense account and a company car. By the age of thirty I was mortgage free and at thirty-five I owned a substantial five-bedroom house in the country complete with games room, gym, sauna and indoor swimming pool. I had kept a large part of my earnings on deposit with *KAS Clearing*, a subsidiary of *KAS Bank Amsterdam*. But I had kept too many eggs in one basket, and when *KAS* went bust due to overexposure in the options market I suffered a massive setback. I was the first of my family to enter the world of finance and at a relatively tender age did not have a mentor to guide me safely through, or to avoid, this type of pitfall.

The trading floor was a crazy frenetic environment, made up of people from all backgrounds equipped with the various skills that made this monster function efficiently. The phone booths would house the more intellectual talent with smooth tongues for the clients and an octopus-like ability to juggle five handsets. The "pits" would be where the rougher element lived, defending their territory whilst awaiting buy or sell orders from the booths. The talent this particular part of the process required was to divide 500, 1000 or perhaps 10,000 "lots" (shares) into varying denominations between two hundred screaming adversaries in seconds, and at the same time remember exactly who you'd traded with and the amount. To give you a better idea I will give an example using "product" to replace the real name of the financial instrument, such as the *German Government Bund* or *UK Gilts*. A trader would raise their hands in the air and say:

'I have 100 product to sell at 18 dollars.'

Other traders, with interest in buying, would scream back at you the price that they were willing to pay. 'I will pay 16 dollars for the product.'

Then some news would come out indicating the market will go higher and there would be an immediate deluge of people trying to buy your 100 lots. Mnemonics of three letters were used to differentiate between traders. MKY, the mnemonic for a lad nicknamed Monkey, would want to buy 15 of them. PPT would want 27. KNL would be after just 3. SLM would buy 50. Most of the others would have to be disappointed because, if you had calculated correctly, you would only have 5 left to sell. Any mistake would be a costly one and it was this accuracy and speed that dictated your worth to a company.

As this was a London-based market and the rougher barrow boy element occupied the pits, cockney rhyming slang and London talk was often used, for instance:

'I'll buy a score off you' [I'll buy 20], or 'I'll let you have a glove' [I'll sell you 5].

One day an American trader from Chicago (where futures began) was in the pit. He was getting very hot under the collar trying to understand the banter and eventually he snapped, screaming, 'Hey you cockney assholes, speak proper English. I used to be a big fish in the States so show some respect!' It was the worst thing he could ever have done. From that moment, every time he entered the space, he would be met by a football terrace chant of "Tunaah, Tuna, Tuna!" Not the type of big fish he had in mind and each time people traded with him they would use any alternative term available in our adapted vocabulary other than something he would understand. Someone purchasing a "one lot" from him would state that they will take a

Valerie, after the news reader Valerie SINGLEton. Another person might sell him a McGarratt, meaning 50 lots after the program *Hawaii 5-0*. A couple of months later he returned to the United States.

Some of the traders that were particularly good at this seemed to have a form of autism. Outside of the trading floor they could hardly spell their names but give them a pencil and trading card and they became a human supercomputer. A very good example of this was a guy that worked for *Tullet and Tokyo* called Darren. One day he was feeling unwell and decided to call his GP but hit the wrong speed dial button on his phone. When the recipient answered, he said in a surprised voice, 'Hello, Sis. What are you doing at the doctors?' On another occasion the same guy was driving to a friend's party and called the host to advise that he would be turning up much later than expected.

'Well how long do you think you will be?' asked the host.

Darren then gave the incredible reply: 'It depends on traffic mate. I missed your turn off on the M25 and it could take two or three hours to get back round to the right exit.'

The M25 is, of course, the orbital road that encircles London and, instead of taking the next exit and coming back on himself, he continued to complete the 118-mile circuit back to the correct exit.

By 1990 I had set up my own broking operation with a guy called Nick Sharp. His mnemonic was NOT, as in *not so Sharp*, the implication being he was not too clever. Names were rarely complimentary but efficiently served as a way to identify between the 200 Daves or 150 Nicks working on the floor which housed some three thousand people.

My code was DOE but actually meant Donut. It came about after an occasion when I was heading home from work, slightly merry and famished, needing food to soak up some of the alcohol. All the sandwiches at the station cafe were sold out and I didn't have time to go back outside as my train was due any moment. So, I bought their three remaining stale donuts and was making my way back to the platform when I suddenly tripped, stumbled and fell, ending up on the track. As the train rolled into the station, I had to lay totally flat, pressing myself into the gap between the rails. When the vehicle overhead finally came to a stop, I clambered back through the gap and onto the platform, jam oozing through the fingers of my shaking hands still holding the doughy delicacies. I've had prouder moments but that was the moment my colleagues christened me with my DOE identity code and my badge became a constant reminder of this incredibly lucky escape.

A less lucky escape, though not life-threatening concerned a friend of mine called James, or Jabba, after the *Star Wars* character. He was super intelligent especially in the options strategy space, but he also managed a broking line for his clients trading the FTSE Future. He had slightly misaligned eyes, or "football eyes" as some of my less PC colleagues used to quip - one home and one away. One day, acting on a client's wish to buy five hundred FTSE futures contracts, Jabba signalled this to one of the pit brokers. Unfortunately, because of his infliction two different guys thought he was looking at them and thus a costly duplication of the order took place. I must say that Jabs is a great friend, and I hope this (Rumoured story) does not offend.

Shortly after that, Jabba and his girlfriend decided to take a vacation to his parent's Spanish villa. However, they had a slight problem; they needed a dog sitter. One of their friends had been suffering with both alcohol and drug addiction so they thought it would be a good idea to offer him the chance to escape the influences ever present in his usual environment. They lived in the country and suggested that he could stay at their house, take the dog for long healthy walks and enjoy some solitude in a nice house, fully stocked with two weeks supply of food. He took them up on their offer and they duly headed off to Spain. All was well for the first few days, checking in by phone every evening to make sure their friend and their beloved hound were well. But after five days the phone stopped being answered. Jabba called another chum and asked if he could check in on the house but there was no response to the doorbell either and a couple of days later they decided to cut the vacation short, return to their home and see what the problem was. On entering the house there was a pungent smell. No one responded to their "hellos" and as Jabba passed through the lounge to check upstairs, he saw his friend lying dead in front of him. At that moment, their dog came bounding down the stairs with a human foot in its mouth. Deprived of dog food, it had been forced to live off their friend's remains.

The next ten years were to produce some incredible highs and some devastating lows. The company was thriving and, while the benefits it provided were great, this all came at a cost to my marriage and personal life, and during that same time a handful of young friends and associates, unable to deal with the pressures associated with this frenetic environment, had taken their own lives.

Without doubt there were obscene extravagances, but this seemed justified and necessary if you were to be taken seriously as a player. We had some thirty guys working for us. They demanded, and received, high remuneration. If you didn't pay up, it would cost you more in the long run; errors made by the less talented staff invariably outweighed the costs of employing the best. When approaching someone to join your company, the meeting would often be held on a weekend, away from prying eyes. If you turned up driving a humble Ford Escort, the young emerging superstar would see no attraction in joining your company. But turn up in a Ferrari and the deal was done. So de rigueur mode of transport were Ferraris, Porches and Mercedes.

And the importance of the notorious "Christmas Party" could not be underestimated. There would be bets on which company or group of traders would throw the best bash. If you couldn't put on the most opulent Christmas party the rumours would start that you were having difficulties and, inevitably, customers would start fleeing like proverbial rats from a sinking ship. As the London futures market and its participants matured, the excesses of this annual tradition reduced to a more morally acceptable level.

These December parties were legendary and at least fifty people would be turned away at the doors having produced forged tickets to the doormen (the tickets were often made from a special card that produced a blue line when folded). These events would set us back tens of thousands of pounds but the benefits to our brokerage always far exceeded this as new clients, desperate to attend the best party, would throw business our way.

There were many business trips during these years which were productive, but they were also an excuse for a raucous jolly up. It was, for many, a by-product of having too much too young or at best the result of very young successful guys and girls having no one to rein them in. The shorter trips were to places like Paris or Amsterdam, but the more coveted longer ones were to Singapore, Hong Kong or Chicago.

One of the Chicago trips sticks in my mind most of all though for a number of reasons. My friend John was working for a company called *First Chicago* and was invited to visit their offices in the States with some colleagues. I decided to go along and treat a few of my team to the adventure. There were about ten of us in all meeting at Heathrow, though one of my guys called Steve had a commitment and would have to join us a day or two later. John's company had arranged everything and would be meeting us at O'Hare airport. The flight was uneventful but when we landed, I asked John where we were meeting his American counterparts. He declared that he wasn't sure, but everything would be fine.

I said, 'Don't worry, I'm sure we will spot him as we come out of arrivals. What does he look like?'

John replied, 'Er, I don't know'.

'Don't worry', I said, 'We can make an announcement on the Tannoy.'

John giggled before sheepishly admitting, 'Well the thing is, I only know him as "The Moose", and he only knows me as "Gripper"'.

After unsuccessfully spending quite some time looking for somebody that appeared to be looking for us, we eventually convinced the airport staff to make a strange announcement over the system:

"Could the Moose from Chicago please meet the Gripper from England by exit 24 of Terminal Three."

It worked and later that evening we went to dinner and then on to a pool bar on the corner of the popular Rush and Division in downtown Chicago. On entering we couldn't believe our eyes. There, hogging the pool table, were another ten guys from the London Futures Exchange. A complete coincidence; neither us nor they were aware of the others' plans. The night was about to get very messy! Those guys were lucky to be there at all though, having been severely reprimanded by the airline staff for playing a drunken game of strip poker on the flight to Chicago with a group of American girls who were on their way home from a trip to Europe. It was just another example of the "we can do what we like" attitude that prevailed during the unsavoury and extravagant Nineties. As it turned out, jet lag kicked in so we all retired quite early, agreeing to meet at the same place the following evening.

The next day, after concluding our meetings, and making a visit to the *Chicago Mercantile Exchange* as well as the *Chicago Board of Trade*, we freshened up and headed to the *Lodge* on Rush and Division. There had been a slight change of plan as to the exact venue, but it was just across the road from where we had met before. The party was in full swing when I got quite an unexpected surprise; Steve, who'd been due to follow us on a later flight, had decided he could not make the trip and had given his plane ticket to one of our female back-up staff called Emma. So now there were twenty guys and one girl, and she was basically my responsibility. I was not overjoyed because this was a trip to reward the team and Emma had not been with us long enough to have necessarily earned the perk. Everyone was ready for a pub crawl to sample the watering holes of the "Windy City". Everyone apart from Emma. She was exhausted, didn't know where she was going, and as I also needed to change the hotel reservation to her name from Steve's I said to the boys I would take her to get settled in. I said I'd be back as soon as possible and asked them not to go on without me. I was only gone about forty-five minutes but when I got back to the bar, they had all left, maybe believing that I would be occupied for the evening. I was livid but decided to sit and have a few drinks by myself in the hope that they would check back in.

There was a local man sitting at the bar next to me who was clearly well into a drinking session of his own. On hearing me order my next beer the inevitable happened.

'Hey, where are you from? England?'

'Yes,' I replied, keeping the answer short so as to not encourage him.

'Let me buy that beer for you,' he said.

'Thanks, but you don't have to do that.'

As it turned out he seemed quite a nice guy and we got chatting. He was celebrating as he had just got a big promotion in the Meat Packers' Union, and this meant a big pay rise too. The more he consumed the more insistent he was that I should not pay for any drinks.

He said, 'Listen, when you're a bit older and earning the big bucks like me, you can do the same for some other young guy on the way up'.

Money to Byrne?

I didn't know how to play it. I didn't want to take advantage, but he was insistent. I also didn't think it would be wise to advertise the fact that I had a good job and had plenty of money. A few drinks later and me feeling far more comfortable, he asked what I would most like to see in Chicago. I had many friends in the city and had been there a number of times. I'd been to the top of the Sears Tower, watched the Venetian boat show from Navy Pier and had lost an evening or two listening to the Blues bands in the famous *Kingston Mines*.

After a short pause I said I'd like to see a *real* Chicago bar where *real* people drink, not one of those jazzy establishments where all the businessmen and tourists go.

He said, 'Get your coat, I'm going to take you to one'.

I threw caution to the wind and thought, why not. After all, it seemed my friends had abandoned me anyway. We took a taxi for about twenty minutes and I was starting to doubt the wisdom of my decision when we pulled up outside a seedy looking establishment, complete with broken window and flickering neon. As I walked in I was met by suspicious stares from the clientele and immediately started thinking of my escape route and how quickly I could get back out.

The locals only relaxed their surprised expressions when "Big Toni", my new friend said, 'It's ok, dudes, he's with me'. I had a sudden need for the bathroom; to splash water on my perspiring face, release my bladder and think of an exit plan. As I stood at the urinal, I heard a voice behind me saying, 'What ya sellin? Ain't seen you here before'. I turned my head to the direction of the sound. There, sitting on a toilet with trousers fully lowered, was a scruffy urchin complete with matted beard and a crudely repaired scar across his forehead. He was in full view as the cubicle door laying against the wall several feet away with its broken hinges hanging jaggedly. This was not good. Not good at all!

I returned to the bar where a beer, courtesy of Big Toni, was awaiting me. No sooner had I taken the first sip when the main door came crashing open. Four Chicago cops burst in guns drawn.

Everyone lay face down on the floor. Now!

Twenty of the twenty-one occupants complied in seconds; clearly not unfamiliar with this routine and undoubtedly wise to the alternative consequences. Only one person remained standing, frozen, unable to move. The instructions were repeated, but this time directed at me alone, as were the chunky barrels of their police issue revolvers. I snapped out of my trance and assumed the same position as Toni, flattening myself to the grimy, sticky, beer-stained floor.

'Now, a friend of ours has told us that you guys are going back into the business of robbing wealthy folks from downtown, and we told you what would happen if you did that', drawled the dark-haired thick-set cop. 'I want you all, very slowly, to empty your pockets.'

I could hear the jangle of stolen jewellery dropping on the wooden floor and the mumbles of "goddammit" as cash was piled beside it. There were a few watches and necklaces, and the wads of cash were really quite small.

Once again, I had not followed instructions nearly quickly enough and the cop, giving me his full attention snarled, 'Are you deaf boy? Empty your pockets.'

I did as I was told and deposited my gold Cartier along with five thousand dollars on the floor between myself and Toni. I was only carrying that amount because I was expecting to treat the whole team for a great year's effort and back then, cash was king, not credit cards. Toni's mouth opened in surprise and his eyes flicked rapidly between the pile of money, the watch, and my face. I think he wanted to beat the living crap out of me there and then. Another officer leapt down and placed me in cuffs, retrieved the valuables and frog-marched me to one of their vehicles. On the journey to the police station I tried to explain what had happened. They asked me all sorts of questions: what I was doing in Chicago, where I was staying, how long for, even where the Dow had closed the previous night.

They were in constant contact with base, checking every answer I gave, but eventually they seemed satisfied I was telling the truth and they removed the cuffs and drove me back to the *Drake Hotel* at the top of the "magnificent mile", Princess Diana's favourite hotel. The cops accepted my offer of coffee but spent a while lecturing me on how incredible stupid - and lucky - I had been.

These trips were not just jolly ups though. All the time I was expanding my knowledge of the financial markets and the nuances and idiosyncrasies of how different cultures did business. In Chicago or New York, it was always coffee chats, meetings in a huge boardroom and, if things went well, a Saturday afternoon at a country club. In Paris it was treating them to a dinner at the restaurant of their choice, usually the most expensive.

On one occasion a guy I knew that worked at *Lehman Brothers* took several French clients to a top Parisian eatery having heard that he may be losing that account to a competitor. The clients allowed him to wine and dine them knowing that they would be moving on, and a small fortune was spent on the dinner for four. It was not until they had ordered a rare bottle of dessert wine that his clients finally delivered the bad news; they would no longer be requiring his services. With calculated dignity, the guy then ruined the wine by topping their glasses with soda water, declaring that they should enjoy their spritzers before paying the bill and leaving.

Conducting business in Asia, however, is a completely different experience. There is always a very impressive reception demonstrating elements of their culture and they usually make some sort of gesture or presentation to show that they have taken time to learn about your own country. And there is always, without fail, a gala dinner to conclude proceedings. It really is a fantastic place to do business where respect and politeness are such important elements of the deal process.

Chapter 4. Learning my trade

Having started my working life in insurance and spent some time in the back office of investment houses before trading in the Futures pits, my overall knowledge had increased exponentially. I had also been studying hard in my spare time achieving examination passes in subjects that would benefit my career, including the Stock Exchange exams. To that I added some accountancy qualifications and learnt how to interpret company reports and accounts. My education was enhanced further by going onto electronic trading and diversifying into other products such as Foreign Exchange, and it was this in-depth and rounded understanding of markets that was to make me an ideal speaker and potential figurehead for any future employer.

Of all the jobs I've done, the old Futures Exchange was the most highly pressured and demanded the quickest learning curve. Back in 1994, after a very successful year for our brokerage operation on the exchange, our phone brokers occupied a triple booth on the top tier of the trading floor, precisely midpoint between the Bund (German government bonds) and the BTP (the Italian equivalent). These were two of the busiest and most volatile products being traded at that time. I had secured a good chunk of business from *Salomon Brothers* who, along with *Goldman Sachs*, took massive positions in these markets. The phone booths were designed like a theatre or stadium, where the cheapest location was at eye level with no clear sight of the overall scene being played out. The best and most expensive booths were those on the upper tiers directly in front of the action. It wasn't just a case of affording the higher price demanded by the exchange for the best view, you were only considered for one of these high-status locations if you could justify this by market presence and activity.

Ted Erser, or Badger as he was known, was the floor manager of *Salomon's* at the time. He was also one of the high-profile characters often asked onto a panel to adjudicate on disputes between traders. The result often meant that one or the other of the companies would be wearing a significant loss, and the losing trader possibly forfeiting his job. One of my team was involved in such a dispute and I was a witness to what happened. Ultimately, I would be wearing the 90k loss if we were deemed in the wrong. It was an unusual case because I was summoned to the panel for my account of events, even though the outcome would have a personal effect on my pocket. Pretending I did not see what happened would have meant that the remaining evidence was stacked very much in our favour. But I did see what happened and, as painful as it was, I knew we were in the wrong. I told the truth which resulted in our trader and my company losing the case, and a lot of money. I was drowning my sorrows in *Deacons Bar* near the Exchange at Cannon Street when I was once again summoned. This time it was by Badger, holding his own personal court with his loyal entourage. He explained that he was very impressed by my honesty and there and then offered me the opportunity of servicing the needs of his company, *Salomon Brothers*. Even though they had their own trading team on the floor, it was common practice for them to use a number of brokers in order to disguise their sizeable activities. This was an elite club and our company was now a member.

There were associated costs though. The first time I encountered this, Ted was saying that he hoped I was keeping my books and records straight with all the increased volume I was now achieving for my company. The implication I thought was that his ego was seeking my verbal acknowledgement that our growing success was directly because of him.

'It's ok, Ted. I'm on top of things', I said. 'But I must say, the workload has increased considerably since you directed some of 'Sally's' business our way. I am really, really grateful.'

He massaged his chin as if deep in thought and then his hands simultaneously started itching the grey streaks that adorned either side of his head and that gave him his Badger-like appearance.

He looked straight at me. 'Are you sure you don't need some help with the paperwork. David? The thing is, I know this lovely lady called Kate. She's lost her job and I more or less told her that you would be needing a secretary. She's coming into town this Friday and I took the liberty of booking an interview with you. If that's not too presumptuous.'

The penny dropped. This was neither a suggestion, nor was it a request. It was a condition. The interview was just a formality with a pre-determined outcome if I wished to continue servicing this particular client. It was a good call though; Kate started working for me the following week, was very competent, had a lovely personality and over the coming years I doubt whether I could have managed without her. Ted never asked for any personal financial reward for the many thousands of pounds worth of business he directed my way each month. You were though, on occasion, expected to foot some dining or entertainment expenses, which seemed reasonable for any industry professional in the interests of retaining a lucrative account.

One US Independence Day the markets, as usual on such holidays, were extremely quiet and I was preparing for an afternoon off when my phone rang.

Money to Byrne?

'Byrnesy! It's Ted. What are you up to?'

'Hi Ted', I said. 'Actually, I'm just about to head for the station. Thought I'd have a few drinks in the garden. Markets are dead and the sun is out.'

'I've got a better idea David. You can take me to the *Guinea*. I'm downstairs in a cab. The meter's already running so get a move on.'

The *Guinea Grill* is a small "olde-worlde" pub in Bruton place in Mayfair. It serves traditional ales in its cramped bar area but it's the restaurant out back that commands the attention of the wealthy, the rich and the famous. The walls are adorned with pictures of the owner or the head chef posing with film and pop stars, and royalty. In fact, there is one photo of the late Queen Mother pulling a pint behind the bar. Not many people are aware that her daughter, Queen Elizabeth, was actually born only a few hundred yards away in Bruton Street. While the *Guinea* is famous for its pies, it's the steaks and racks of lamb that are particularly spectacular, both in quality and price. An afternoon with Ted was always an expensive one, with just one bottle of *Margaux*, his favourite wine, often costing more than the entire meal. Ted was neither being pretentious nor taking advantage of his dinner companion, it's just that he preferred venues with an extensive wine list, fine wine being his passion. He often returned the compliment, although my choice would usually be to share a decent bottle of house red and an equally good steak somewhere humbler, such as a pub close to Smithfield meat market near Clerkenwell.

The two brokers in the booth for *Salomon's* were Ian Murrell and Howard Marks, though not the infamous drug smuggler of the same name. Ian had a couple of affectionate nicknames attributed to him: Mario, because of his likeness to the computer game hero; and Ronseal, makers of varnish and wood stain whose slogan is, "It does what it says on the tin." You knew exactly what you got with Ian. He was honest, reliable but incapable of keeping a secret. If you wanted a rumour to circulate quickly you confided in Ian and asked him not to tell a soul. He was capable of helping a story go viral long before Twitter, Facebook or Instagram were even thought of. He was also very cautious, and it would take some considerable time before he would take anyone into his confidence. As such, most of my initial dealings were with Howard. Howard was a very pleasant person and a bit of an unlikely ladies' man. He was a fairly quiet, cheeky chappy and an easy listener with a good ear for anyone with a problem. This was one of the traits that enabled him to be a silent assassin where the opposite sex was concerned. They would feel much better after confiding their problems to him over dinner and would later feel completely reassured but confused as to how a simple dinner with a friend ended in the hotel bedroom for the night.

Back on the trading floor, when deals came down the phones from customers, they were very clear and precise.

Client: 'What's in the Bund?'

Our phone clerk: 'There are 300 on the buy side at 1.26, and 500 on the sell side at 1.28.'

Client: 'Sell 300 at 1.26.'

Money to Byrne?

It was all very clear with no room for ambiguity as this would inevitably lead to costly errors, and a mistake was always the broker's loss not the customers. *Salomon's*, and Howard in particular, were very different in their approach and I remember the events of our first day of doing business. I had placed myself in the booth instead of my usual place in the BTP pit. Every customer had their own dedicated numbered phone line for secrecy against prying competitors. I was watching line sixteen, *Salomon's*, like a hawk, ready with my rehearsed script of where I thought the market was heading and who had been the main players so far that day. Sure enough, the red light on line sixteen started blinking fast and regular like a car indicator at double speed, emphasising the importance of the call.

I spoke into the mouthpiece, 'Good morning, Sir. It's been fairly busy so far toda ...'

Howard cut in, 'Buy me some Bunds!' Brrrrrrrrrrrr. The line went dead.

'Ok', I said to the vacant handset and launched myself down the gangway and into the pit. An average size order for a decent size bank was between 50 and 100 lots. But this was *Salomon's*, so I reaped in a total of 500 and ran back to the phones feeling very pleased with myself at my speed and efficiency. I hit line sixteen and the corresponding secret button flashed in the client's booth.

Howard answered, 'Yep?'

I said, 'I've bought you five hundred at an avera ...'

Howard interrupted, 'Is that all? I said, "buy me some bunds!"' Brrrrrrrrrrrr.

I proceeded back to the pit and bought another 2000 lots. This time, on relaying the purchase amount and price to the client, the response was far more satisfactory and gave me an idea of what I would be dealing with. This was a whole new level

Howard: 'Yep?'

Me: 'I've now bought 2500 bunds in total.' This was a huge amount.

Howard: 'That's more like it. Now go back and do it again.'

Howard had turns of phrase such as, "sell it until your balls ache" that could send the markets in to a frenzy so, on answering his line, it was not unusual to be met by an instruction like this:

'I want to see the BTP trading 300 points higher by ten o'clock. In case you can't tell the time that's in three minutes. Oh, and I've got two other brokers doing the same, so you'd better be quick if you don't want to look a prat.'

This was like moving a currency 20% in 180 seconds all by yourself. It didn't matter how many you bought, you just needed to get the price up there. Over the coming months we became good friends and I developed an understanding of his unusual instruction method, and "Sir" became a simple "H".

Since those heady days though, things had been changing rapidly. Mathematicians were combining their skills with a new breed of computer genius to create black box systems; essentially computer algorithms that collated data and acted upon pre-defined instructions or conditions, to place trades without any further human intervention. This did not happen overnight as the one component that was difficult to factor in was human behaviour. There were often situations where a market, expecting bad news, would be selling off only to rally again once the news was released as there were too many sellers. In the old days this was called "sell the rumour, buy the fact." How could you instruct a computer to identify panic short covering? Of course it was possible but back then the world of traders and computer geeks did not speak the same tongue. A trader would instruct a programmer to build a system, using trader talk that, to him, was quite clear. Often though, the instructions would be misconstrued resulting in costly or ineffective systems that quickly became redundant. Eventually their worlds were forced to merge but during this courting period there was little respect for each other's talents. There were two jokes circulating around this time that demonstrated the opinions of both sides very well.

The first pitches the trader against the geek and goes as follows:

A woman asks her computer geek husband to go to the shops for a loaf of bread. As he leaves the house she says, 'Oh, and if they have eggs, could you get a dozen'.

The husband returns later with twelve loaves of bread having taken the instructions literally. What she ought to have said was: "If they have eggs, could you get a dozen of those *also*'.

This was the sort of misunderstanding between traders and programmers that cost companies hundreds of millions during the transition or incubation period.

The second joke pitches the geek against the trader at the latter's expense:

Three good people have unfortunately died but there is a delay at St. Peter's gate to enter Heaven. God tells St. Peter to keep them occupied while the problem is sorted out.

St. Peter explains that there is a slight delay and asks the first person, 'What is your IQ?'

This first person is a computer programmer and replies, 'My IQ is 168'. St Peter engages in some small talk about black holes, coding and algorithms, and gives him a copy of *Mensa* magazine to pass the time.

He moves on to the second person and again asks for their IQ. This person says, 'It's 112', and tells him she was the founder and CEO of a PR company. He gives her a copy of *The Times* crossword.

Lastly, St. Peter approaches the third person and asks him what his IQ is, to which the reply is, '38'.

So St. Peter asks him whether the FX markets are up or down today.

As time moved on, the men in coloured jackets dealing face-to-face became a distant memory and a new breed of trader emerged. These were computer literate, had high mathematical skills, and were able to build systems that included the factor of the human psyche. When it came to this new world of computing, Asia was recognised as the world leader. Be it Japan, South Korea or China, they were all considered to be ahead of the curve.

Chapter 5. Life after Liffe

Although derivatives trading developed and matured in Chicago during the 1970s as a means for farmers to protect themselves against unexpected price movements in agriculture, it was Europe that made the transition to electronic trading first. The days of waving hand signals and throwing trading cards crammed with counter party names was rapidly drawing to a close. It quickly became evident that the intentions to be innovative and more efficient leaders in trading technology was way ahead of developers' software capabilities available at that time. Even major institutions were inadvertently moving markets by selling 100,000 shares instead of 10,000, just by pressing the wrong button. Many losses were still incurred by inefficient risk management or server failure. However, over time significant improvements in risk management were introduced: Managers were able to implement limits to the size of trades placed by juniors, and senior traders would have an "Are you sure you wish to sell this amount" alert in case they had "fat-fingered" the keyboard. We were all still young and prepared for a challenge, but highly educated university graduates were making great strides with black box and automated systems that mere mortals could not match for speed. It felt like the train containing my previous earnings was leaving the station very quickly and my connecting train carrying future earnings had been delayed, indefinitely.

By the early 1990s, the United States was also speeding up its transition to electronic trading and it wasn't long before I was contacted by an American ex-employee who had returned to his homeland. He told me that trading rooms in Chicago were crying out for European traders that could help them avoid the pitfalls during this period. So, I headed to Chicago and joined the team at *Borsellino Capital Management.*

Lewis Borsellino and his brother Joey were very big floor traders in the *Standard & Poor's* futures market on the *Chicago Mercantile Exchange*. The *S&P*, the US version of the *London Stock Exchange*, the *FTSE*, is widely regarded as a more accurate measurement of the US economy than the *Dow* as it represents the top 500 companies, as opposed to the top 30 represented by the *Dow*. The *S&P* was traded on both the floor (open outcry) and electronically. This created an arbitrage opportunity which was my responsibility to help set up. Many of the terms used in financial markets seem to be very complicated or confusing to the outsider but, in reality most are very simple. By replacing a financial instrument with an instantly recognisable product, arbitrage can be easily explained.

Imagine a town has two stores that both specialise in buying and selling one identical product, for example tins of beans. The only difference is that one shop buys and sells the beans to people that enter the store while the other manages all of their bean transactions online. The price of beans in both stores should be the same. However, if there is an influx of people walking into the shop wishing to sell and there's a greater number of people trying to buy online, then there will be a separation in price. So, arbitrage traders try to buy the tins from the shop and sell the beans online at a higher price. There is a short window to make a profit before the price inevitably comes back in line.

After about a year I was thanked for my assistance and told that they could handle things themselves from there on in, so I returned to London and spent a number of years continuing to network and getting involved in various market activities. I was a regular stock picker on *Bloomberg*

Television, and I did some personal trading as well as completing a course in Technical Analysis. None of these produced any real opportunities to get back to winning ways and my situation was becoming increasingly precarious. I was trying to build a brand called the *Intermarket Group* but lacked the funds to fly around or entertain like the big players. I did have some limited success that was stopping the rot, if not replenishing the coffers but then, in the summer of 2009, I got a transatlantic phone call from James Bowe. We had become friends many years before when he was President and CEO of the *New York Board of Trade*. He had since retired and was missing the buzz of the markets and putting deals together. His relaxed and confident drawl was instantly recognisable.

'Davey, it's Jimbo. How the hell are ya, buddy?'

I was overjoyed to hear from him, which no doubt came across as I yelled down the phone, 'Oh my god, Jim! I thought I'd heard the last of you when you sailed off into the sunset on your boat. What was it called? Oh yes, I remember. It was "Sea Ya"'.

Jim chuckled and said, 'I should have called it "Sea Ya Soon". To be honest, I'm bored. After a while one wave looks like any other, so do the beaches. So, what's happening Davey, Still making your millions?'

'Hardly Jim', I replied. I didn't want to cry on his shoulder, but I didn't want to pretend things were hunky dory either, he knew me too well.

'I'm actually having a bit of a tough time, mate', I said in an appealing voice, hoping there could be something interesting behind the call. 'I seem to be making little bits here and there on too many small deals. It's like I'm a sort of jack-of-all-trades and I can't command the fees of a specialist.'

'Well, let's specialise and do some bigger deals! How would you like me to come on board your boat and turn it into a cruise liner? I wanna come back but don't want the politics or lack of freedom associated with the big corporates', he said in a matter-of-fact, but serious tone.

We had a lengthy discussion where Jim agreed to become Chairman of my company. It was a great honour and would immediately elevate the status of the *Intermarket Group*. Of course, there is much kudos associated with history and completed deals but having someone of Jim's stature and reputation join a small company was also a VIP pass to the big boys and girls.

Jim asked, 'So what deals are hot at the moment, Davey?'

I named a few that were around the £4-5 million mark which were met with silence. Then I decided to go for it. I have been a West Ham fan from the age of five. They were in deep financial trouble after their Icelandic owner, *Magnusson*, went bust leaving the club needing a new owner. Their debts were estimated at £50-60 million, but the potential was enormous. They owned their current ground, Upton Park, and were favourites to take over the massive new stadium that hosted the 2012 Olympics meaning their old ground could be sold. It was a no-brainer and I relayed the information to Jim, who loved the idea. John Henry, a big US bond trader that Jim knew, had just bought Liverpool FC so the topic was on everyone's radar.

'So, Jim', I said, 'How about I send your contract first thing for you to become Chairman of the *Intermarket Group*?' I held my breath.

'Sure, why not', he said.

Then he laid out his plan of action: He was going to run the circuit in the US, letting everyone know he was back working as Chairman of a new and exciting company from the UK. At the same time, he would be informing them of the first deal to be undertaken and for which he required backing. He was pitching for £100 million to purchase West Ham United outright - small change in his circles, and an amount they would be comfortable with knowing Jim was at the helm. My task was to get as much information as possible to him on the club and at the same time announce his appointment to the London Mayfair fund manager belt. I also had to make our interest known to *Rothschilds*, who were handling the sale, as well as the media. Before long, I was appearing on TV and was being hounded by the tabloids. The fund manager doors were now also open to me.

One day in the late summer of 2009 I was having lunch with a colleague, Abdelhadi Rhiti in *Shepherd Market* in Mayfair when he spotted a large group of investors and legal people that were known to him and were all clearly good friends. One man in particular was very chatty and very pleasant. He had a broad smile, rosy cheeks and a sweep of silver hair. He had recognised my picture from the tabloids and offered to give any legal consulting assistance I needed.

'David, even though you are not at the stage of needing full representation, it would be wise to have some legal consultancy during these early discussions with *Rothchild's* and investors. I would be happy to help and, quite frankly, the work would be most helpful at the moment.' He said this with confidence but there was a hint of desperation in his eyes.

'Ok', I said, thinking to myself that this was perhaps a very sensible idea. I suggested he give me his card and I would call the next day to arrange a meeting. He reached into his suit pocket and produced a business card. It read: *David Orchard. Legal Consultant.*

We met a couple of days later and got on like a house on fire. He confided that he had also been going through a tough time recently, so I tried to secure further work for him with City associates of mine. He accompanied me to many meetings over the coming months. Meanwhile, Jim had secured a letter of intent from one of his many contacts for the £100 million to buy West Ham. Then, just days before Christmas in 2009 I received a late night call from America.

'Hello? I'm sorry for calling so late. Is this David?' asked a quivering female voice.

'Yes, this is David Byrne. How can I help?'

'It's Mary Bowe. Jim's wife', she said.

'Oh, hi Mary. Happy Christmas,' I said, with a slight slur after some decent wine with that evening's dinner.

'Jim's gone', she said, before bursting into sobs.

'Gone? Gone where?' I said, trying to make sense of the brief declaration.

'Jim died in his sleep last night of organ failure. I'm sorry, I have to go but I thought you should know as soon as possible.'

I sank back into the chair still holding the phone with the dialling tone telling me she had hung up. I knew instantly that the West Ham deal was dead. I also knew that the bright future that beckoned for the *Intermarket Group* was dead. But the greatest sadness of all; one of my dearest friends that I adored and respected was also dead.

Things went back to how they were, jumping from one small deal to another whilst trading a small personal account, wondering if I would ever get another chance at the big time. This went on for the next three years until one day, in the summer of 2012, I was heading up the escalator at Fenchurch Street Station in the City on my way home. Coming down the opposite escalator, smiling, was a familiar face. As we crossed paths and we spotted each other, recognition dawned. David's eyes lit up…so did mine.

'David! Wait at the top of the escalators. I will come back up to see you', he called. Orchard used the stairs instead of the escalator packed with commuters unwilling to give way. He bounded up the stairs like a man half his age. The silver hair, broad smile and the rosy cheeks were there, but there was a noticeable difference in almost every other aspect. The tie was eye-catching, the shirt crisp, the suit was dapper and there was no sign that his eyes were attempting to cover desperation. This was a man that had clearly turned the corner that I simply could not navigate to.

'How are you Mr Byrne? he enquired with mock formality.

Like two old Etonians bumping into each other, I replied in the same manner: 'Very well, Mr Orchard', although it was clear that I still carried the demeanour of a man carrying many worries.

'What are you up to these days?' he asked. 'Still involved in foreign exchange and trading?'

'Yes, indeed I am, although only some small own account stuff.'

'Would you be interested in doing some consultancy work? I have a big private company from Asia looking to set up in London. They have all sorts of questions and I think you could be a great help', he said.

'I would be delighted!' I bellowed as I almost ripped his hand off during our parting handshake.

'Ok, I will call you next week and arrange lunch and we can have a proper catch up', he called back as the distance between us increased.

'Oh, David!' raising my voice to be heard over the throng of people that had filled the space between us. 'What's the company called?' I couldn't really hear his reply but, assisted by a limited ability to lip read which we all possess to some degree, the words formed in my head: "EURO FX".

There passed a few weeks of emails going back and forth which consisted mostly of market-related queries from his client. What is the best software platform for trading Foreign Exchange in the United Kingdom? What would you recommend as the best disaster recovery set up for a FX broker? What is the process for being accepted by a liquidity provider and what spread would you consider appropriate?

The questions went on and on every other day. I was imparting my advice and knowledge but as yet had not been paid a dime. I eventually sent a polite email reminding David of this and the fact that asking me to do some consultancy does imply payment of *some* sort. His reply was an invitation to discuss an exciting opportunity over lunch the following day. He told me to join him at the *Island Bar and Grill* next to Lancaster Gate Tube Station. He was already seated when I arrived and had taken a guess that I still enjoyed a glass of Sauvignon Blanc. The décor was modern and stylish with neat sharp furniture, subtle colours adorning the walls, and there was an overall warm yet minimalist feeling to the place. We took our time ordering whilst having a proper catch up on what had happened in both our lives in the preceding four years. The starters arrived and the scallops melted in my mouth, the gentle lemon butter dressing making it almost impossible to resist the urge to let them slide down my neck before fully savouring their delight. The Sea Bass too was equally delicious, simply grilled with a subtle aroma of eastern spices, which got my mind refocusing on the matter at hand; his Asian client.

David asked me if I would consider the position of Consultant Chief Executive Officer for the newly formed London division of this company. I was overjoyed. This was totally unexpected, and I felt like all of my Christmases had come at once. It was explained that the initial salary would not be fantastic for a CEO, but that I would have very little to do in the first year. The client did not quite have everything in place yet but were so impressed with my knowledge that they wanted to secure my services at an early stage. He went on to say that dealing with them may be a bit strange at first as they were very secretive and protective of their investors and did not necessarily do things in a manner that I might be accustomed to. I said that I was eager to accept the offer but that I had very little experience as a CEO. He said that he would watch my back and make sure everything was done correctly whilst I learned the ropes.

I appeared to be exactly what they needed: I had an in-depth knowledge of the markets; I had previously enjoyed substantial media coverage and I had never fallen foul of the regulators. I had never even had a speeding ticket. But most importantly for them, which they did not say: I had never been a CEO and I was desperate for another chance to be a success again.

Chapter 6.   My new job

The first thing that needed to be done was provide all of the necessary information relating to me such as passport, proof of address and my NI number to Companies House. This was handled by a lady called Julie Cook who, at the time I did not know, was the sister of one of the biggest alleged fraudsters in the world. With the information provided to Companies House, I now became a director of the newly formed *Euro Forex Investments Ltd*. Even without David Orchard's guidance, I saw no problem putting my name to this subsidiary. It was to be a UK company, the sister company of "*Euro FX*". It held no bank accounts and was conducting no regulated activity so what could go wrong? I was summoned to 17 Hill Street, Mayfair, home to the offices of *William Grosvenor & Partners*, David Orchard's Company. It was here that I finally met Julie Cook and we proceeded to the *Punchbowl* for lunch, a very popular (and pricy) gastro pub, famed by the owner at the time, film director and then husband of Madonna, Guy Ritchie. After a sumptuous lunch accompanied by fine wine, pleasantries and face-to-face introductions were completed and we headed to Bruton Street. This is a very exclusive address just across Berkley Square from Orchard's office, and was to be my base during my short tenure as Consultant CEO and director of *Euro Forex Investment Ltd*. Our office was on the top floor and as we exited the elevator we were greeted by a very modern piece of art; a large silver orb with water cascading into a silver bowl, around which there was a Chinese inscription etched inside the rim. It translated roughly as:

> *When we reach the top of our world of*
> *prosperity, we must allow some wealth to flow*
> *down to the less fortunate.*

This area lead to a second reception accessed through a glass security door. This is where we were to later greet the many coach parties visiting from China, its walls decorated with a number of paintings and artworks (that I found out later had been rented at great expense from a local gallery). A second security door was off-limits to the clients. Through this door was to be the Operations Centre, though at that early stage the area consisted of a few sparsely furnished offices where a couple of staff and I had little to do for large parts of the day. I decided to install my own multi-screen set up to monitor the major currency markets in preparation for the client migration to the new, soon to be regulated, *Euro Forex Investments Limited*.

About one month into my year-long contract, I entered the office at Bruton Street. Sitting in one of the smaller meeting rooms was David Orchard, deep in discussion with a slightly portly mustached gentleman. I was beckoned to join them and was introduced to the stranger, Bryan Cook. Cook was a confident but fairly laid-back individual. There was a definite rapport between the two of them; the type of relaxed banter that only comes from years of knowing each other. They also had something else in common; the ability to talk for hours without really saying anything of substance. David explained that Bryan was there to outline the plans for the company over the coming year. I was told that his sister Julie Cook, whom I had already met, would be basing herself in New Zealand to oversee the setting up of a subsidiary to the London company. Being an offshoot of London meant that it would fall directly under my responsibility, so I was eager to find out as much as possible. It was explained that the intention was to apply for regulation by the New Zealand Financial Authorities. This was music to my ears as moving client monies from a totally unregulated environment into a regulated one can only be a good thing. Although I was aware that New

Zealand did not carry the prestige of the FCA in London, it was the quickest way to start steering the ship in the right direction. Bryan Cook also told me that I would need to visit New Zealand at some point once the client monies were ready to move over. In the meantime, he said he would like me to attend a number of events so that the clients could meet me as the person that would eventually be running the business proper. This seemed enough information for now as I felt that I would surely receive a detailed plan of action at some point. But this never really happened, and I was never to meet Cook again.

Two weeks later I received notification of my first trip. My email pinged and my inbox contained confirmation of a first-class ticket to Bangkok.

I arrived at Suvarnabhumi International airport at the beginning of January 2013. Once through customs I was greeted by an executive limousine service and taken to the *Peninsular Hotel* on the Chao Phraya river in central Bangkok. As I entered the lobby it was clear that I was expected as a rush of staff and porters descended on me and my luggage. I had expected to proceed to the reception for check-in but, relieved of my bags, the manager led me directly to the elevator and up to the top floor. The heavy mahogany double doors to the rooms along the corridor were spaced well apart, indicating substantial accommodation within. I followed the manager through a very plush reception room, through another set of doors and into a fully equipped office suite. But the tour didn't end there. Another set of doors led into an extravagantly furnished lounge area complete with sumptuous sofas, a dining table fully laden with crystal and cutlery, and a bar area stocked with a full complement of spirits, champagne and mixers of every description. It was only when I was told that the bedroom was through yet another set of doors that I realised this whole expanse of rooms was to be my base for the next few days. After the many facilities were explained to me in a speedy but thorough fashion, my host left me to my own devices handing me a gold heavily embossed envelope as he left.

I opened the letter to find an invitation to dinner at eight o'clock that evening in one of the hotel restaurant's private dining areas. I still had three hours, so I decided to unpack and take a shower. I deposited my bags on what can only be described as a super double king size bed and rummaged around for my toothbrush and other personal items (it's never the same using those provided by even the best hotels). I was dead on my feet and the thought of ordering a tuk-tuk to transport me across the huge bedroom to the equally large bathroom did not seem like an unreasonable idea. As I approached the bathroom door there was a small telephone on the wall with its light blinking at me. I was a little perplexed as to why I did not notice the message indicator on the larger phone beside the bed. I glanced back over my shoulder to find no matching alert on that device. So, I picked up the phone and was immediately greeted by a gentleman's voice.

'Good evening Mr. Byrne. Welcome to the *Peninsular Hotel*. I will send two of our very finest ladies along to assist in your bathing requirements.' Although this seemed like a very enticing idea, I was still a bit in awe of the grandeur of everything and who would be picking up the tab, so I politely declined the offer. The huge room had floor to ceiling clear glass panels affording a view straight across the bedroom and out through the panoramic windows of the Presidential Suite to the bustling streets of Bangkok. Although the room was way too high up the building to be seen into from the street, as I removed the last of my clothes my instinct was to flick the light switch to the off position. In my haste I actually hit an adjacent switch and all of the glass panels turned immediately opaque. I was fascinated by this and, like a child, spent several minutes just changing the glass from clear to frosted and back again!

I headed to the *Mei Jiang* restaurant down at the garden level of the hotel. I was initially surprised to be eating in a renowned Cantonese restaurant for my first meal in Thailand but when I was greeted by the *Euro FX* sales team who were all Chinese-Singaporeans, it suddenly made sense. There were ten of them in all and every one of them treated me with absolute reverence. The first thing that struck me was how young they looked. I assumed that their ages hovered either side of the thirty mark and one or two considerably younger. I guessed that this group had been instructed to make me feel welcome and that the tone of the evening should be one of boundless fun. The conversation was lively, and the drinks were already flowing by the time I had arrived. Most of the attention was directed towards me with one person holding out the chair where I was encouraged to sit as another questioned what my choice of beverage would be. Their attentiveness was extreme and I'm certain that if I didn't feel like washing my hands after the bathroom one of them would have handled my equipment for me before proceeding with his own post bathroom cleansing. A little later an eleventh member of their team turned up. He was introduced simply as Panda. I waited for an explanation of the cute nickname and perhaps his real name but nothing more was said. He too looked incredibly young at first glance, but on closer inspection he must have been in his mid-forties. His watch looked noticeably more expensive than those worn by the others around the table, and the expensive cloth of his suit had a beautiful sheen to it and hung perfectly. As Panda took to his seat his chosen drink was poured; sparkling water as (I discovered later) he was tee total. As he sipped from his glass, I couldn't help noticing an incredibly long nail extending from his little finger. This was a status symbol and established him as the most senior. In Ancient China, a man that did manual labour would have rough hands and short fingernails whereas wealthy or important people would have the opposite, soft hands and long nails. In the modern world long nails would not be practical, so the tradition adapted to having just one long nail on the least used digit, the little finger. It's not dissimilar to Elizabethan England where the wealthy would powder their faces and avoid the sun to prove that they were above manual work.

Panda was obviously the head honcho and one glance from him had his minions quaking in their Gucci shoes. They were all dressed head to toe in designer names, but in styles and decorative additions that I had never seen in Bond Street or Knightsbridge. A classic tailored Armani suit would, for example, be embellished with glittering embroidery across the shoulders, or gold braiding down the lapels and sleeve cuffs

The dinner was meant to be an ice breaker, but it took quite some time for me to relax. I was aware that not every joke or quip that I made deserved the raucous applause and cheering that it received. Far from making me feel comfortable I found the exaggerated adulation quite disconcerting. I am quite adventurous when it comes to trying new dishes and there were plenty arriving that I had never seen before. Although I sampled pretty much everything, I did have difficulty with the crispy whole sparrows, revealed by the removal of a domed silver lid that displayed their shrivelled bird-like forms only identifiable by their mangled beaks and twisted feet.

As the meal finished, we were then informed that our cars would be arriving in fifteen minutes to transport us to a surprise venue for an evening of fun. I asked if the owners of the company would be joining us but just received confused looks. We sipped cocktails in the lobby until a convoy of four blacked-out Mercedes Limousines arrived at the hotel. I was chaperoned into the first vehicle and, once all staff were seated in the accompanying vehicles, we were silently whisked away. We arrived at what looked like a plush office building, far from the bright lights of central Bangkok where we proceeded to the lift which managed to accommodate only half of our group. The button for the 20th floor was pressed, and we were elevated to our destination. Everywhere I had been so far seemed to involve the top floor and when the doors slid open 30 seconds later, I was confronted with the most elaborate and sumptuous reception area I had ever seen. There was colonial style furniture everywhere and every surface that could be was adorned in gold leaf. There were four enormous security staff, two either side of the double doors that were located at each end of the rectangular lobby. Directly in front of the lifts was a *Louis XIV* desk occupied by a stunningly elegant lady who, despite clearly approaching retirement age, had retained much of her beauty. She delivered what was far more than a practiced welcome smile; she clearly knew this group of high rollers.

A bell sounded and, as if by magic, two enormous doors glided open revealing a luxurious lounge area. Everything was as elaborately decorated as the reception area we had just left behind except this room contained double-depth soft seating positioned below silk tapestries that depicted exotic dragons soaring over mountain tops, ready to swoop on an unsuspecting village of beautiful women attending their gardens. In many parts of Asia and in their artwork, a man's appendage is depicted as a fierce dragon while the woman's equivalent is represented by a beautiful, fertile garden.

Money to Byrne?

The entire centre of the room was filled by tables brimming with literally hundreds of full shot glasses. The end of each table housed fresh bottles of vodka and whiskey waiting to be cracked. Staring down from the back wall was a three-metre television screen begging us to request the lyrics for the first Karaoke song. Much to my surprise the first words displayed were not that of any song. It simply said "Philippines". Then a secret partition concealed by a full-length waterfall painting slid aside and ten Philippino girls entered the room. They strolled around in a practised catwalk fashion before coming to a halt in a straight line with military precision. They were all smiling and trying to catch your eye, repeatedly raising their eyebrows as if trying to remove a fly from their forehead without the use of hands. Nobody made a move, so I just sat there and followed suit. Then the words "Hong Kong" appeared on the screen and the first girls silently left the room to be replaced by another ten Chinese girls. Two of my entourage seemed to have the same flying pest problem, before I realised that this was the signal that they liked a particular girl. Immediately two of the parade left their line and joined my colleagues on the sofas as the remaining girls left the room, no longer smiling. The contrasting looks on the faces of the chosen versus those not suggested that only the selected girls would be getting paid. After visiting another five regions of South East Asia all members of our party had a companion. All except me. Given my VIP status I was required to be chaperoned by two, and while I felt a little uncomfortable with their attentions, I was only human. They were absolutely stunning.

As the drinks flowed and inhibitions were forgotten, members of our company started singing. Overall it was great fun and not some sort of orgy. I was taught a popular game involving two dice and a leather cup. It became clear to me that all of the girls were experts at this game and my two companions were no exception. I soon realised that their task was not only to keep the drinks topped up but also to manage the situation. They needed us merry and spending, but not too drunk to take them home at the end of the evening. This would result in a reprimand or even losing their position at this prestigious establishment. Each time I lost a game I would be required to sink a shot. After easily winning three or four games, my companions would mysteriously land a bad roll allowing them to enjoy a drink. After several hours of this entertainment I was a little fuzzy. I felt I'd had enough, and I didn't want to embarrass myself, but at the same time I felt that not participating at the same rate as my colleagues might offend. One by one they would insist on a toast with me saying:

'Today is for fun and tomorrow is for work and success.'

At around 1am, Panda announced that we would be leaving. Ten staff of *Euro FX*, Panda, myself, and thirteen girls headed back to the hotel bar and shortly after arriving I seized the opportunity of a bathroom break to slip back to my room. I would not be missed.

Chapter 7.   A celebrity in focus

The next day was one of relaxation. The Singaporeans were nowhere to be seen. I was later to find out that being spoiled by year-round high temperatures and humidity they would choose instead to lounge around in air-conditioned spaces during the day or have meetings in the cool of their hotel suites. I myself preferred to do a little exploring of the local vicinity and to experience the culture of the Thai people and their buzzing markets.

Immediately upon leaving the refrigerated confines of the hotel I was hit by a wall of extreme heat. Within one hundred metres of the hotel my clothes took on an appearance that they had been worn in the shower, clinging to every available expanse of skin, like over-pasted wallpaper on a damp wall. Each moisture-laden particle of air carried its own aroma of local life. Amazing spices and chillies seemed to demand their own pocket of space between the stalls of the street markets. Periodically my nasal cavities were invaded by the smell of the inefficient drainage system or the recently caught fish rapidly succumbing to a heat-induced rotting process. Within half an hour an inexplicable exhaustion set in, regardless of how lazily I had been meandering around the streets, and the lure of a cool swim became overwhelming. Back at the hotel pool I was soon to get my first taste of the Beckamesque celebrity status that would be afforded me over the coming months. Although all five-star hotels around the world have a certain sanitised feel about them, the extreme difference in East/West culture still leaves plenty of room for the senses to be stimulated. It truly felt like I had finally achieved the A-list lifestyle that my ego had always craved. I was travelling first class, staying in the best suite in a fabulous hotel and there was no ceiling on my room tab. I was floating on my back, starfish mode, when two hotel staff came rushing over to the pool and pointed to the exotic native trees providing some welcome shade, whilst another two seemed to be shouting up at the branches. Voices were being raised and other guests were now sitting up to see what the commotion could be. After several minutes of the shrubbery being vigorously shaken, a Chinese man was unceremoniously deposited from his elevated hidey hole, his camera complete with zoom crashing to the floor. Seconds later two more photographers climbed down of their own free will and all of them were escorted from the premises having had their camera memory cards confiscated which, no doubt, contained pictures of me in a less than flattering pose.

Upon returning to my suite there was a message laying on my pillow. It was instructions for the big event that evening. I was to meet the team in the hotel lobby at six o'clock that evening for transportation to the convention centre at six-thirty. I showered, donned my dark blue suit, crisp white shirt, and red tie for good luck. I sat on the bed to rehearse my speech one last time before heading downstairs. I picked up my notes, but my reading glasses were nowhere to be seen. I looked behind the bedside table, under the bed and quickly scouted around the room. But they were gone. Time had now run out and I needed to head for the reception. They were all anxiously waiting for me and a few minutes later two police motorbikes arrived with blue lights flashing. As I stepped outside there were no less than five stretch limos with another two police bikes at the rear. As we glided away, I was told that the roads to the convention centre had been temporarily closed to ensure our swift journey. This now felt utterly surreal.

We were deposited at the rear of the event building and led by management to a holding area where there was comfy seating, canapés and an assortment of drinks laid out for us.

I scanned the room looking for any elderly statesmen-like characters that could be the owners of *Euro Fx*, but none were present. While I was still being treated as a VIP there was none of the previous evening's jovial banter. The mood was quite serious and each of the Singaporeans was organising everyone from the security to the caterers in a well-oiled professional fashion. Bear, the name used by another of the team who had been throwing up on the previous evening, was directing operations with sober military precision. After sipping one vodka to steady my nerves I surprisingly needed the bathroom. Not knowing exactly where they were, I headed for a set of double doors and as I opened them I was confronted with hundreds of guests in ball gowns and black-tie attire. Everyone started pointing and some made a rush towards me. I felt a pair of hands on my shoulders and I was dragged back into the safety of the holding room. I was in shock at the number of guests as I had been given no forewarning as to the size of the event. I had spoken at numerous functions over the years but only knowing these guys for one day brought on the feeling of being very alone. It was now 8pm and I was told it was time to make our entrance. The previously off-limits doorway was now swung open on silent hinges revealing a huge open space minus the lavishly attired guests. There were, however, four huge bodyguards and ten stunningly beautiful, petite bunny girls. I was instructed to take my position in front of an even bigger set of doors. The bouncers took their positions, two at the front and two at the rear. My female colour guard lined up, five either side of me and, as these doors finally opened, I was confronted with over a thousand guests applauding and cheering my name. There was a central aisle leading to a huge stage and above it, covering the entire back wall of the dining room, was a gigantic screen with my own incredulous image staring back at me. Fanfares began and the back of the room was lit up by a display of lasers and pyrotechnics.

We took to our seats which were stage front with a security cordon declaring that these few tables were for VIPs only, the middle one of which was reserved for the guest of honour: Me! The pre-dinner entertainment commenced with eight giant kettle drums being played with traditional ceremony and micro precision. It was a deafening spectacle. The horde of guests flooded to the cordon that was protecting us, eager to take closer photos of the celebrity entertainers, similar to *Blue Man Band*, but playing with an almost religious fervour and intensity. I suddenly felt arms around my shoulders again and camera flashes lit up our table. It was then that I realised they were trying to get photos with me. Further security personnel arrived to control the throng. Eventually everything calmed down to some sort of normality and at last it was time for the speeches.

Earlier I had informed Panda that I had lost my reading glasses and would have trouble reading my script without them. All the young consultants had 20/20 vision so borrowing a pair was not an option, and even if there was a pair that I could borrow it was unlikely they would match my particular prescription for short-sightedness. Panda came up with a solution and requested that I hand over my notes. He summoned Eagle, yet another animal nickname, and told him to take my speech to guest services and have it scanned and printed in a much larger font.

I felt panic setting in as the MC was coming to the point where she invited me onto the stage for the main event. I missed much of what she was saying, including the fact that I was being introduced as the CEO of *Euro FX* (not that of the sister company *Euro Forex Investment Ltd* from London that was my official role). As I heard my name announced Eagle appeared from behind me and thrust the speech into my hand. The much larger print meant that I was now carrying ten pages to the podium as opposed to the three that the original point twelve font had required. Quickly regaining my composure, I took my position, staring down at an expectant audience of over a thousand investors and I began my speech in English. Because each sentence required me to pause while it was translated to the audience by an assistant, the speech ended up taking some forty-five minutes to deliver, way longer than in my rehearsals. I couldn't tell if the language was Cantonese, Vietnamese or Thai (though it turned out to be Mandarin) and the speech seemed to be very well received. But there was something niggling at the back of my mind. The sentences that received the most raucous applause were the very same parts that I had insisted be removed when I had first reviewed the transcript. This enlarged script that Panda had given me made some pretty fantastic predictions. Ones which I was not comfortable with, but I had no idea how this mistake had happened. However, as the applause grew these concerns drifted from my mind and as I ended my delivery the audience leapt to their feet cheering as loudly as fans of the winning team in a World Cup final. After what seemed like a million photos I returned to my table and the security once again formed a protective line around the VIP area. A sumptuous dinner was served and an array of pop and TV stars from around Asia provided the entertainment. At the end of the evening I was encircled by ten security guards and a protective blanket was placed over my head to prevent my adoring fans from tearing hair or clothing from me as a memento of their encounter. Sitting in the back of the blacked-out limo I felt on top of the world.

Chapter 8.   Why can't I sleep?

As I boarded the plane for the flight home to London, I felt very strange. There was a knot in my stomach and a restlessness nagging at the back of my mind, akin to wondering if you turned off the cooker hob or closed the upstairs windows when you left the house. I took to my seat, indulged in a glass of red wine, ate a more than acceptable meal and waited for the usual drowsiness to set in. I was still restless, and the food had failed to remedy the uneasiness in my stomach. With plates, glasses and cutlery safely collected, the lights dimmed, and the cabin staff having asked those seated closest to the windows to lower the shutters, I changed into the unflattering complimentary pyjamas and reclined my seat to the full flatbed position.

Although there was a vast selection of films and on-board entertainment, these marathon three- or four-day business trips, including flight time, were exhausting. I needed sleep badly, but it simply would not come. My eyes were glued shut but my brain would not close down and I couldn't figure out why? I was so tired but felt if I succumbed, I would miss something of great importance. I could sense that this feeling of unease had a much darker undertone. Why was I feeling like this? It was then, after hitting a touch of turbulence, that my reading glasses slipped from my lap to the floor, and as I reached down to retrieve them everything fell into place:

When I had returned to my hotel room after the event, I was dead beat but had wanted to check my emails for anything important - in particular, messages from my kids. I remembered lying on the bed with my knees bent to form an easel on which to perch my laptop. I'd reached my hand out to the left, fumbling for my reading glasses. And this was the problem that was nagging at me: they were precisely where I had left them. They weren't missing!

I know it sounds fantastic and possibly paranoid, but could this have been orchestrated? I remember Panda looking disturbed that I had insisted on changing the speech. Could he really have instructed that I be given the original non-amended text when I was handed the enlarged font version of the speech at the conference? Were my glasses deliberately moved from my room, forcing me to rely on this non-approved version? I questioned my assumptions, telling myself that perhaps one of the maids or concierge had found my spectacles and returned them. But this was, to my mind, highly unlikely. Hotel staff depend on tips to supplement their meagre incomes and would almost certainly have made sure I knew who had found them. At the very least there would have been a note or a message on the phone informing me of their discovery.

I landed back at Heathrow with a list of questions for the Orchards that required answers. After a far more satisfactory sleep back at my apartment I headed to Bruton Street with the first thing on my 'to do list' being a phone call to their secretary to book an appointment. The Orchards always appeared to be the busiest people in the world and as such one had to follow protocol in order to see them. I called their number and spoke to the young lady that handled their hectic schedules. I was informed that both father and son were on business travels in Hong Kong and would not be back for a week. This just added to my frustration and confusion. The frustration is obvious, but what did give me pause for thought was, why were they not at the event being hosted by surely their biggest client? Country hopping around South East Asia is a very easy and common practice, with few destinations more than a couple of hours flying time. David Orchard could and should have been there.

I was booked in for a meeting upon their return in a weeks' time and when it came, I felt it went well. They explained that they were only involved in the running of staff and offices for *Euro Forex Investment Ltd* in London, and as such had no reason to attend the *Euro Fx* functions in Asia. Everything therefore seemed in order and then I was informed that we had been approved by the regulators in New Zealand. This was great news and one step closer to completing my first task of providing a safe vehicle to accept all the client monies from the parent company.

Chapter 9.   The gang of five

Time moved slowly as I waited for information I had requested from the Singaporeans as well as keeping tabs on the currency markets and sending financial reports to the consultants for distribution to our trading rooms in Asia. I eventually received notification of the next event that I was to attend. My tickets were booked on British Airways but this time the destination was to be Macau via Hong Kong.

I arrived at Hong Kong International, or Chek Lap Kok airport, on the 12th of April 2013. Chek Lap Kok opened in 1998 after the closure of its predecessor, Kai Tak Airport. The new terminals are mostly built on reclaimed land and, although still providing a very impressive visual approach to Hong Kong, it is not the same as the adrenalin rush delivered by the sweeping approach to the old airport. I came through customs remarkably quickly but then had to endure a long wait for the connection to Macau. Hong Kong was returned to Chinese ownership on the 1st of July 1997 and is increasingly ruled by Beijing. It is in fact known as a special administrative region with British citizens still being afforded a great amount of respect.

It was 7am as I headed for the hydrofoil transfer terminal. The first departure for Macau was not until 11am so I had quite some time to while away. After doing several tours of the duty free and food outlets my eye was drawn to a glass structure in the middle of the concourse. It appeared to have smoked glass windows and nothing to advertise its purpose. There was a constant flow of people entering and leaving, so my curiosity was piqued. I strode to the entrance and pulled on the glass door which immediately turned from opaque to clear and a vast plume of smoke billowed out into my face. It was in fact a smoking room of about ten square metres with at least fifty occupants puffing away.

Eventually the time came to depart for the turbojet ferry which takes about an hour to reach Macao. There is now a bridge system near completion that links Hong Kong, Macao and mainland China, greatly reducing travel time. After an uneventful journey along the Pearl River delta, and having cleared the minimal customs, I was met by my personal carriage that would take me to yet another five-star hotel.

This time my accommodation was in the *Four Seasons Hotel* on the Cotai Strip where all the main hotels and casinos are based. Once again it was a fabulous suite on the nineteenth floor, but it was not the best room. This was reserved for Panda, the head of the consultants. Why he required such opulent surroundings became clearer later, but for now I unpacked and decided to go for a walk to get some sort of idea of my bearings. There was a strange familiarity about the Cotai strip. I had been to Las Vegas on a number of occasions but didn't expect to see so many of the same hotels in Macau. In fact, turnover in this gambling mecca far outstrips that of its counterpart in the United States. At the end of the strip were less well-known hotels that offered other sorts of entertainment and, although not blatantly advertised, it was common knowledge that any sexual desire could be accommodated in this area. Just a short stroll over a bridge led me to the old part of the city which still retains its Portuguese influence. In fact, the territory was only returned to China by Portugal in 1999 after being used as a trade port since the 16th century.

Even though this part of Asia has a far more temperate, kinder climate than that of Thailand, I soon became weary after the long flight and I hailed a cab back to the hotel. I entered the elevator to find myself surrounded by Chinese gentlemen in what looked like a cross between modern expensive attire and that worn by ancient noblemen. I was curious why the two mammoths in black tie gave me scrutiny but did not join the strange ensemble in the cubicle. I was further surprised to see that the only button lit on the panel was for the nineteenth floor. My floor! I exited the lift and took three strides to my room, almost directly opposite the elevator doors. I pretended to be hunting for a lost key in order to see which room these guests were going to although my instincts already knew it would be suite 1949, the number that corresponds with the year the communist party finally took full control of their country, and the room that Panda occupied. At either end of the corridor on our floor were two more mammoths guarding the emergency exits. It didn't take much imagination to work out what the angular bulges in their jacket pockets were.

The event the next evening was another spectacular occasion. Magnificent indoor fireworks, celebrity entertainers, hostesses and a similar amount of guest as at previous events. Once again, I was kept hidden away in a holding room until my grand entrance as the keynote speaker. However, on this occasion there were five more VIP tables than usual, one for each of the gentlemen in the elevator the previous evening plus their guests. Their elaborate multi-coloured silk attire would not have looked out of place at the courts of the Ming Dynasty. The camera flashes were giving them more attention than me for a change, with a permanent gathering of people restrained by the security ropes and guards. Later that night I was personally led and introduced to each table in turn in another change to the normal proceedings. Usually people queued patiently to be presented to me at *my* table but his time it was *me* who had to use some shoe leather to do my rounds of these five tables. All of the guests stood and bowed at my approach, but not the main guys. They were clearly of some great importance, but none spoke a word of English and I was told next to nothing of who these people were, just that they were "very important dignitaries".

There was another addition to the proceedings which was greeted with great fanfare. There were ten names read out from the audience and these people were invited onto the stage. They were, apparently, the ten most successful introducers raising money for *Euro FX*. As each name was called that person was presented with the highest quality three carat diamond to rapturous applause. I have no idea what each diamond cost, but they were truly stunning and seemed to be dancing out of their presentation boxes, coming to life under the flashing lights and glitter balls suspended from the ceiling. I was then invited back on to the stage and thanked for all my hard work in steering the company to imminent greatness. Eagle, the number two consultant, appeared on stage holding a painting which was then delivered into my hands to thunderous applause. It was a landscape by Wu Guangzhong who died in 2010 and is considered to be the founder of modern Chinese painting and one of the top ten artists of all time from that part of the world. When I returned to my table, one of the consultant's gofers took the painting to be carefully wrapped and sent to my home address. That was the first and only time I laid eyes on the painting.

As the event drew to a close the five dignitaries and their entourage were ushered away, chaperoned by their personal security and Eagle. The other consultants were arranging transport to yet another high class KTV to feed their appetite for booze and girls. I decided I needed some "me time" so returned to my hotel. I wasn't really tired; I just needed some space and time to think about the night's events. In the end I descended to the lower floors which housed an enormous casino. Despite having been involved in the financial markets for some thirty years and contrary to the implied stereotype, I was not much of a gambler. In fact, a day at the races or indeed the casino felt very much like a busman's holiday. However, this night I fancied a small flutter on the roulette table, remembering a basic system told to me by a friend.

It involves blocking off sections of the wheel, with number 32 as the banker. I put a few chips on 32, split a few chips on 0 and 3, split 32 and 35, and placed one chip on 15, and one on 19 and 26. This basically blocks off a stretch of seven numbers on the wheel. If a single number comes in it pays odds of 35 to one, paying for the whole bet. If 32 comes in, then its payday. I meandered around the roulette tables looking for three things: First, a spare seat, which were few and far between; second, a spare seat at a table where the minimum stake was not too high, as twenty-dollar chips while looking pathetic in comparison to these high rollers, were plenty big enough for me; and third, a board devoid of evidence that number 32 had recently hit. I found my space and five rolls later I had accumulated just over one thousand dollars. Even when trading, I do know that luck can play a part, so I had no problem in quitting while I was winning. I counted my lucky stars and walked away with a healthy profit.

I took the elevator to the nineteenth floor and headed to my room. I heard voices from room 1949 and thought I would look in and maybe have a nightcap with the boys. I poked my head through the door but could see no one in the first reception. The conversation was clearer now and, although in Chinese, was most definitely of a cheery nature so I proceeded to the room that was the source of the noise. As I entered, I saw five tan briefcases laying open on the dining room table. Each one was packed with hundred-dollar bills. Each must have contained two hundred thousand dollars, so perhaps a million in total. Just sitting there. Just then one of the consultants came out of the bathroom and froze. He shouted something in Mandarin, though not directed at me as indicated by the slight turn of his head toward the bedroom door. There was some bumping and crashing accompanied by girls' voices and the piercing illumination given off as the bedroom light was frantically turned on. Panda appeared in the doorway wearing nothing but a mixed look of surprise and rage. He strode forward seemingly unaware, or unashamed, of his personal valuables on display. I was escorted out of the suite and the door was slammed behind me. I stood for a moment wondering if I should try the bell and make my apologies for the intrusion. But I decided to mind my own business and returned to my own room.

The next morning, I woke and made myself coffee still amazed at what had occurred the previous evening. The concierge knocked on my door and handed me an envelope. I opened it and withdrew two tickets. The first was my hydrofoil pass back to Hong Kong, the second my flight ticket back to London on British airways. There was also a short note signed by Panda which read:

"Dear David, I am so sorry if I seemed rude or disrespectful last night. I did not want you to think bad of me for liking to play poker with my important guests. I was very, very lucky and believe this is because you bring us all good luck. Have a safe journey home and thank you for your efforts."

I showered and packed my bags before heading down to breakfast. I saw Michael, the very friendly concierge that had been most helpful during my stay and the same guy that had delivered my tickets. I gave him a decent tip and asked if he had seen any of my colleagues that morning. He told me that they had all left for Singapore earlier and that the other special guests would be leaving shortly as he had just arranged their transportation. He told me that they were very important politicians from mainland China. I thanked him and took to my table in the restaurant for a full English breakfast. As I was dipping my self-sculpted bread soldiers into my over-easy eggs, I saw the five men heading for their Limousines. Each of them carried a tan coloured briefcase.

Chapter 10.   Time for some advice

Once back home, life soon returned to a period of boredom and frustration. Information I had requested seemed either incorrect or simply didn't arrive. I decided to call a couple of friends and book one or two luncheons. Apart from a well-overdue catch-up, I also wanted to get their take on what was happening at *Euro Forex Investment Limited* and *Euro Fx*. The first lunch was with a good friend, a super intelligent guy and someone I've known for over twenty plus years. We were to meet at the *George and Vulture*, one of the oldest restaurants in the City of London. Although a very famous establishment it was rarely visited by tourists due to its almost clandestine location, tucked away in a series of alleys just behind Cornhill. In fact, the entrance to the alley is almost directly opposite the *Royal Exchange*, which is where the Futures market was housed in 1982 and where my career proper began. It is also where I first met my friend when he was an options trader and market maker. The *Royal Exchange* has a long history of facilitating the dealings of the City. The original building was destroyed in the Great Fire of London with the current structure being rebuilt in the 1800s. It is indeed a grand building and has often been mistaken for the Bank of England, the "Old Lady of Threadneedle Street", which is just across the road. We would frequently cross paths during our day-to-day dealings and I would often seek out his no-nonsense counsel. Although he was born in Zanzibar and moved to England as a child, his Cockney accent is as authentic as that of someone born within earshot of the chimes of the Bow Bells (the widely held definition of a "true" Cockney). He also had a tendency to deliver his views and assumptions in the most direct manner. And that is what I needed: The point of view from a trusted friend who understood the complicated world of finance.

Money to Byrne?

I entered the restaurant and my friend was already seated in a corner booth, his senses already perceiving that I might have things to discuss of a private nature. There was a gin and tonic waiting for me, and a bottle of house red had been de-corked and allowed to breathe. There is a limited choice of wines in the *G&V*: Red or white. That's it! The menu is also fairly limited but consists of traditional fare that has been served at this establishment for centuries. A plain grilled steak accompanied by bubble and squeak would be a typical meal. This side dish of mashed potatoes and vegetables refried on a pan was originally a peasant dish but is now a firm favourite with the City suits. By the time we had finished dessert of Welsh rarebit, basically a roux textured version of cheese on toast drizzled with Worcester Sauce, I had relayed all of my suspicions and concerns.

'Ok', he said, 'How well do you know the people that gave you the job?'

'Pretty well', I said. 'I met Orchard some years ago and he did some legal consulting when I was trying to buy West Ham. He was a really nice guy but had had some bad luck and was desperate for work'.

My friend then asked, 'Where are they based?'

I told him they had an office in Mayfair close to my own office in Bruton Street.

He said, 'Honestly Dave, if you are not completely comfortable you need to think really carefully about continuing. Set a deadline for delivery of the things you've been asking for and for God's sake, copy every document you can to your private email.'

As we left the restaurant, he shook my hand, made the usual, "See you soon" pleasantries and then paused. 'Dave, watch your back. This doesn't sound right to me. What if it's a bloody big scam and you are being set up to take the fall!'

Over the following week or two I was getting uneasy and decided something needed to be done. I acted on his advice and began Bcc'ing myself on any correspondence from the group, but unexpectedly, things looked to be taking shape. I had confirmation from Julie Cook that the bank accounts were now open in New Zealand and were ready to take in funds. The regulation to accept and manage client monies was active and we had secured an office space, complete with a manager to get things rolling. Once again, I felt excitement about the coming year, a part of me still believing that I was to be the head of a global powerhouse.

Chapter 11.   **The final event**

I then received another fantastic boost. I was told that I would soon be delivering good news to the clients; the systems and banking were in place and we were ready to receive the transfer of monies from Asia to the new regulated vehicle in New Zealand. I was elated and satisfied that my concerns were almost certainly just phantoms in the dark corners of my mind. I was sure that my friends had all misjudged the situation.

The next trip was planned for the beginning of August 2013 in Manila and I was really looking forward to delivering this good news. I felt once again very comfortable to be talking at these gala events. However, there was a bad hurricane that had swept across the Philippines causing mass disruption and flooding, so the consultants decided to rearrange the event to take place later that month, but back in Bangkok. This was a problem for me as I had already arranged to take a vacation with my youngest daughter. She was twenty years old at the time and I had not decided on a suitable destination. Panda contacted me and suggested that she accompany me to the event. They offered to pay for her flight as well as our extended accommodation in Thailand as a gesture of gratitude for disrupting our family plans. We were over the moon to be spending time together and, although there would be a few days of work to be done first, it was a great location for a vacation. I was also excited for her to experience the event, with her dad as the VIP guest of honour. The trip got off to a great start. A limo from home to the airport, the first-class lounge and seats on the plane, the usual blacked-out top of the range Mercedes to greet us in Bangkok complete with uniformed driver.

But that's where things began to change from my previous adventures. As before, the car delivered us to the *Peninsular* in downtown Bangkok but this time the driver delivered us to the back of the hotel and took us straight to our rooms through what only can be described as the service entrance. We were greeted by Bear who explained that the clients had been gathering in the reception, hoping to obtain photos and autographs from me. He said they were arranging to have them moved on to ensure our privacy. At the time I was wondering just how much further my celebrity status would reach though of course later I found out that this was far from the truth of the real reason for their presence.

There was noticeably increased security surrounding the whole group as we travelled to the venue. An armed guard rode in each limo that was transporting us. We still had the police escort fore and aft of the procession but never before were individuals actually sitting opposite us in the cars with firearms visible and ready in their hands. This was passed off as a precaution because there had been some recent demonstrations by the People's Democratic Reform Committee, which on occasion had been violent. That movement, led by MP Suthep Thaugsuban, eventually resulted in the removal of the incumbent Prime Minister, Yingluck Shinawatra. As with everything involving the *Euro Fx* collaborators, every concern was met with a plausible explanation.

But there was another oddity: we were heading to the venue a full three hours before our usual departure and some four hours before the event actually started. Once we arrived though, things seemed almost back to normal. We were taken to a holding room which was embellished with a greater and even more lavish variety of food and beverages. There was Beluga caviar with Crystal champagne, and a selection of fine whiskeys served from a special table by a Scottish gentleman complete in kilt and a knowledge that spanned the centuries.

Money to Byrne?

Two chaperones entertained my daughter as I was summoned to a smaller private room where Panda was waiting. His greeting was warm and affectionate unlike the last time I saw him in all his glory at his suite in Macau. After the usual introductory chit chat the mood turned serious. He explained that in the interest of the clients, and being prudent with their monies, the new course of action was to continue the dual hedge strategy once sufficient funds had been procured. He went on to say that to continue successfully would involve the doubling of staff that were capable of managing the investments in both Singapore and New Zealand. As such, a decision had been made to suspend all trading accounts for a three-month period while half of the funds for the Asia accounts were transferred in full to the regulated vehicle in New Zealand. They also informed me that I had a very different speech to deliver, this time containing the shocking information that had just been disclosed to me. I leapt off my seat in a rage, virtually screaming in each and everyone's face including the head honcho, which more than surprised his lackeys. No-one had ever spoken to the main man in this way. As I glared directly into his eyes, he remained calm and smiling. He told me not to worry and that everything was fine.

He explained that any of their loyal clients could opt out and reclaim their investment at any time, with the cleared funds back in their personal accounts within three days. I asked why this piece of information was not included in my proposed speech. It was then his turn to be outraged. But his anger was not directed at me it was directed at his underlings. He told me that this was an unforgiveable oversight by his staff and that my speech would be amended immediately.

Having reviewed the amended version, I was happy to go ahead. I was also told by him that an additional statement would be made by Eagle, explaining that any investors with less than thirty thousand dollars deposited could visit a designated desk at our hotel in the next two days, where staff would reimburse them with cash, or a pre-paid debit card linked to their account should they wish to withdraw from the program. Those with more monies invested could attend the same desk and fill out a withdrawal form or, if heading home, could complete a form on our website. How could this be a scam with such open accessibility to retrieve investment in such a short period of time?

I returned to the main holding room to be reunited with my daughter before it was time to enter the main hall. This time, however, we did not go through the double doors to great fanfare but were taken via the service corridor, where all the chefs and waiters were lined up as if on some sort of military inspection. There must have been two hundred event employees; one hundred either side, at attention, backs against the walls. It felt like a cross between a wedding procession and a troop inspection; they were all clapping in unison but with their eyes avoiding mine, focused directly in front of them. It was only as we neared the end of the alley that senior chefs and managers were permitted to step forward to shake my hand. I'm sure now that this entry route was taken for my own safety and to avoid the possibility of irate investors demanding answers from me.

We arrived at curtain right and were announced on stage. There was much applause though nothing like at the previous gala dinners. And as I concluded the speech, I asked the audience to give a show of hands if they were happy with the situation. My invitation was met by almost total silence. No hands were raised. Gone were the cheers and standing ovations that usually accompanied my deliveries. No camera-toting fans were rushing to snap my picture. The tension in the room was palpable.

Rather than exiting the stage via the steps in front of the podium, I was ushered off by the same route that I'd entered. Then, as I reached the wings out of sight of the guests there was quite some commotion going on. I turned my head to the source of the noise and saw some security guards pinning two men in dinner suits to the ground. Another guard had a rifle trained on the back of the protesters' heads while two more were securing their wrists in handcuffs. I was taken to our front of stage table where we were served food and entertained but the atmosphere was somewhat flat. We all left the event much earlier than on previous occasions and to much less fanfare. During the drive back to the hotel I was informed that my daughter and I would be transferring to another hotel more suited to a vacation in Thailand, and that the Singaporeans would be heading home the following day. The next morning as I went to check out, I was asked to pop into a side room to show my face for a few minutes. The team were assembled at desks providing statements of accounts and, in some cases, debit cards to those clients wishing to withdraw their funds. Despite the strange occurrences of the past few days - entering the hotel by the back door, the guests' muted response, the altercation in the wings and the early exit - it looked like *Euro Fx* was honouring its promise to its clients.

I had a wonderful few days with my daughter doing all the usual touristy things including a visit to the floating market, an elephant ride, an evening watching the Thai Boxing, and lots of sight-seeing. The trip was over all over too quickly and the memories of this exclusive time together gave me strength later but, as we headed home to London on another thirteen-hour flight, sleep would not come easily.

Chapter 12. Should I stay or should I go?

Never had the lyrics of this iconic Clash song, *"Should I stay, or should I go?"* been more poignant in my life. Something still felt very wrong, but I desperately wanted this to turn out well. Was I in too deep, swimming against an increasing current of possible corruption, slowly drowning? Was I was kidding myself that I could sort everything out and quash any incorrect practices? How much did the Orchards know? I never seemed to get a straight answer to a straight question. At best they must have known more than I did. After all, they were paying the staff, paying for the offices and the day-to-day running of things. But It was me that was standing up in front of investors and it was me who was the potential target for everyone to shoot at if things went to the wall. By September 2013 I had the growing feeling that I should resign. Everything was in place in New Zealand to accept and regulate the *Euro FX* clients and I continued to perform my duties, attend meetings and prepare for either an exciting future … or give my reasons for leaving. I set a six-week deadline for things to right themselves. This simply did not happen and on 15th October 2013, I decided to tender my resignation. The Orchards stated that they thought things were at best unusual or not in perfect order, and they supported my decision to resign. My last day at the company was the 31st of October, completing my initial one-year commitment.

Pol, one of the staff told me that the website stated that *Euro FX* was being bought out by a bigger entity. When I opened the webpage, this statement was posted by senior management. I had not been told anything about this and there were no actual individuals named. I asked Orchard what he knew, and his reply was, "very little" but he did state that Bryan Cook wished me to remain at the company for a few more months for a considerable increase in remuneration. This was to expedite the transition, tidying up *Euro Forex Investment Limited* and handing over the reins … to whom, I did not know. I declined the offer. Orchard respected my decision saying he totally understood my reasons. The next day, 1st November 2013, I found out that *Euro Forex Investment Limited* was to be wound up. Why would the sister company of an entity that was being bought out be wound up? I figured that I had made the right decision as the apparent mess was too complicated for a debutant CEO to address.

I visited both offices one more time and sat down with the six staff individually. It seemed no surprise to them that I had resigned as I had given enough hints in recent weeks that I was less than comfortable. There was a dark cloud hanging over both offices, the type of sombre mood that grips any company when things start imploding. The staff at *Lehman Brothers* must have felt the same way before they were told to gather their belongings and exit the building at Canary Wharf back in September 2008 when the first fall-out from the financial crash became publicly visible.

The client visits had ceased and there were no more functions planned. On recent visits to the Orchard offices there were different clients being entertained and there seemed to be no activity relating to *Euro Forex Investment Limited* at all. Staples, pencils, stationery, even coffee was no longer being replenished. Nobody checked to see if staff were where they were supposed to be. Unlike myself, whose contract had expired, the staff were to be paid another few months' salary and they were no longer required to turn up for work. Each one of them seemed happy with that and the mood immediately picked up. Little did I know they were already attending interviews for new jobs. This was to be a good Christmas for all of them, starting new jobs and being paid by two companies. Unlike me, however, none of their names would appear in negative social media and no disgruntled investors would be hunting *them* down.

In February 2014 I decided to take a trip to Singapore to see if I could find any of the consultants who had organised the events. I was still unsure who was responsible for what? I had a number of friends still working there and I arranged to meet with a couple of them to catch up and also to see if there were any work opportunities available. I would suggest the venues for the meets, being establishments that I had frequented with the consultants as I had hoped to run into one of them. I knew it was a long shot as all their phone numbers had returned an unavailable message, but I still clung to the thought that this could have been because they were company devices and been subsequently returned or disconnected. A good friend, Jason, said that there were many work opportunities in the region but, if I was associated with a massive scam, this would be the last place I should be based.

It was a Friday morning and I was due to meet Jason at the *Raffles Hotel* the following Sunday. Its location on Beach Road can be confusing as the shoreline is some distance away after years of reclaiming land from the sea. *Raffles* is one of the great hotels of the world and exudes a charm that more modern establishments, with far better facilities, seem unable to achieve. The white marble winged façade with arched windows and red tiled roof gave an immediate impression of walking back in time. This feeling increases as you pass the doormen in military-style white jackets with matching turbans and black trousers. There are shaded walkways with gently rotating fans designed to give welcome relief from the heat and humidity in the days before air-conditioning. Most rooms are arranged around a central courtyard with passageways leading to the hotel's fine eateries and bars, the most famous being the Long Bar where a certain Ngiam Tong Boon invented the Singapore Sling cocktail a century ago when this island was part of Malaysia. The fare offered in *Raffles* is outstanding, in my opinion, and the equivalent would come at a horrendous cost were we in London or Paris. The brunch was fabulous and after catching up on old times, our stomachs full to capacity, I confessed my concerns to Jason.

I said to him, 'When I joined *Euro Fx* in November of 2012, I was keen to add my market experience and input to their system and, if at all possible, improve the trading program to produce greater results'.

I explained that I had been spending many hours analysing the markets, sending my observations to the team, hoping that I would be contributing to the overall success of the company. Now, after leaving, I was unsure if there was a "black box" system that placed the trades or whether that was carried out by data crunching human geniuses. The huge events I had attended, full of happy investors, suggested that money had been pouring in, that profits were good and that the introducers were being paid (or at least being shown impressive amounts of dollars accumulating in their accounts). Incredibly though, it now seemed that client money had simply been stolen. Was there one rogue trader, or were darker forces at play with a criminal plan from the beginning? The biggest unanswered question for me though was how many people were in collusion? Was it a couple of senior guys or was everyone, except me, part of a massive scam?

Jason asked if *Euro Fx* had a dealing room in Singapore. I was certain they did. In all my time with *Euro Fx* I had only been taken through a dealing room on one occasion. It had appeared to be a very impressive setup, located next to Orchard Towers on Orchard Road in the luxury retail district of Singapore. I remember thinking how strange a coincidence the location's name was. It had been just before the last event and had had convinced me that this was a proper professional operation. I decided that the following day I would go back to see if there was still some activity.

I approached the reception and said that I might be interested in leasing some space, asking what options were available. I said that I had visited the premises the year before and particularly liked the office space on the 20th floor. The receptionist told me that this had always been the show office and was only used to attract customers. When I told him that when I had visited it was a fully functioning office with at least fifty staff he insisted that I must be confused and asked for the specific dates. Then, after checking his records, he assured me that for the week in question a film company had hired the 20th floor space as it was making a short movie about trading and dealing rooms.

Surely, he must have been mistaken. I had seen enough dealing rooms in my time and was convinced that I'd have spotted any anomalies. TV shows and movie makers never quite get it right to the trained eye. On my previous visit the office had been filled with dealers and phone brokers. There had been screens with live prices flashing away. It had looked like an authentic dealing room with traders busy talking to clients, although admittedly not speaking Mandarin I had no idea what they had been saying. I decided to take a tour of the show-office anyway to see for myself and a sales representative escorted me to the elevator. I entered the office for the second time in my life to find it mostly empty. There was an elaborate Chinese tea set arranged beside a modern coffee machine with biscuits placed on mock Ming saucers. But there was no electronic ticker tape flashing currency prices and no whiteboard with the day's upcoming financial data. And there were no phones or computer terminals, no dealers, in fact no evidence of the operation I had witnessed months previously. I returned to my hotel, called Jason and told him of my discovery. He asked if I was sure that I had the correct location. I assured him I had. Then he said:

'Dave, with the amount of money they had at their disposal, it would have been easy for them to stage the whole scene. That ties in with what the reception guy said about a movie being made'.

He suggested that they must have contrived the deception for the benefit of reassuring both me and the investors and recommended that I take the next available flight back to England.

I was shocked by their audacity and the lengths to which they had appeared to have gone to convince me of the authenticity of the operation. I acted immediately on Jason's advice and booked my flight home for the following morning.

....

Just prior to the Singapore visit in 2014, I had spent a wonderful Christmas, enjoying family time and basically doing very little as I contemplated my next move. Once the new year arrived, I began jobhunting but was quite sure that I did not want a Chief Executive role just yet, or if that was even possible. I felt that the experience at *Euro Forex Investment Limited* had, at best, left a bad taste in my mouth. At the time, and even immediately after my departure, I thought that perhaps my guidance or business directives were not clear enough, that this was why everything seemed to be slow or off track at the company. I now wished that this had been the case and not what was being alleged, a massive scam. I was doing some small, own account trading as a stop gap and had applied for several senior positions with City institutions. Not one of my applications had got past Human Resources, and the replies were unusually curt, the typical response being something like, "Unfortunately, you are not a suitable candidate for our company", rather than, "We are looking for slightly different skill sets", or even "You are overqualified for this position." It could only mean one thing; the scam had hit social media.

I googled *"Euro Fx"* and the page just filled with Wikipedia descriptions of the Euro currency, such as when it had replaced the individual tender of many European countries, which countries had adopted the new centralised system, and some comments on the British Pound remaining outside of this Euro club. I then typed in *"Euro Fx scam"* and my jaw almost hit the floor. There was a whole page of headlines and it took me a good five minutes before I summoned the courage to click on one of the headlines.

"Thousands of potential victims ask British police to investigate Euro Fx and Euro Forex Investment Ltd (EFIL)."

Then the next:

"Chinese authorities look for assistance from British to unravel smoke and mirrors pyramid scheme, Euro Fx."

And another:

"Takeover of Euro Fx by FX Cap just another attempt to hide a scam."

Money to Byrne?

As I clicked on each one, I saw my name included in the first paragraph as a key figure. There were pictures of me on stage at gala events, pictures of me with the Asian sales team that organised the functions, and even some videos of the events. These videos made me feel physically sick. I was making promises that I believed to be true based on the information that I had been given. But the information that the speeches didn't contain was that a high proportion of the yield return was being derived from a corporate bond that was helping the company expand globally. I had easily swallowed this lie as the two plush and expensive London offices seemed to be clear evidence of the expansion. The omission of this information in the speeches only served to incriminate me.

I was still in contact with David Orchard, the person that offered me the position and paid my salary throughout my tenure. Was his legal consultancy firm part of the whole debacle? I contacted a Moroccan friend that had introduced me to Orchard in the first instance. He no longer lived in the United Kingdom and during our phone conversation he told me that they were no longer friends. He warned that I should be careful but refused to elaborate any further.

I called another old friend and briefed him on the current situation, asking if I could bend his ear over a pint the following Saturday. We had kept in touch over the years and he had not changed at all since school, thirty-four years ago. He worked in the City in London, but I knew that a pint and a burger down his local would be far more appealing to him than a posh meal near his workplace. We agreed to meet at *The Drill* pub in Essex which suited me, as the clientele would not know or care what we were discussing, unlike many of the nosey, incestuous rumourmongers in the Square Mile. I entered the pub to see him standing there with two pints of Stella on the shelf and a stack of one-pound coins on the pool table. It's not that he did not intend paying full attention, it's just that the mild distraction of potting balls had always helped our discussions to flow easily.

We smashed the balls for the first frame before he said, 'Looks like you've got yourself in a bloody big hole, mate'.

I poured it all out, with only the occasional interruption between shots. When I'd finished, he simply gave me two short pieces of advice: Go to the police and offer any cooperation possible, and do not go to Orchard. He wisely stated that it would only be a matter of time before the Serious Fraud Squad came knocking and it would be better if I went to them first. He added that, in his opinion, it seemed obvious that I had been set up as the fall guy, and if the people that gave me the job were part of the scam then they were the last people I should speak to.

I took his advice and the following Monday I contacted someone I knew at the Serious Fraud Office just off Liverpool Street. When we met, he told me that there had indeed been contact from a foreign victim's group and the Chinese authorities about my old company. He said that initial inquiries had concluded that there was no evidence investments had been procured from these shores, that no UK citizens had been affected, and that no regulated activities were unlawfully being conducted in this country. As such, they would be taking no further action at this point. This was a great relief, but I felt a tremendous pang of guilt that these poor trusting people who had been scammed were to receive no assistance from the UK.

I had worked my way up the ladder the hard way. It now looked like thirty-three years of study and toil would culminate in the end of my financial career. I decided to keep a low profile. Perhaps I had no choice. I felt sure that over time, after the next headlines grabbed the attention of the backstabbers and gossipmongers, *Euro Fx* would soon be long forgotten.

Chapter 13. Two years and counting

By the end of 2015, two years after resigning from *Euro Forex Investment Limited*, I had been making a modest living, providing technical analysis to companies in the City, doing some small own account trading and dipping my toe into a number of ventures, both as an introducer of investments to money and vice versa. Since the demise of open outcry trading, where hordes of brokers shouted and screamed prices face-to-face, the participants had dispersed into many different jobs. Those with no desire to embrace the new computer era went back into the education system, several became, and a couple joined the Financial Conduct Authority, while others retrained as electricians or taxi drivers. There were a number of occasions on my way home from the City when I had been engaged in conversation by my cabby asking if I remembered them from the trading floor. The funny thing is they looked far happier and content than back then.

Those that stayed in the investment business had tried to adapt as best they could, but some were ruthless. Knowing you had contacts but were suffering from bad publicity was an opportunity for them. They would be happy to meet; buy you lunch and make a promise of looking after you for any introductions. But, gone were the days where the trader's motto of "My Word is my Bond" was honoured. You would set up a meeting only to find out later that the two parties had done the deal, cutting you out as the middleman. Even to this day, supposedly reputable companies welsh on Introducing Broker Agreements (IBAs). A deal would be done, and you would receive remuneration for a period of time, but increasingly the agreements had small print containing a get-out clause where the company could keep the client but no longer pay you commission.

Money to Byrne?

This happened to me whilst in China the following year. I had introduced a long-standing client to a broker (who shall remain nameless) who did just that. My client was from Chicago and a friend of many years, and much work was done by all to accommodate the complicated structure of their company's business. Once my situation hit the news, the broker exercised their right to cancel the agreement stating that I was not of suitable integrity to have a relationship with their company. I had not been charged with anything and I was not barred by the Financial Conduct Authority. However, they correctly assessed that I would not have the funds to instigate a legal case against them. My client and his customers were happy with the service and I would have lost face disclosing these events to them. These days this is a common practice and, unless you have the funds to fight them, you just have to accept that your commissions have a limited lifespan before the client is lost. The term "legalised theft" springs to mind.

Many years before, I suffered a similar setback but, on that occasion, I was forewarned. A contact named Fuad put me in touch with some very high-ranking Saudi advisers. Fuad's business was to arrange special visas and passports, concierge services, and every other VIP luxury to visiting dignitaries coming to the UK. He presented a fantastic opportunity to spend a couple of months in Morocco where I would meet many people that controlled billions of dollars. Half my time was spent in the *Es Saad Hotel* in Marrakech. As well as the standard hotel rooms and executive suites they also had a number of private villas in the grounds. I was staying in the Sultan's Villa, a huge apartment with a butler and private pool which, apparently, Mick Jagger had checked out of just the day before. I was summoned to the *Robinson Hotel* in Agadir some three hours' drive away and a car was sent to pick me up. As we left Marrakech, the Atlas Mountains disappearing into the distance, I was extremely excited about meeting these dignitaries and their Royal masters. We arrived at the *Robinson* around midday. It was a nice hotel but, surprisingly, not quite as plush a residence as I had been expecting. It turns out that the Saudi Royal entourage were staying here being very close to a palace owned by one of the Saudi Princes. I learned that Morocco was a common stop off for the party en route to, and from, European visits. They would be able to let their hair down, drink whisky and partake in other activities banned in Mecca or Riyadh. When I had checked in, changed and showered, I headed down to the marble-floored reception area. It had been totally transformed. Tonnes of sand had been piled onto the floors and there were mannequins on surf boards suspended from the ceilings. The Saudi host had decided that a beach party was in order for that evening, but as he did not fancy a chilly night outside, he had the beach brought to him. Fuad picked up the fifty-thousand-dollar bar tab that night. The following morning the reception, complete with gleaming marble floor, was back to normal. There was no trace or evidence of the previous night's festivities. Not even a grain of sand.

This was not an isolated example of such extravagance that I witnessed whilst among this oil-rich entourage. I had become friends with the nanny to one of the senior dignitaries' children. She had left some hair serum and a treasured hairbrush, a gift from her mother, back in London. The normal situation would be to contact the hotel and ask them to forward the items to your current address. But no; a two-hundred seat Boeing aircraft with one sole passenger was sent back to London to collect the items and return to Agadir!

I suggested a number of investments opportunities to these people, several of which were executed, but I was rarely paid in full. Fuad's warning was this:

"They will try to make you wear many of the previously agreed costs, threatening a cessation of future business if you do not agree."

You would have little choice but to comply if you wanted to continue servicing their needs. I knew I had accumulated an immense amount of knowledge when it comes to markets and investments but, doing the deal with these people and protecting your interests was a whole new ball game. Even in the strictest regulated environment, wheels would just stop turning without the employment of a certain level of trust: Trust in your colleagues, trust that requested information would be forthcoming in a timely fashion, and trust that any bad eggs would be exposed. It was this type of trust that was to be the root of my problems whilst at *Euro Forex Investment Limited*. I was told that I would be guided and protected, assured that anything I was asked to do would be checked and rechecked by Orchard, and that anything I was asked to sign would be scrutinised by compliance advisors. To a point this did happen; company formations, applications to the regulators, health and safety documentation and so on. But the speeches I later delivered contained misinformation that had been backed up by falsified documents from Asia. I did not know, nor did I suspect, the things I was promising to be non-truths.

Chapter 14.   What am I to do now?

Having attended many job interviews and been completely up front about my previous employer, each occasion was now met with a polite thank you for attending and an apology that I was not suitable for the position. I knew what was going on. Most brokers were heavily relying on acquiring new business from China. That is where all the new business was to be found and having someone on the team associated with *Euro Fx* could be very damaging to the acquisition and retention of client process. I was way overqualified for a minor position that would be far from the attentions of Chinese clients, but they could not afford the potential fallout by offering me a frontline directorship. To pay the bills I did some consulting and managed some small funds, but if my name appeared on any company's websites, the victims would file a complaint and my services would be abruptly terminated.

I did still have quite a number of good friends and sympathetic associates who valued my market knowledge and expertise. Through one of these contacts I was introduced to a gentleman from Hong Kong by the name of Leo Sui. Leo was almost a caricature of the atypical Chinaman from a time gone by, cringingly depicted in Hollywood movies as a wise and happy sage with answers to all of life's mysteries. His face was coursed with laughter lines and his permanent grin made his lips struggle to keep purchase on the ever-present cigarette. It was always difficult to tell if he was about to offer some profound advice or crack a joke, though either would always be worth waiting for. Having met in the summer of 2015, we had really bonded over the next six months and he tried to help me out by introducing me to his many contacts. I would often meet him for Dim Sum in his favourite Chinese restaurant in Bayswater, *Royal China*. The lunchtime dim sum menu was by far the most popular, with queues for a table spilling out onto the street during the lunch hour. On each visit most patrons were of Chinese descent, a sure sign that the food was both high quality and authentic. In fact, one of the most popular dishes there is crispy chicken feet, a dish I had not seen in any other oriental establishment in the UK. Leo was married to an English lady and spent a few months a year in his London apartment which was his wife's permanent residence. I discovered that Leo had been Chairman of the Hong Kong Gold Exchange for some twenty years but was now retired. He was held in high regard by senior members of many institutions both in London and Asia. As with many retired people from the world of finance, especially those that reached a senior status, turning your back on power lunches was difficult to do. He thrived on discussions about the price of gold or the Dollar Index whilst dining at an old haunt. It was in December 2015 that he asked me to meet some representatives of a new Chinese broker that would potentially be interested in paying me for some consultancy work. After an initial Skype call and several emails, it was arranged for a group of senior officials of the company to visit London from Shanghai. This took place at the *Grange Hotel*, Tower Hill in January of 2016, close to where I was then living in East London close to the City. The company was called *ABS* and their party included the head of marketing and the head of sales as well as one of the senior partners. We got along very well and they seemed impressed with my advice and my answers to their many questions. A month after their return to Shanghai I was contacted and offered the position of Chief Executive Officer for *ABS Group*, London.

Leo was fully aware of the *Euro Fx* debacle and I asked him if I should appraise *ABS* of that situation as this had not come up in our meetings. He advised that I mention the situation, but only to elaborate if asked. I had nothing to hide and brought the subject up in an email, explaining why I had resigned from *EFIL*. Their only question was how long ago this occurred? After hearing that it was a few years ago and that no action had been taken against me, they swiftly moved on to when I would be available to start working for them.

Part of me was so excited to be given another chance, but there was also a massive knot of concern that I could be jumping out of the frying pan and into the fire. I truly believed that I had much to offer and that I could do an efficient job as a CEO. I knew in my heart that it was a clever collaboration of crooks at the centre of the *Euro Fx* failure, and my doing anything different would not have changed the outcome. But this was another opportunity from China and the narrative was much the same: Wealthy investors, a top-notch team with ambitions to take the financial world by storm and a request for my expertise in leading the London operation. The whole scenario was almost identical to that of *Euro Forex Investments Limited*. There were obviously alarm bells going off, but the overriding factor was that I was in desperate need of this opportunity and the introduction was from Leo, whose reputation was beyond reproach. I pondered things for a couple of days and came to a decision. I would take up this job offer if they were prepared to meet my conditions. I told them that I would happily sign on the dotted line once I had met the directors, the senior staff and visited all of their offices, both front line and support. If they would show me fully staffed offices, introduce me to the key people and provide enough background for me to perform due diligence, then I would be overjoyed to join the operation. They agreed to this in an instant and I was invited to a gala dinner in Shanghai on the 23rd of April 2016.

It had been many months since I had my last communication from the victims. I was still nervous but felt that I could prove beyond doubt that I was not knowingly complicit in any fraud. I went back over the emails and press releases. I put all these communications along with supporting documentation into one file that would show that I was in no way a fraudster. I then confidently relaxed and began to look forward to the Shanghai visit

In the days leading up to the Shanghai visit I couldn't help but re-read the note containing the shocking accusations that had been stuffed under my apartment door in 2014, and another later email from an Outlook account, titled "UK Fx Victim", a request to meet in London. At the time I did not think this would be a good idea. Surely, if they were in London they would have spoken to authorities, and it would be that safer environment where I would be called to answer questions. The people behind the emails had still not identified themselves and I was worried that any victim wishing to meet me without a police presence might have more dangerous intentions than just asking some questions. I remember speaking with friends, and even David Orchard, as to what they thought I should do regarding the request. All of them agreed I should avoid this confrontation and instead wait for the UK officials to conduct any interviews. Therefore, I decided not to meet them out of fear for my own safety. In response to this decision I received an email in April 2015, and this time it was signed: "Chao Ma".

(Exact copy of communication)

Subject: RE: EuroFX

Dear Mr Byrne,

I reckon this is to say you have decided that you will not meet with me.

I have to say that I am disappointed with your decision, but I respect you must have had your own considerations. Your 'consultants' – whoever they are – might have told you that there are nothing you need to be worried about because you are 'innocent'.

Here are what I want to tell you - not to your consultants, not to the company but just to you.

First of all, you will not be able to just walk away from this, at least not as easy as you thought. Remember, you were the director and the CEO, you served as the spokesman for this fraudulent company. You might not know the conspiracy at the time when you joined, but you will be a key person during the investigation. If there has been no fund made to you as promised and that's the reason why you resigned, why didn't you perform your duty as a director and tell the stakeholders about the company's status and your concerns? Instead faking facts that you slept only 4 hours a day because you were too busy managing the money.

I believe you recognise a few faces in the arrest warrants I have sent you - you once shared wines and glories together. They were your 'colleagues' and 'managements' who looked after your business in China. Do you think they knew about this fraud in the first place and decided to go ahead with this operation? No, they did not. However, as a consequence they are captured by the police for interrogation now. The only thing they did wrong was listened to you and referred too many people. Do you have any idea how many victims know no one in this scheme but you? Almost everyone has some pictures or video evidences about you. Even if you are innocent, you will be the first person who takes the blame.

It is true that most of the victims are in China and you are in the UK. Frankly speaking this does added a layer of difficulty to the case. However, I believe you are not naïve to think no investigation will be made on you. Especially when the UK and China is trying to form a good international relationship now. China and the UK have already signed the treaty of Mutual Legal Assistance in Criminal Matters. Sooner or later, you will have to face the consequences. It is going to be a time bomb for you and l assure you, it will explode.

In the meantime, we will start looking for media exposures. We have not done so because we did not want media to interfere in yet and we wanted to get more time for you. Since you do not want to cooperate, I hope you are ready to get famous again, for the same company, but with different titles.

*Saying this***, I hope you understand I do still believe you are innocent and was framed.** *That was also why I wanted to meet you and know the truth and are still writing to you right now – I can communicate with the police, so they do not investigate in you but look for the real criminals. Why was William Grosvenor & Partners hired you? Who promised you that you would have funds? Who instructed you to give all the speeches?... Even if it turned out you are innocent in the end, do you really want to go through all these investigations, questioning and media exposure? As a finance manager I believe that is not the kind of risk you would like to take and affect* *your career.*

I understand we may not meet each other before I leave, but I would still like to leave you the choice of explaining everything and providing supportive evidences to us. Feel free to contact me at any time if you ever change your mind.

Regards

Chao Ma

Chao Ma claimed to represent many hundreds, if not thousands, of Chinese victims and seemed sincere in her intentions to obtain some answers. At the time I was still of the mindset that it may have been a trap; likely some sort of assassin, or at least someone with the intent of doing me harm. That is why I had decided against meeting. Chao Ma said she was an elderly lady from Shanghai and as such presented no direct threat. Her email clearly indicated that she had returned to London and had no intention of giving up the pursuit of justice. I did take heart from the fact that, although there were many accusations in the text, she also showed clear indications that she believed me to have been tricked into making false representations on behalf of *Euro Fx*. Had I decided to meet this lady I would have been better informed and perhaps taken a different path in the future, including accepting this latest job offer, but instead I decided to keep my head firmly in the sand, hoping, but not truly believing, that it would eventually go away. Of course, I knew that the bad publicity and my involvement in the company would forever be in the public domain, but I also knew that yesterday's news soon became old hat. My life was currently in limbo and I was convinced that I either had to take the risk of the visit to China or just walk away for ever from the world of finance. I didn't feel I could throw away over thirty years of experience and start anew at the age of fifty-two. It was just not a viable option, so I packed my bags and applied for a travel visa. Even this application process had my mind playing games. If I was on a watch list would they refuse me entry, or would they relish the opportunity to arrest someone who, to their mind, was a potential criminal? Would I be met at passport control by security guards, or by Interpol waiting for my plane to land? As strange as it may sound, I think there was something deep inside me that hoped for a situation where I could prove my innocence; hoping that perhaps then my life would return to normal and I could finally put the whole episode behind me. The express visa arrived with a two-year multiple entry pass. Part of me was excited that I was given the all clear, perhaps a moral victory. But there was also a feeling that I would have welcomed a refusal as that would have taken the decision out of my hands.

I arrived at Pudong Airport, Shanghai on Thursday the 21st of April 2016. As I approached the border control my heart rate quickened considerably. The intimidating military-style checkpoints reminded me that if the Chinese authorities had a problem with my involvement in *Euro FX*, then this is where I would find out. On doing a quick double check of my landing card I realised that I had no idea where I would be staying and there was a blank space demanding an answer. A young silk trader that had been my new thirteen-hour companion on the plane was still within sight. He had built a fantastic business buying exotic high-quality materials very cheaply from remote areas in China and then selling them at a considerable mark-up to the fashion houses in the south of France where he lived. I spotted him ahead of me and made my way through the throng of impatient bodies shuffling towards immigration and relayed my dilemma. He provided a pen and the address of his hotel which I rapidly filled in on the form. Problem solved.

Immigration was incredibly slow, and several people were apprehended at the passport desk. My heart now felt as if it were trying to jump straight out of my chest and onto the inkpad of the Chinese official stamping the passports. However, in spite of my trepidation, everything went smoothly. Even so, once cleared for entry, I had to rush to the bathroom to splash water on my face, calm myself down and stop myself emptying the contents of my stomach in the sink.

I reminded myself that having been offered the CEO position with a new rapidly growing Chinese brokerage, I would insist on seeing every part of their operation and meet every member of staff before accepting the role. I would take nothing on trust ever again

After leaving the bathroom, taking deep breaths and allowing my pulse rate to normalise, I scanned the crowd for the plaque saying "David Byrne, ABS Group." There he was, directly in front of the exit waving enthusiastically and holding the sign in one hand whilst his eyes and head did rapid movements between my approaching mass and the photo that he was juggling in his spare hand to confirm that I was his intended passenger. As the distance between us shortened, a big knowing smile spread across his face, satisfied that he had found the right person.

'Sir, Mr David Sir. Can I take your case, Sir? We have a limousine waiting, Sir', he said with an almost imperceptible bow accompanying every mention of the word "Sir".

I was humbled but ego dictated that I assume the posture and conduct of a very important person. It's one of those things you look back on and cringe at but have an inability to refrain from repeating whenever in these situations. I think it's a way of convincing oneself that the tough times are finally over, that you have arrived in more ways than one. My small suitcase was deposited in the trunk of a very smart long-wheelbase Mercedes AMG. There was enough space for ten more cases of the same size as my compact wardrobe consisted merely of two suits, two shirts, two tee shirts, a pair of swimming shorts, sandals and my highly polished *Church's* work shoes. I was, after all, only anticipating a one week stay in the Peoples Republic of China. We drove in silence for the one-hour journey to the centre of Shanghai and as we approached our destination and crossed over the river, the Bund in all its magnificence came into view. Futuristic buildings reached for the sky, drawing the observer's eye away from ground level where majestic architecture from a not-too-distant past defiantly retained their pride of place. We arrived at one of the many five-star hotels out towards Beijing Road West, halfway between the financial district and the area that housed the foreign embassies.

Things were looking good again. I was in a fantastic hotel and I had a potentially bright future with *ABS Securities*. The hotel was wonderful, but it was with some relief that the extravagances lavished on me by *Euro Fx* were not in evidence. It was a comfort to me that while my accommodation was luxurious, it wasn't over the top and this prudent expenditure indicated this to be a legitimate enterprise, not a free-spending scam. I was still very cautious though as there were a number of similarities with the reception I'd had with *Euro Fx*.

For instance, our first engagement was a "meet the top team" dinner which reminded me of the time when I first met Panda and his entourage. Although *ABS* had hired an entire restaurant, on this occasion it was quite a small, humble establishment and certainly not the most expensive in town. There will always be certain things in evidence when at any function in China: Bottles of Chinese wine, more akin to schnapps, branded with the company logo and placed on each table, the obligatory branded goody bag with a brochure, some logo'd pens and other useless novelties. The food was traditional and of a very good standard but once again could hardly be described as lavish. The evening drew to a relatively early close as we had a busy schedule planned for the next day. All in all, I was pretty happy with how things were developing. The team seemed very pleasant and their attire was of a business nature with no evidence of bespoke Gucci suits emblazoned with diamante. Also, several of the staff were proud of their background, moving to *ABS* from institutions such as *FXCM* and *Abu Dhabi Securities*, well known establishments in the financial industry.

The next morning, after a light breakfast in my room, we assembled in the Lobby. I accompanied one of the partners, Anthony Yu and Joe Li, a director and head of sales, on a short stroll to the impressive Coca Cola building in the financial district. On entering their offices, we were confronted with a large reception desk complete with a giant *ABS Securities* logo on the wall. A sharp left turn revealed a bank of meeting rooms on the right with the boardroom straight ahead. There was a smoked glass wall on the left blocking off the noise from some one hundred telesales brokers. I was led to the last room on the right where the majority shareholder, Mr Liu, was waiting with the rest of the senior staff. They were all seated on comfortable sofas which were arranged around a traditional Chinese tea service. They take tea drinking very seriously in China and the whole process was quite ceremonial. I was handed my business cards which read, "*David Byrne, Chief Executive Officer, ABS Group, London*". This was a little presumptuous of them, but it was difficult to keep an ear-to-ear grin off my face. Gazing out of the window, I took in the vastness of Shanghai for the first time. There was a distinct point in the distance where the highly illuminated city buildings gave way to literally thousands of grey, drab, high-rise blocks of flats. I was told that approximately twenty-eight million people live and work in Shanghai and that this number often exceeds thirty million when taking tourists into account. To put it in perspective, that's almost half the population of the entire United Kingdom. In one city!

After about half an hour, where heavy discussions were conducted in Mandarin leaving me in an awkward position of feigning interest but understanding nothing, the first non-Asian member of the team entered the room and was introduced to me. His name was Brad, a very amenable and suave Australian. He informed me that in the afternoon we were to visit the second *ABS* office in the region, a much bigger office but, in the interests of cost-saving, situated in the suburbs. Brad took me to lunch before we met an *ABS* chauffeur in the car park of the main office. On our ride to the suburbs, Brad opened his briefcase and took out a pad and pen, informing me that he needed some more detailed information from me as he was handling the regulatory application with the Financial Conduct Authority in London. It was quite refreshing to see a slightly old-school approach, scribbling notes with a fountain pen as opposed to tapping on a tablet. I gave him great detail about my experience and work history, elaborating on my time spent with major institutions. I brought up the situation with *Euro Forex Investment Limited*, saying that I had been a consultant CEO and that I had left within one year. I knew that this subject would have to be revisited when, or just prior to, the application for regulatory permissions were submitted in London. I did not see this as a problem as I had not been barred from registration and I would also have some time before that to prove my value to the company.

We arrived at the second office building which was not exactly what you would call impressive on initial inspection. The paintwork and décor had seen better days and there were no glitzy lights adorning the entrance. Once inside however, I was blown away with the size of the operation. There were two full floors of phone brokers with upwards of one hundred bodies on each level. Apparently, the rent on this office was less than half than that of the smaller office in the centre of the city. I was now not only happy but more excited than I had ever been. I would definitely accept the job offer. I was told that the team would be dining at a Moroccan restaurant that evening and the following day would be one of rest. During the dinner I was seated next to Joe Li and I confirmed my decision to him, explaining that I was more than happy to accept the post having seen their operation. Joe laughed, telling me I had only seen the tip of the iceberg. He said the next day, Friday was to be one of rest and on Saturday we were to hold a gala dinner at a resort in the outskirts of Shanghai where I would be expected to make a speech prior to being presented with my contract on stage. He then went on to tell me that starting on Monday we would be going on a two-week tour of China visiting all their offices. I needed to change my return flight as I had originally planned to return to London no later than Tuesday.

I had been to Morocco on a number of occasions and the food in this restaurant was as authentic as anything served in Marrakech. Even the dancers looked to be true Moroccans, though this was more of a party where guests were encouraged to join in with the gyrations and gesticulations. I have never been one to partake in dancing, even at weddings. But Brad and the rest of the team had no such inhibitions. I always take great pleasure in seeing others do so and secretly wished I could sometimes let my hair down in the same way. It was a truly wonderful evening and I was in a superb mood.

I spent most of the Friday pinching myself whilst calling and emailing friends and family with the good ne

Chapter 15.   Heaven for a day

It was Saturday 23rd of April 2016 and, once again, I found myself in the back of an executive saloon being driven towards the resort for our gala event. I discovered from my driver that the company owned three of these corporate limos (which was another difference to *Euro FX*, who must have just hired cars and drivers as and when, knowing that they would only be needed for a limited period).

As is the norm in Shanghai during April and May, the heavens had opened, and torrential rain was bouncing off the windscreen creating a deafening aqua applause. The hotel complex was in a beautiful setting with lakes and waterfalls surrounding the main building. Several Koi ponds were threatening to burst their banks, spilling their treasured gold and red inhabitants into the path of the cars approaching along the palm-bordered driveway. The building itself, being of a low construction, was camouflaged behind a multitude of plant life with only brief reflections of glass invading the spaces between the leaves.

As we pulled up under the sheltered car port in front of the lobby and the chauffeur opened my door, there was an unmistakable feeling of déjà vu. A crowd of investor 'groupies' were waiting by the glass sliding doors; cameras and iPads held high above their heads like the winners of the World Cup showing the Jules Rimet trophy to their fans. I was a "celebrity in focus" again and my stomach became a lepidopterarium, housing a thousand butterflies. Under normal circumstances I wasn't prone to nerves, but at this very large event the possibility of a *Euro Fx* victim being in attendance seemed a real possibility. Yes, there are millions of people in Shanghai, but this was a specialised event for the nouveau riche and that increased the potential of a confrontation immeasurably.

Money to Byrne?

I checked in and headed to my room on the fourth floor, next door to Brad's. We freshened up and made our way, in casual attire, to the main ballroom where a buffet had been laid on. At each turn en route I would be approached by an investor to have their photo taken with me, and each time my heart would skip a beat. We arrived in the ballroom to see hundreds of clients, filling their plates and glasses. As we sat down to eat, the word had spread that ours was an important table and soon enough a crowd had gathered, photographing every moment as each morsel was transported from plate to mouth via chopsticks. Most snaps were taken of me struggling with the traditional utensils, causing a flurry of camera clicks and laughs every time a prawn or mushroom slipped from my amateur grip. I was still nervous that at some point an irate investor would break through, screaming about my previous employer. However, everything went smoothly; no potion slipped into my beer, no poison darts firing from a camera lens, and no stiletto slipped between my ribs as I mingled in the crowd! My paranoid mind had gone into overdrive seeing potential dangers where there were none.

Following the buffet, I unpacked and relaxed for a while before taking a self-guided tour of the hotel and its grounds. It was truly magnificent. I could only imagine what a wonderful time one could have if it were not for the miniature Niagara Falls spilling from the clouds. In fact, if you closed your eyes, the huge raindrops seemed to be playing a timpani ensemble as they crashed down on the wooden bridges and lily pads.

I headed back to my room, showered and slipped into my business suit for the evening event (to be held in the main ballroom). Entering the room for the second time that day, I was struck by the transformation of the place; the casual buffet arrangement set out for the lunch was now rearranged for a formal dinner with silver cutlery and crystal glasses. There were one hundred tables each with place settings for ten people. At the front, and parallel to the stage, was one straight table, where the *ABS* team and I would be seated for the pre-dinner speeches.

One by one, existing senior staff took turns on the stage, delivering proclamations of future success for the company and its clients. I was uncharacteristically nervous as usually by this point adrenalin and focus would have taken over. But, knowing that my new employers would be watching the attentive crowd, I was gauging the reaction to my first delivery on behalf of the company, wondering if their money had been well spent. I did my best to give a strong performance knowing that spaces between sentences for translation could kill the momentum of my message, a scourge suffered by many a President or politician. The trick was to speak slowly allowing the interruptions to assist the power of suspense of your next sentence. And it worked. After receiving a standing ovation, I walked back to my seat and for the first time truly relaxed. Surely if there was to be an outburst from any victims that moment seemed to have passed and, after the post speech dinner, Anthony Yu asked me to join him on a round of the guests' tables. I was told that at each and every one of the one hundred tables we were to drink a toast of Chinese wine. I thought I must have misheard. A hundred drinks? This was not humanly possible! When Anthony confirmed the instruction, I asked if we would be dividing the task by visiting fifty tables each. Maybe we would be drinking water at some or perhaps only toasting at random tables. He explained that treating guests differently would be taken as an insult, so we were to drink the same at every table. I was relieved to find that the amount of Chinese wine in our two glasses was so minimal as to be a gesture, but that what mattered and we progressed through the audience, table by table, toasting and sipping. By table ninety-nine though, my eyesight was becoming a bit blurry. Not only from the wine, but also from the hundreds of camera flashes I had had to endure. But then the strangest thing happened, and even Anthony seemed confused. Table "100" had left the event. Their food untouched. The wine bottles uncorked yet full to the top.

Chapter 16.   The Arrest

The next morning, I packed my bags having arranged to meet Brad for breakfast. Before I left my room there was a knock on the door and I opened it to see a lady from the reception desk. She asked if she could quickly take a copy of my passport. This normally happens on check in not when you are about to leave, but I thought nothing more of it and went down to breakfast. I apologised to Brad for keeping him waiting and explained about the passport. He told me that he had not received this request and I wondered why I'd been singled out; perhaps they would ask him as we passed reception. As we finished our coffee and headed for the lobby everyone was waiting outside for our transportation to arrive. We were about to join them when Joe Li told Brad to wait with the others, then asked me to join him for coffee.

I took a seat. The conversation seemed strained, and other than the usual pleasantries he didn't really have anything to say. I heard a sound, glanced to the window and suddenly saw blue flashing lights. Four police cars screeched to a halt on the concourse and eight officers exited the vehicles, guns drawn, and sprinted into the hotel. The colour drained from my face, my breakfast was making its way back up my throat and my hands started shaking. I knew that they were here for me.

Two officers waited by the reception while two more walked to the back of the hotel café where we were sitting to block off any attempted escape. A couple more approached our table.

One of them told Joe Li to explain that I was to accompany him to the police station while the other took hold of my bag. I didn't need anything to be translated as it was clear what was going to happen. I was relieved not to be placed in handcuffs but, as the policeman holding my small travel case was still brandishing his gun, I'm sure they knew that there was no need. As we exited the hotel there was a group of ten Chinese, both men and women, waiting for me to pass by. They were pointing fingers and saying things in a muted but animated fashion. These people that had called the police were evidently the same people that had left the event early the previous evening, presumably victims of *Euro Fx*. One of the men stepped forward and said in broken English, 'You are a criminal and are going to prison'. He later dishonestly stated in an interview with Reuters that it was *he* who grabbed my suitcase and wouldn't let me leave. He also said that I had seemed incredibly calm. I have no doubt that it must have looked that way to the throng of onlookers, but I don't remember feeling calm at all. The truth is I was in shock. Moments later I was in the back of the nearest of the four officer's cars and en route to the local police station. On arrival a few minutes later, I was guided to a small interview room and was relieved when Joe was permitted to wait with me, as not one officer spoke a word of English. We sat patiently for several hours whilst victim after victim arrived at the station to make statements against me. I was then questioned about these allegations for another couple of hours. At this point I was treated quite well and part of me still believed that once I had answered all the questions I would be allowed to leave. I needed a bathroom break and the toilets were out in the public area of the building. Four officers chaperoned me and, as we passed through the security doors, it became obvious that this was for my protection rather than to stop me from escaping. A lynch mob had been gathering and the number of victims waiting to vent their anger had now risen from the original ten to over fifty. I later found out that another vigilante group had raced to the departure gates at Pudong airport with the intention of preventing me from leaving the country should I be released. After using the less than hygienic facilities I came back through the door to be confronted by a news reporter from Reuters thrusting a microphone into my face and requesting a statement. I gave the obligatory "no comment" and returned to the interview room. All I could think about is what my family would do when they saw me plastered across the news channels and in the tabloids, the way Nick Leeson's had in the wake of the Baring's Bank collapse a few years earlier. The thought of my family finding out about my predicament on British TV before hearing a word from me was unbearable and my concern now was for my loved ones and the victims, no longer for my sorry self. Another two hours must have passed before I was told I was being taken to another police station, one that handled major crimes. My heart sank even further as I was led out of the back doors with a coat over my head and a ring of five policemen surrounding me.

On entering the second police station any hope of being allowed to return home soon quickly evaporated. This was a very scary place and the attitude of the officers was far more intimidating. Even the original officers seemed reluctant to make eye contact with my new charges as they passed responsibility. Added to this, Joe Li was no longer allowed to stay with me. I was in deep, deep trouble and completely alone.

I was taken to a cell area which could easily have been a prison from Victorian times; everything was filthy, including the ill-fitting uniforms of the four guards supervising the ten cells, seven of which were already occupied by an assortment of scary, pitiful characters. One particularly dangerous looking individual repeatedly threw his whole body at the cell bars whilst trying to deliver a saliva bomb across the fifteen feet to the guards' desk. A lady, probably in her thirties, sat rocking back and forth mumbling away to no one, a small trickle of blood oozing from one of the many puncture holes in her arms. It was like Bedlam. I was unceremoniously deposited in the cell at the far end of the room which thankfully left two empty spaces between me and the next detainee. I had to hand over all my possessions as well as my shoes, jacket and belt. It was damp and cold and it was now twelve hours since my arrest. I was exhausted; physically and mentally spent and I soon found myself dozing on the single bench in my ten feet by six feet cage. After a while I was roused from my fitful slumber by a clinking noise as one of the guards entered my cell. He spoke to me in broken English.

'You are a very lucky man. Come with me, you are now free to go.'

I leapt up off the bench, my relief palpable. Then the guards burst out laughing.

'This very funny joke, yes?' They were playing with my mind. I was going nowhere!

I lay back down but could not find the escape of sleep again and eventually I was led to an interview room where I was told to sit in what can only be described as a giant baby's highchair. I climbed onto the seat with my feet dangling a good ten inches from the floor. The legs of the chair had steel braces attached which were then secured around my ankles. This overgrown baby chair also came complete with the fold-down tabletop which, when lowered, put pressure on my stomach. This wooden surface was thick and solid, designed for restraining adults not babies having dinner tantrums. The handcuffs, secured by chains, were clamped tightly to my wrists; tight enough to cut off some circulation but not cause visible damage. There were six people in the room including myself. The lead investigator sat directly opposite me. His side kick, ready to type the questions and answers on an old PC, sat to his right. An interpreter sat on a single chair to my right and another strolled around the room puffing his chest out like a peacock. Another officer would occasionally leave the room, returning with more files and documents.

It felt like everyone wanted to be in on the arrest of the century. Peacock and the officer seated to my left had clearly been watching too many old American cop shows;

whilst peacock strutted around, preening and brushing down what, to his mind was very snazzy attire, the guy on the PC just stared at me, scowling, playing the latter of the good cop/bad cop cliché. The lead investigator could only be described as evil. He had mastered a practised stare that immediately made you feel as if everything you were saying was a lie. His eyes were pitch black with no trace of white surrounding the iris. I couldn't help thinking that he resembled an alien from a 1960s movie about *Area 51*. The blackness that filled the over accentuated almond shaped eyes were all the ammunition he needed to have you quaking in your boots. The interrogation began and set the mood for what I would be facing.

Alien: 'Why did you think you could come to China knowing you had stolen millions from our citizens?'

Me: 'I was tricked and believed I was working for a genuine company. I was also not aware that the investors were Chinese.'

A slap around the head from Peacock!

Alien: 'You are a thief, a trickster and a liar. We know you stole the money, but are you saying that you can't tell the difference between Thais, Filipinos or Chinese? To you British we are all the same; servants to your fading empire, with funny eyes.'

Me: 'Not at all. I know I am not well travelled in this part of the world and do not speak any of the languages, so I do have difficulty differentiating between citizens of the individual countries. Also, I did not think Chinese nationals were allowed to invest in a foreign exchange product.'

Although I spoke no Mandarin, the interpreter's translation seemed overly animated, with the odd English word or phrase thrown in, such as "British", "Queen", and "not scared". Whatever he said, it was definitely some way different to what he should have translated. Ugly Bad guy leapt from his seat and drew his pistol, pointing it at my head, screaming, projectiles of spittle flying from his mouth. To warrant such a reaction the interpreter must have said something like, "I am British, you do not scare me, now let me go before you are in serious trouble with the Queen of England!"

Alien's face grew sterner and his eyes seemed to become even blacker if that were possible, like deep sunken orbs of tar. He was like a man possessed by the devil. He did, however, reprimand Ugly Bad cop telling him to vent his anger at the shooting range and giving him a life-sized mugshot of my head on which to practice. If that wasn't intimidating enough, the shooting range was the other side of the wall directly behind me in the interview room and, as the questions continued, there were repeated thuds of bullets hitting the wall behind my head. To my great concern there were spears of light piercing from the crumbling wall that was expected to protect my cranium. Perhaps it was an adjacent wall he was shooting at as no one else in the room flinched or seemed worried about a rogue bullet. The interrogators retrieved bottles of chilled water from a cooler and began to relieve their thirst after hours of talking and the stifling heat. I, on the other hand was given a cup of boiling hot water poured from a kettle.

My handcuffs were released, and we all sat in silence. I had not been provided food or water since arriving at this facility and I was parched, but the temperature of the water made it undrinkable. Just as it had reduced to a temperature that would not blister my lips, and as the officers finished their cool bottles of fluid, Alien took my cup away feigning surprise that I was not thirsty. The questioning then resumed.

Alien: 'You spoke in Hong Kong and held a very big event in Macau. Why did you not think that there were Chinese investors in the audience?'

Me: 'I knew there were probably people from Hong Kong and Macau, but I didn't think there were any from China.'

This was a big mistake. This time it was Peacock that lost his rag and he slammed a fist down on the top of my head. The interpreter told me that citizens from Hong Kong and Macau are Chinese and no longer part of the British, Portuguese or anyone else's Empire for that matter.

The verbal attacks and accusations went on for what seemed like an eternity before two new people entered the room. They had guest passes hung around their necks from red ribbons adorned with Chinese stars. Their names were printed in Chinese, but the English underneath in bold type stated, "Euro Fx Victim". Peacock removed his pistol from his holster and placed it on the desk. Another officer removed a cattle prod from its charger plugged into the wall by the door and placed it on the desk next to the gun. Then the policemen left the room for a break leaving me alone with the two victims. I was now sweating profusely, fearing for my safety, perhaps even my life. They had left me alone in the room to be tortured by the victims, possibly killed.

At that moment, Peacock came back into the room, mopped my brow with his tissue and said, 'I think all of the interviews for the rest of your life are now over my English friend'. Then he left again.

After ten minutes of sitting in front of me and staring, one of the victims menacingly said, 'We are not animals. We will not torture you. Just admit what you have done, and you will have a swift death with a single bullet to the head'.

I knew this was a lose-lose situation. If I denied everything, they were not going to believe me; if I admitted guilt then I was going to die anyway. The gun was raised and placed against my forehead as he began a slow steady count from one to ten.

'Ee, are, san, sur ...'

Pictures flashed through my head of my children, of my parents and my sisters. The room was spinning with flashing images and memories appearing and disappearing from focus; when my babies were born, their first day at school, me starting work, passing my driving test ... My whole life managed to squeeze its way into those few seconds. When he reached "sure", Chinese for ten, he paused. Then he pulled the trigger. There was a loud click, but the chamber was empty. At that point the officers returned to the room. The victims removed their false identification cards, replacing them with their true police IDs and I was led, shaking, back to my cell.

Money to Byrne?

I lost track of time as there was no clock in the cell area, but my detention had to have been approaching twenty hours or so. The cell guards seemed to be not so bad after all and provided water, albeit from a kettle, whenever I asked. One of them even shared half of his stale pastry with me. It was probably fresh when he started his shift but the intense heat of Shanghai, aided by the semi subterranean prison area, ensured a rapid deterioration of food … and one's spirits. Three of the four guards visibly relaxed and became far friendlier when the elder of the quartet took a break. He was obviously their senior and afforded me no special treatment as a foreign national, giving his subordinates a stern glare if he thought they were being too nice.

It turned out that the youngest guard spoke very good English, with a distinctly American twang achieved through the self-taught method of watching as many English language movies as he could lay his hands on. He seized every opportunity to practice his language skills on me. Jason, his adopted English name, was a strikingly handsome young man that would not look out of place gracing the silver screen. He told me that he worked twelve-hour shifts with the police to help provide for his parents and to pay for his private evening classes in economics. He told me that he had read about *Euro Fx* and seemed genuine with his questions, his face not betraying any sign of trying to catch me out. Before he finished his shift, he told me that I would be interviewed again but I may have quite a wait as officials from the Head Department for Public Protection were taking over the case. They were currently flying in from Anshan, a city in the north east of China bordering North Korea. When the new shift arrived, it was clear that these guards were far less approachable. When I asked for water they would reluctantly walk to the kettle, fill the plastic cup and plonk it down on the floor of my cell without saying a word. They understood some English making comments to each other intended for my ears such as, "No soft bed for the Englishman tonight", letting me know that I was regarded just the same as the other unfortunates in the dungeon. One of the guards had spent some time in an adjacent room that, judging by the smell, could only have been the toilet. Having had virtually no food and only a couple of cups of water I had not yet needed to use this facility but, as the guard re-entered the room, I indicated through a simple motion of charades that I too now needed the bathroom. He opened my cell door, pointed in the direction of where he had just been and gave a vicious smile. His hands were red, covered with what appeared to be blood and I feared that he may have been some sort of interrogator. I gave him the name "Nasty". As I walked towards the opening where a door had once hung, the smell was overpowering and, on entering, was immediately grateful that I only needed to urinate. The hole in the corner of the room was filled with and surrounded by stinking piles of excrement. The walls were filthy and there was fresh red graffiti, still dripping in places like blood seeping from the cracked wounds in its surface. The words were in English and conveyed messages of hate such as: "You will die", and "Help me". Nasty had been painting these messages with the ink used to refill the fingerprint pads. The graffiti was clearly for my sole benefit as it was highly unlikely that any of the other poor wretches in this sewer could speak or read any English. I tried to get a grip on my emotions and apply logic to the situation; to keep my metaphorical mental glass half full, not half empty. I reasoned that if they wanted to hurt me then they could have already. If they wanted or intended me dead, then I would be. I left the room pretending to be uncontrollably affected by the messages. I figured that if they believed their desired goal of intimidation had been achieved then perhaps, they would cease tormenting me.

Who knows how long I waited but eventually I was once again taken to the interview room and secured into my highchair. The usual suspects were in attendance again; Ugly Bad, Nasty, Alien and his sidekick, and the interpreter. However, this time there were two new additions that took centre stage; the new head honchos in the room. These were the visitors from Anshan and, although asking many of the same questions, they were directed in a way that demanded more concise and precise answers. They were completely poker-faced, emotionless, not intimidating. I could not figure out if this was a good or a bad thing.

The lead investigator's name was Inspector Liu. He opened an enormous file, quickly flipping through to a glossary of photos which he extracted from the pile. One by one his assistants showed me a picture and asked if I knew the person. Each time the answer was 'Yes', as close-ups of Orchard, Cook and the Singaporeans were placed in front of me. I couldn't remember any real names of the Singapore group and Liu became agitated when I referred to them by the only ones I knew; "Eagle", "Panda", "Bear" and so on. Even to me this seemed ridiculous and I know how stupid and unbelievable it must have sounded to my interrogators. I was then shown photos of Chinese citizens, mostly women, and asked if I knew who they were. I didn't recognise them. They then placed photos of me posing with them after one of the events but still I couldn't remember their faces, let alone their names.

Inspector Liu then stood up sharply pointing to the Chinese flag which took pride of place on the wall directly opposite me.

'Do you know what this is?' he demanded.

'Of course,' I said. 'It's the National Flag of The Peoples' Republic of China.' I hoped that giving it its full and proper title might afford me some small mental favour.

He then showed me the picture again where I am standing with a group of investors, all ladies.

'Can you tell me what each of these ladies are wearing around their shoulders?'

I looked again at the picture with disbelief as I could see each of them proudly wearing a red shawl with the stars that make the Chinese flag displayed as clear as day.

He said, 'You have been telling my colleagues that you were unaware that Chinese citizens were at your scam events and yet you instantly recognise our country's flag? You are under arrest pending further investigation. You are free to stay in a hotel but the penalty for trying to leave the country is ten years in prison without trial'.

He left the room and I was escorted back to the cell area.

This time though, I was taken to a smaller room and told to stand on a block of concrete. On the wall behind me was a measuring chart waiting to capture my height and width for the camera that was being set up. I had to hold a board across my chest which reminded me of the prison mugshots published after the arrests of major criminals such as Al Capone or the more recent New York Mafia boss, John Gotti. I then had my fingerprints and palm prints taken in red ink. They even took my feet prints, first with shoes on and then without. I was then presented with my possessions and told I could collect my passport in a day or two, providing I furnished a ten thousand Yuan bond.

I was also required to sign a document stating my understanding of the charges, that the statement records were accurate, and that any attempt to leave China would result in an instant jail sentence. It's the quickest document I have ever signed, even though it could have said absolutely anything. In hindsight this may seem a stupid thing to have done, but I had had no embassy representative visit me, I'd not been allowed a phone call, so I figured my only chance to organise some help was to be out of there. I was led to the front of the police station panicking about how I was going to get back to Shanghai with no money and without the corporate card that had been supplied by *ABS Group*. To my great relief and with eternal thanks, Joe Li was waiting for me by the exit.

Chapter 17.   No Job, no money

When we finally left the police station it was well past midday on Tuesday the 26th of April. I'd endured over fifty hours and had consumed just half a stale pastry and a few cups of water. Joe Li said he would take me to lunch and that he had booked us into a local hotel for the evening. It was very thoughtful as I was starving and exhausted, but he must have been tired also after the long wait. The local town was quite small but very pretty with postcard traditional buildings and beautiful gardens at every turn. Even in this tiny suburb of Shanghai, albeit some two hours by train from the centre, *ABS* retained introducers here for their foreign exchange business and one of them joined us for lunch. The establishment was quite large and very pleasant. The menu had no English translation so I told Joe to order for us knowing that I would wolf down anything placed before me. The meal came and seemed to be served in reverse order; first a Chinese custard tart type delicacy followed by a bowl of opaque soup made with sweet rice and cornflour. Thereafter it returned to something more familiar with dishes of meat in black bean sauce or sweet and sour chicken. It was quite remarkable how quickly the mind and body recover once it has received life's essential fuels. Yes, I was still tired and aching, but I was thinking clearly again and eager to organise a plan of action. The introducer drove us to our hotel and said his goodbyes. After checking in and depositing our luggage to our rooms Joe said we should go downstairs for a coffee.

'I guess you will be wanting my contract back along with my unopened batch of business cards', I said.

'I'm afraid so, David. We would also like you to sign a letter stating that you falsified your CV.'

I was not overly happy about this as I didn't think I'd falsified anything. I had been consultant CEO to *Euro Forex Investment Limited* and was also consulting to a couple of other companies at that time. I had brought the subject up on a couple of prior occasions before accepting the position, but not naming them individually on my CV was all the excuse they needed to divorce themselves from this toxic association. Joe explained that if I were to sign the document as laid out then they would pay me one month's wages. I needed every penny I could get so had no hesitation in putting pen to paper. After all, this situation had caused them considerable embarrassment and they had a reasonable argument for not paying me a bean. Joe's company had a lot of work to do in order to minimise the fallout. Immediately after the speeches, before the gala dinner, I had been interviewed by several television networks and these interviews had to be urgently retracted. One thousand attendees and many more of their clients would have to be told why I had left and why *ABS* did not know about my previous employer. I couldn't blame them. Joe and his guys had been extremely helpful and, quite frankly, I don't know what I would have done without their assistance.

In keeping with the rest of the town, our accommodation for the evening was a small traditional boutique hotel, prettily painted with its own Chinese water garden in the centre courtyard, sloping roofs, and a multitude of different sized pots containing native exotic plants and flowers. The rooms were quite small, comfortable but simple, with the bare minimum of modern facilities.

The following day inspector Liu arrived with my passport and I was able to give him the ten thousand-yuan bond. He reiterated that should I try to leave the country it would result in an immediate jail sentence. I'm quite sure that victims were using connections at Pudong to alert them, or perhaps keeping vigil themselves, should I show my face. After the inspector had left, Joe and I took a train back to Shanghai. At the station Joe instructed a taxi driver to deliver us to any hotel close to the British Consulate. It was beginning to dawn on me just how alone I was about to become. Without Joe being present I would have had no chance even buying a train ticket from our rural outpost back to the more cosmopolitan city centre. There was not a single English sign, nor was there anyone official that spoke anything but Mandarin at the station. We found a hotel about half an hour's stroll from the Embassy and I got out, waiting for Joe to exit the car and assist me at the reception. But he remained in the passenger seat.

'I'm sorry David but the time has come when you are going to have to stand on your own two feet. I'm not going to be around from here on in, so you've got to start taking control of your situation. Good luck.'

It was tough but necessary advice and not delivered with any malice as we said goodbye. I saw him briefly the following day when he delivered the promised months' salary in cash but that was the last time I ever saw him. While his hotel was only ten minutes away from mine I was clearly not welcome back in the room that they had already paid for. I stayed at my new hotel for two weeks, still believing I would get the all clear at any moment. However, thinking ahead and just in case things did drag out, I started my search for something more affordable in the longer term. I felt so alone, and this area of Shanghai did not exude the buzz that is so infectious in the tourist areas. I knew I would be moving hotel soon but, for the moment, I needed to be here, and I decided to map out the walk to the British Consulate. I guessed that I would be making many trips to the embassy as they flexed their political muscle in order to secure the safe release of a British citizen. This turned out not to be the case as they seemed to have little interest in my plight, only providing counsel by junior staff on rare occasions. Even the consulate premises were somewhat different to what I had been expecting. Given the colonial past, and the remaining influence of the British Empire's trade magnates, I was anticipating a grand stuccoed structure with a sweeping drive through manicured lawns, perhaps some marble pillars and a polished Rolls Royce or two parked out front. This image was far from the reality that greeted me. The British diplomats occupied one section of the 17th floor of a 1970s tower block in Garden Square, West Beijing Road. The first time I entered the reception I was told that I could not visit the consulate without an appointment, emergency or not. I returned to my hotel and sent an email explaining my plight and requesting an urgent appointment. I received an immediate automated reply explaining that someone would address this request in the next five to seven working days. The realisation dawned on me that I was the only person that would get me out of China and the odds of that happening were beginning to look bleak.

Over the next week or so, in order to pass the time, I ventured farther afield, exploring this vast city while I waited for some good news, *any* news from the consulate. Everything was much as I expected; high-rise buildings with spectacular lights typically associated with the skylines of the Far East. Things were changing though. Corner street tailors and discount markets were being closed on a daily basis to make way for modern boutiques or department stores selling the likes of Gucci or D&G, though the authenticity of the products was very much in question. News channels reported Chinese government officials making loud noises about no longer being a "cheap copy" nation. However, there was still a market on the outskirts of the city with a thriving tourist trade, proudly proclaiming the quality of their rip-off merchandise. There was also a prominent stylish store modelled on Selfridges, whose top floor sold genuine lower price-range watches. However, if you were introduced to the manager by one of his trusted street hawks, a secret panel in the wall would slide open to reveal a room full of fake Rolex, Cartier and even Patek Phillipe watches. Their price range started in the hundreds of dollars, reflecting their amazing quality, unlike the lightweight, tinny copies sold in the markets starting at ten bucks though the more expensive ones in the market were often packed out with clay to give them the weight of the genuine article.

Another thing I discovered was that the emergence of self-propelled prosperity for China was no accident and had been well planned for some time. Within commuting distance of many major cities there are enormous newly built towns with hundreds of modern tower blocks just sitting empty. These were built in preparation for the relaxation of the one-family-one-child rule and are unlikely to remain unoccupied for long. Likewise the ready-built schools, universities and hospitals because the baby boomers are just that; still babies. If the city planners and developers had waited until the population hits two billion, as surely it will, then there would be a massive housing shortage in the future. The real worry though is that not enough is being done to address the pollution problem or the ongoing environmental problem: Great rivers like the Yangtze are being dammed to provide power, and lakes are being dredged for fine sand to supply the massive building projects.

My second hotel in Shanghai, close to the Embassy, was some way from the bright lights and buzz of the river district, named the Bund, with its meandering waterway reflecting the bright city lights. It's this image that the world most often sees on pictures of this sprawling city. As I succumbed to acceptance that I would not be returning home anytime soon, and that I would no longer have any income, I realised that I would shortly have to temper my expectations of where I would be able to afford and downgrade again.

I had been using the metro system on a regular basis to visit Bund and I used these excursions to scout for more affordable digs. The metro system was immaculate and modern, and a typical journey of four or five stops would only cost the equivalent of about thirty pence. An hour and a half journey to Pudong International airport would only cost about one pound. If you wanted to splash out fifty Yuan, six pounds, there was also a Maglev (magnetic levitation) train servicing the airport. This train would take an astonishing eight minutes to transport you the thirty kilometres to the departure terminal travelling at over three hundred kilometres an hour. I found a very basic hotel close to the centre of activity for two hundred-yuan, a saving of six hundred yuan per night from my current plusher digs. Many of the cheaper hotels in China are only permitted to accommodate Chinese citizens. In some cases it's because the facilities are substandard or, to be kind, very basic and designed to provide a roof for the many rural workers now making a living in the big cities and only returning home once a year to deliver their savings to their families. In other cases though, it's simply that the hotels employ cheaper, less educated staff who only speak Mandarin. This is a good thing in that it provides employment for locals who may not normally get the chance to work in that industry. I was pleasantly surprised by the simple but clean and comfortable room containing a small double bed with crisp white linen and a wet room complete with a sink, toilet and shower housed in a sealed plastic-shelled cubicle. There was also a twenty-inch flat screen TV perched on the wall that would air a Schwarzenegger or Stallone blockbuster film at ten pm every night.

It was a one-minute walk from a large outdoor plaza that housed a number of tented bars and eateries. April and May are very warm months that can see some days of exceptionally heavy rainfall but during the dry periods I would frequent these establishments, sipping a cool beer whilst reading a book to pass the time and enjoying the sun. It was also only a short walk to the beautiful People's Park, just past People's Square, down People's Road past People's Memorial ... I think you get the picture!

The first thing that really grabbed my attention in Shanghai was not a pleasant one. There is a culture of spitting, whenever and wherever they feel the need. This is not a mere whisper of sound followed by a glint of saliva flying through the air. This is full on hoiking followed by a jellified green globule hurtling towards the pavement. Everybody does it, and when your first sight of the day is an eighty-year-old lady removing her teeth to avoid them accompanying her deposit, your appetite for breakfast is somewhat diminished for an hour or so.

Another thing evident in epidemic proportions is the hawks and street sellers. The hawks are the ones that want to take you shopping or, more to the point, bring you to a particular establishment where they have a commission arrangement with the owners. They all use the same approach line, "shopping, shopping, watchee, watchee, handbag, massage". You could be carrying two handbags and wearing six watches whilst being tenderised by a twenty-five-year-old Swedish model, and they would still bombard you with the same pitch. Each morning I would play a game in my head to guess how long before I heard these lines directed at me. The record from leaving the hotel reception was a mere three seconds. Once seated comfortably at the outside cafe with my pint of Tsing Tao and book at the ready, it was the turn of the street sellers. One after the other would come to my table demonstrating their wares. Anything from mini face fans and mobile selfie sticks to torch lasers that were powerful enough to light a cigarette. There was a seller who regularly approached me, a girl called Lily. She and her young daughter were living with her parents, while her husband was serving three years after being caught with twenty fake watches worth only about one hundred pounds.

One day, sitting at the café I noticed the craziest of things. There was a tourist train that would take people from one end of the mile-long shopping street to the other. Hanging off the back of this train was a seventy-year-old American man on a skateboard. He was a beast of a guy but displayed a childish grin through a grey handlebar moustache. The braided locks that escaped his Texas baseball cap trailed behind him giving a false impression of immense speed. He noticed me watching and the inevitable happened. He released his grip and headed for my table.

'Hey dude, you American? TJ's the name.' The slow drawl suited his ageing, hippy/WWF wrestler/retired surfer boy image.

'Hi, Dave from London', I said, secretly hoping that would be an end to it.

'Can I join you?' he asked. It turned out he was really very nice, and a welcome distraction and we soon became firm friends, frequently meeting at that spot over the coming weeks. He loved a debate and often directed the conversation towards a friendly confrontation. He was also very religious and disclosed that he enjoyed being a guest speaker at his local church whenever he was back in Texas. I was telling him how I thought the spitting was disgusting.

His Christian view was, 'Maybe they think we are disgusting for not doing it. It's part of their culture'.

'If it's not disgusting or deemed incorrect, why do we not see any actors or news reporters hacking up on Chinese TV?' I countered. Round One to me!

He then switched the subject to food.

'You must be missing home and family, but I bet you're not missing the terrible English food!'

I responded as one would expect, defending our culinary expertise and mum's home recipes, but he continued:

'If English food is any good, show me one English restaurant in Shanghai. You won't be able to because there aint one! I can see two MacDonald's and two KFCs from where we are sitting.'

I was stumped for an answer and it looked like Round Two was his. After a period of allowing his guard to drop I said:

'Where do you find it in yourself to see the good in everyone? It's very admirable.'

He replied, 'In the good word of the Lord, my friend. In the Holy Bible'.

I then asked if there was a shop in Shanghai where I could buy a Bible. I explained that I had plenty of time on my hands and might see the light and become a better person. He said that he doubted I would find a shop in Shanghai that would have one, but he would try and find out.

I said, 'Don't worry, it can't be any good!'

He looked mortified and asked why I would say such a terrible thing. I simply replied that I used the exact same reasoning that he had applied to English food. Realising I was baiting him, he relaxed, and a knowing smile soon returned to his face.

Another group of street sellers included the shoeshine merchants. These were the poorest group that I came into regular contact with. They were generally older gentlemen with crooked backs and leathered hands; bodies that had succumbed to the rigors of constant stooping and scrubbing at the feet of wealthy tourists. I would have my shoes polished to a gleam every day. If I couldn't afford the fifty pence for a shoeshine, I shouldn't be drinking beer at five pounds a pint. Even so, I had to draw the line with the other two shoeshine guys that were waiting for him to finish so that they could offer their services. If I said yes to them all eventually the leather would be gone, and I would have had tanned, shiny feet. Shanghai had caught up with the West in respect of food and drink prices that were comparable to any major city, but the rich/poor divide was far more evident, and I found it quite disturbing. The very poorest people, while collecting cardboard from dustbins or eating scraps from the road, would often have to dodge a passing Ferrari or Maserati.

Chapter 18.   "The Irish Pub"

I am not one of those whose first mission abroad is to find an English or Irish pub serving traditional food. In fact, I'm quite the opposite; "when in Rome" and all that. One afternoon I was leaving the hotel for my usual escape from boredom at the plaza, but the slight drizzle and gathering clouds were a forewarning of the impending downpour. The streets were still busy but with a very different implied agenda to people's movements. Crowds with purposeful looks on their faces were busily heading back to their accommodations. The novelty sellers and shoeshine merchants wore resigned and disappointed faces as they packed away their wares knowing there would be no tourists buying their goods or services today. The only smiles I saw were spread broadly across the faces of the umbrella vendors as they restocked their empty pitches.

I spotted Lily who confirmed that there would be heavy rain for the rest of the day and evening.

'Bad storm no good for Lily's business selling. People go to the Irish Pub.'

I asked how close it was and what it was called.

'The Irish pub close, that way, near Fuzhou road.'

That was fine, but she still hadn't told me the name. The stupidity of my frustration was instant; it would almost certainly be called O'Tooles, O'Neil's, Flanagan's or possibly O'Grady's. So I set off, trying to spot a shamrock sign swinging in the rapidly increasing breeze, the universally recognized Irish native clover leaf. As I passed the plaza, one of the waitresses called out to me.

'Mr. David, you come see us when the sun comes back, yes? I think you are going to the Irish pub.'

I confirmed that was indeed my destination but cut myself short of asking again what it was called. I would stick to my spot-the-shamrock methodology. My eyesight had deteriorated considerably over the previous few years and I even needed my glasses to read the three-inch letters that would tell me I had reached Fuzhou road, and the rain was causing my spectacles to mist up so that any green neon sign had the distorted possibility of being a shamrock. After several short but false detours, it was my ears that would come to the rescue. There was the distinct deep growling pitched whine of U2 on the peripheries of my sonic range. This had to be the place. As I homed in on the sound and I drew closer to my destination, the irony of Bono's lyrics made me laugh out loud: "Well I still haven't found what I'm looking for." I reached the entrance and sure enough, hanging above my head was a large green shamrock, and next to that was the elusive name of the bar, "*The Irish Pub*"!

It was a big buzzing establishment but still managed to exude a warm welcoming cozy ambience, a skill the Irish are world leaders in achieving. In the brief lapses of noise, as one song ended and the next began, you could hear the dull thud of darts piercing the board or the clack and kerplunk of pool balls clashing before dropping into a pocket. The combination of the above on one's senses had the effect of fooling the brain that at the end of the evening you were in London and would be hailing a cab for the familiar journey home. Rather than being upsetting, I would leave with a feeling that I had been granted a brief sabbatical from my enforced exile. I asked the owner, Michael O'Leary, why he chose to call the place simply "*The Irish Pub*". His rosy cheeks and bushy grey sideburns wagged from side to side in disbelief at my question.

'Jeysus, we're in a feckin city, with twenty-six million feckin people, and I'm the only feckin Irish pub! An de English tink we are tick? Jaysus!'

There was a group of guys seated next to me at the bar and snippets of their conversations established that they were from the north of England and worked together in Shanghai. Upon returning to my seat after a short visit to the bathroom I discovered my previously full pint was nearly empty. It was quickly ascertained that one of the guys, Jim, had made a genuine mistake. He replaced my beer and I was inevitably drawn into the small group of expats. They were really friendly people and perfect ambassadors for our country, unlike the hordes of drunken reprobates that so often mar the UK's reputation abroad. A few weeks later they even threw an unexpected party for my birthday.

Jim explained that he worked for a company that supplied packaging to European retailers and supermarkets. This could be anything from polystyrene-filled boxes for toys or chinaware, to the protective cartons for eggs. His company were about to reduce staffing levels as they had been losing business to competitors. The manufacturers from the factories in China would place sales reps in the big cities. It would be these reps that competed to offer the lowest price to produce the supplier's goods. The production quote would plummet if the right incentive (or backhander) could be offered to the rep, ensuring their personal financial security or a luxury that would normally be out of their reach. Suppliers were paying bribes to the sales reps in order to achieve the lowest price and Jim's company was not prepared to do this. On one occasion he showed me a modern apartment building where many of the factory sales reps lived. He said that the basement car park was full of Ferraris, Lamborghinis and other top-end automobiles that had been given as bribes. All the vehicles had virtually zero mileage as the sales guys couldn't afford to insure them or, more importantly, explain to the state and their employers where they'd got the money to buy one. On evenings off they would slip into their snazziest attire, paid for on their client's credit cards, stuff their Gucci wallets full of undeclared cash and head off to the trendiest bar or club. Their tried and tested modus operandi was to grab a prominent bar stool, order a bottle of Champagne and leave the keys to their expensive motor in full view on the counter. This would guarantee the attentions of the most beautiful gold diggers in the establishment. A girl would inevitably accept the invitation for a spin around the streets of Shanghai in a supercar, believing she had found the man of her dreams. Once back at his apartment car park she would get the chance to sit in the car and even hear the majestic roar of the engine magnified by the echo of the underground cavern. The rep would then explain that he had had too much alcohol, describing the dire consequences should he be caught drink driving. The promise of taking her out the following weekend ensured her acceptance of his invitation to continue the evening upstairs in his apartment. Next week it would be a different club and a different girl duped by the promise of future financial security.

A few days later.......

From the very first time that I met Lily she had wanted to introduce me to an English person that she knew. She would insist that my fellow countryman would be very excited to meet me, though we all know this not to be entirely true. I didn't want to meet him and I was pretty sure he would be feeling the same. I was quite happy to sit in the sun, sip my beer and read my book. I had no interest in meeting a stranger to exchange small talk. So, I would reach into my mind's invisible library and pull out one of the imaginary books containing pre-prepared excuses as to why now was not a good time. Her street seller's instincts told her that my book of excuses needed updating and today was the day that she could force the encounter that excited her so much. There was no ulterior motive on her part. She truly believed we would enjoy being introduced which would increase her kudos with the pair of us, ensuring further purchases from us by way of thanks.

Street sellers are as tough as diamonds wearing a rhino skin coat and do not take no for an answer. They also have their own selective interpretation of what you are saying. If you say, "No thank you, I do not wish to buy anything today", that to her means you don't want the item she is currently demonstrating and so will only encourage her to reach into her bag for the next product until you eventually make a purchase. As she persisted, explaining her friend was in the very next bar, I decided to just get this thing over with. So, I reluctantly followed her to meet the English stranger, all the while foraging my mind's depths for a new set of excuses as to why the meeting could only be brief. She led me to his table and gave him a gentle tap on the shoulder, beaming with excitement at making this important introduction. As the guy began to turn to face us, I could hear the resigned sigh that confirmed he had the same intentions as me; let's just get this over with. We all burst out laughing as Jim from the Irish bar said:

'Bloody hell, Dave. It's you!'

Chapter 19.   The British Consulate

Time was passing slowly and at least twice each week I would message inspector Liu in Anshan to ask if there had been any progress, hoping for any hint of when I would be able to leave for England. Each reply was short and curt: "We are still investigating!" That is, until the fourth week when there was a much more detailed answer: According to their investigations, it was highly unlikely that I would be leaving China for many months, possibly a year … And if allegations against me were found to be true, then I should not ever expect to leave their country. Once again, I was hit by nausea, giddiness, the shakes, basically the whole shock package.

It was time to Skype my children. My feelings of shock were replaced with dread as I could no longer keep saying, honestly, that I would be home in a couple of weeks. It was going to be best if I told them I may not be back for a year. But even that was an uncomfortable lie. I was protecting them from the possibility that, if found guilty I was facing the highest of sentences: life imprisonment … or a rope.

Before I had moved to my current accommodation, when I had visited the British Consulate on Beijing Road West, they told me that they would keep me informed of any developments and had given me a substantial brochure of what they could and couldn't do to assist me. It was high time I read this manual from front to back. I needed to freshen up, so I took my toiletries into the compact wet room and had a long cold shower. I then put on some shorts and laid back on my bed to read the manual to see what help I could get and what level of assistance the embassy could give. After reading every word from first page to last I was astounded. Of the two hundred or so pages, one hundred and ninety-six were details of what they couldn't assist with: They would not represent you or interfere with police procedure; they would not provide a lawyer; they would not provide any financial assistance; they would not provide an interpreter. It made me wonder what exactly the British Consulate could or *would* do. The four pages where they proffered help consisted of advice on keeping your family appraised of your situation and helping them to send you money. It was beyond belief! There was also a very disconcerting section which they had highlighted for me and which went into great detail of what to expect in prison. It was extremely depressing.

My final visit to the Shanghai Consulate was at the end of May, six weeks into my enforced detention. This time I was met by a young representative who spoke very good English but looked to be fresh out of school. She had pink and blue streaks dyed into her hair, wore three-quarter length jeans with trendy holes ripped into the knees and she sported a multi-coloured pair of *Doctor Marten* boots. After establishing that I had read everything correctly and there was very little they could do, she gave me one more pause for thought. She told me that they would do everything they could to keep me in the Shanghai area, but admitted that the worst-case scenario would be if I was moved to the north of the country. This area, sandwiched between Inner Mongolia and North Korea, is a barren part of the country where many of the long-term detainees were imprisoned. The ominous delivery of the message suggested that this would be similar to the isolation of a Siberian Gulag. I trudged back to the metro station and on to my hotel to read the section on prison conditions in Northern China. It made grim reading: Although direct family members were permitted several visits per year, the prison locations and logistics of getting there made this almost impossible. It went on to explain that there would be sixteen inmates to a cell sharing one television and one bathroom.

I needed a plan, but I also needed to downgrade my accommodation again in order to save as much money as I could.

Chapter 20. An unexpected nap

I was getting hungry and although I had always been a fan of Chinese food, I was feeling like I never wanted to see a rice, dumplings or noodles again. Shanghai is becoming more cosmopolitan and still retains pockets of eateries from its colonial days. However, these were way too expensive on my budget and to my surprise a found myself craving a simple MacDonald's. The closest one was just two minutes from my hotel, so I set off to gorge on both a Sausage and Egg, and Bacon and Egg McMuffin, washed down with a Diet Coke. In China, the vast majority of people are early to rise and early to bed. So being nine thirty in the morning I was hoping to find the place less than full, with most of the populous having completed breakfast by seven thirty. The doorway to the fast food restaurant was the smallest on the square and not having been there before I wasn't sure if there would be any seating. I descended the steps and to my amazement found a five-a-side football pitch-sized seating area. It was like I'd entered Dr Who's Tardis. There were quite a few diners, mostly the younger generation, but plenty of free tables. I ordered my food and headed to one of the vacant alcoved cubicles to read my book in private. Despite the plentiful empty tables, a Chinese man came and sat directly opposite me, placing his diet coke on the table in a type of pawn to pawn opening move in chess. I ignored him and continued to read my book but was aware that he was staring directly at me. Five minutes passed and he was still sitting there staring. I noticed that all the while he had not taken one sip from his drink. Strange, I thought. I did a three sixty on the fixed swivel top seat and spotted an alternative location to enjoy my meal without intrusion. It was a smaller two-seater arrangement, so I pottered over, placed my bag on the only other seat opposite the one I intended to occupy. Problem solved. I glanced up occasionally and, although he remained where he was, his gaze was still fixed firmly on me.

I awoke with my head on the table and the cheese from my cold McMuffin firmly stuck to my cheek. As my eyes opened, I could see a number of people staring at me, probably assuming I was another hungover tourist. The lights from the restaurant sent a searing pain right through my eyes and across the top of my scalp and down my neck. I attempted to lift my head which, after just two inches, flopped back into my food. I tried again with more success and just sat there allowing my eyesight and senses to return. My head felt like a medicine ball balancing on a wobbly foam kiddie's swim noodle. Then I noticed a piece of paper wedged underneath my half-consumed Diet Coke. I cleaned the grease off my glasses and read the note which was in precise and bold English.

"YOU MUST BE TIRED. ENJOY YOUR SLEEP. BE SURE YOU TELL THE TRUTH."

I looked around. The Chinese man had gone. I got shakily to my feet and walked the short distance back to my hotel, where I lay on my bed replaying again and again the episode in my mind. I had been overcome by dizziness on several occasions due to the strain of the situation, so was this passing out just an acceleration of the pressure I was under? This was different though. The lasting headache and grogginess had not happened before, and I had felt perfectly well when ordering my food just minutes before. Trying to make sense of it all, it started to become obvious to me what had happened: I must have been drugged. Maybe the man who had sat opposite me was a victim of the scam and when I had turned around to look for another seat, he had swapped my drink with his doctored one. That would certainly explain why he had not taken a single sip from his cup.

After that I knew that I could no longer stay there, in the same hotel. My mental state was deteriorating, and I was getting paranoid. It was time to change venue again and try to do so in the most clandestine, stealthy fashion. For my own sanity and safety, I needed to disappear from the main square quickly. I packed my bags.

Chapter 21. The Captain's Table

Money was becoming a serious issue after two months living in a relatively expensive city without any means of income. My dilemma was either to remain in the present hotel and not go out at all and become dangerously depressed, or to seek even cheaper accommodation and retain the cash that provided a means of escape and the sanity that can only be gleaned from social interaction?

The events in MacDonald's the previous day had made my mind up for me. My eldest daughter, being ever concerned, had scoured the internet and found a hostel called the *Captain's Table*. It was in good location, close to the Bund, and was only seventy-five Yuan per night, just under ten pounds.

It had a wonderful rooftop bar affording fabulous panoramic views of Shanghai, with all of the beautiful city lights dancing off the water at night. The downside to this though was that the price of food and drinks was based on the view. And many visitors, not staying in this establishment, were happy to pay the premium. The beautiful setting, unfortunately, was all that could be said to be good about the hostel. The sleeping accommodation was of a nautical style, with six sailors' bunks to a room. They looked like they had been salvaged from the 3rd class quarters of the Titanic, seventy-five years *after* its unfortunate encounter with the iceberg. The windows were, admittedly, bigger than portholes, but those that opened revealed the pollution-tainted walls of the buildings next door instead of a panorama. The bathroom facilities were shoddy, with shower heads that varied between the force of a cold fireman's hose and the scorching trickle of a leaking boiler. Going to the toilet or having a wash would involve navigating an endless maze of passageways decorated with varying shapes and sizes of shorts, shirts and underwear, struggling to shed moisture in the ninety percent humidity as they sadly hung from improvised washing lines often constructed of joined bootlaces.

During my two-week self-imposed nightmare in this shipwreck there were numerous comings and goings. Some were travellers spending a night before setting off to explore the Great Wall. Others were more hardened low-budget adventurers, used to this type of place where you could mingle with like-minded backpackers and experience "another China" that mainstream travel agents wouldn't even know existed. The discomfort that was permanently ingrained on my face was probably mocked by the many youthful backpackers taking a gap year before returning to parties in their dorms at one Uni or another, looking forward to returning in a couple of weeks to be pampered at Mum and Dad's cosy home, regaling only the adventures that were appropriate for their parents' ears. I was struggling to come to terms with the fact that my next home, possibly for the rest of my life, could be a rat-infested cell in China's equivalent of Siberia. I was fifty-two and if I couldn't cope with this hostel then I was in serious trouble.

There was one long-term resident who occupied the bunk next to mine and he believed he owned the establishment. He was in his early twenties with an ambition to become a photographer. He spoke very little English but most of what he could speak was offensive, or at the least antisocial: "Old people smell", "I don't like foreigners", "I wish you would all go home". Many other young Chinese staying there were very polite and tried to engage me in conversation. When I disclosed which room I was staying in, virtually all of them hugged me and said to be careful of the strange young "camera boy". I decided I needed to make him wary of me. I'm not a thief so I decided rather than his stuff I'd move his things around. Only slightly but enough for him to notice. Each time he returned to his bunk he would stare in confusion, noticing something was different. Nothing missing, but not quite right. I would giggle whilst reading my book and when he confronted me, I would tell him I was reading a humorous novel, despite the cover depicting a blood drenched knife or a pistol indicating it was a thriller that I was reading. I think I was at this point starting to show the first signs of cracking under the pressure I was under. It was beginning to manifest into a psychological problem. I was starting to feel a bit crazy. I needed to get away from this and on one occasion, on the rooftop bar, staring across at the flotilla of merchant ships, I even considered the possibility of being a stowaway. I knew that this was the last thing a posse of investors would be expecting me to do. It was a crazy idea; it was bound to have strict security aimed at stopping poorer Chinese Nationals from seeking a better life abroad. Being caught, even attempting to leave, would have the same condition attached: instant imprisonment. I began to search for new accommodation once again and it was probably a good idea to keep changing location under the circumstances.

I'm glad to say that "camera boy" was the exception and not the rule when it came to Chinese people. I took to reading a lot more to pass the time and had soon exhausted my limited supply of novels. I was told that there was a foreign bookshop not too far away. It was on Fuzhou Road, but the opposite end to *The Irish Pub*. This time I didn't try to be too clever and just looked for a retail outlet called "The Foreign Bookshop". My search was a success and I restocked my reading material on a number of occasions. It was on one of those visits that, just beside the bookshop, I noticed a bar called *The Max Pub*. It had a sandwich board sign declaring that all beer was on a 2-for-1 happy "hour" that lasted for five hours every day between 3 and 8 pm.

Chapter 22. "The Max Bar"

I decided to take a look in *Max* and was pleasantly surprised. It was run by a really lovely guy called Michael Yang and his equally accommodating group of young Chinese staff. There was a pool table that required no coin payment to play and, when you purchased a beer, you were given a voucher to claim your second pint free of charge. With the price of a voucher pint effectively being two pounds fifty and free pool play, it was a great way to while away a couple of hours each day. There was an even eclectic mix of Chinese locals, ex-pat regulars and the odd smattering of tourists. Many of these people became close friends and, to this day, stay in regular contact. It was one of these friends who told me not to panic when I missed the last of the happy hour at 8 pm. If you paid for two or three pints earlier in advance you could keep the spare tickets for later. This was common practice and not frowned upon at all, unlike the scrutiny you'd be subjected to at a bar back in England.

My reasonably capable talents on the pool table had not gone unnoticed and before long I was invited to become a member of the *Max* pool team. I was a bit reticent at first because the matches were on a Thursday evening, started at 8.30 (which was post-happy hour) and they frequently dragged on late into the night. However, my reluctance evaporated when I was given three important pieces of information. First, that happy hour remained in place all evening for members of the pool team. Second, you got a free pint of beer for each game that you won. And third, the pool team were provided with free food, typically a pizza or something just as easy for them to present en-masse for both teams. This meant that at least one day a week I could have a relaxing evening without spending a thing. My debut was a great success when I won all three matches; a rare win for the *Max* pub. I was the hero for the day and on the next encounter I was promoted to captain of the team. I arrived at the match full of confidence and proceeded to smash the balls around the baize to great cheers from my teammates ... only to see the black ball disappear down the hole before its time, conceding the game to my young female opponent. My second match of the evening saw me lose again, this time without even getting the chance to take a shot. I was duly demoted to first reserve in the pool team and had to surrender my brief tenure as captain, but it was little things like this that helped me retain my sanity and forget my plight, even if it was just for a few hours. As *Max* was one of the few places that accepted Visa I thought there was possibly a trail to follow by authorities if they were keeping tabs on my movements and expenditure. It was such a relaxed atmosphere that I began to dismiss this assumption as a pre-programmed thought process embedded by years of reading spy thrillers about communist China or Russia. As it turns out though, my suspicions were justified.

I was sitting at the bar talking to another acquaintance and regular at *Max*, an American photographer called Bill who was documenting the ever-increasing changes in China. He had amazing observational skills, honed by years of dedication to his craft. He had already completed a five-year stint in China many years earlier and had returned to produce a book showing the rapid developments that were taking place. One day he was retracing the steps he had taken years before, photographing streets that had undergone dramatic transformations, when he spotted a man on a side street repairing shoes. The elderly gentleman was sitting in the very same spot, doing the very same thing as he had been ten years earlier when he had mended Bill's shoes. Bill grabbed his camera, and with his eidetic memory for scenes, waited to reproduce the photo he had taken all that time ago. He returned the next day to show the man the two photos, unsure of what his response he would be, or if his ancient eyes would be able to recognise the two shoe menders that were in fact one and the same, separated only by time. The gentleman began to cry, either from nostalgia or the realization of how cruel life had been, working in the elements day after day and how that had changed his appearance. As it turned out he was overjoyed when he was handed two framed pictures of himself hard at work and he insisted on removing Bill's shoes for a spruce up. The only difference in the pictures, apart from the obvious effects of the gentleman's aging, was the backdrop. The first showed a laundry repair and ironing service, whilst the latter depicted a modern Family Mart convenience store framed by gleaming skyscrapers in the distance.

Bill leaned across the bar and asked when I would be inviting my friends in for a drink? I didn't know what he meant. He went on to tell me that a black car with tinted windows always parked across the street when I arrived and left within a minute of my departure. I looked out for a mysterious car on my subsequent visits and sure enough, he was bang on the money. I can't believe that I had not spotted it. The temptation was to wave or to send out a couple of complimentary sparkling waters, but I didn't need to add to the pile of trouble I was already in. They must have realized by my involuntary glances towards their car that they had been rumbled and the car stopped turning up.

It was not the end of their surveillance though. One time, I was playing pool by myself, getting some practice in, in the hope of regaining my place in the first team, when some young guys in casual attire asked to join in. We had great fun and I was oblivious to their seemingly casual questions about what I was doing in China, and what I thought of the people. Of course, I was on my guard, but these were typical questions I was asked almost everywhere I went. As the evening progressed and the usual suspects arrived for some post-work drinks, I was approached by the one female member of our pool team. Lan Lan was an unusually tall and strikingly beautiful Chinese girl. She pulled me to one side and told me that my new friends were in fact plain-clothes police. I asked how she knew this, and she replied that she'd dated one of them for over a year. It was time to go!

I also became friends with a South African guy named Gert that frequented *Max*. He had relocated to Perth, Australia after a very close call when his head was somewhat more than grazed by a bullet in an attempted carjacking in his hometown of Johannesburg. He was earning two hundred thousand Yuan a month overseeing the construction of a power plant. He told me many stories of how you must be very clear when giving instructions to your Chinese workforce. He told me how they were very loyal and industrious and will do precisely what you tell them, but nothing more. He told me about how he was about to visit home to see his family and had instructed his on-site manager to read the land survey he had just emailed: He was to send lorries to Shanghai docks to collect the steel, then begin work on the footings for the plant immediately.

After three months of building, the construction was having problems with subsidence. When Gert read that the land survey recommended moving the footings, he went ballistic. He calculated the cost in time and money and was livid. He summoned the site manager to his office for an explanation.

Gert described how he was at his desk, "moving anything I might throw or use as a weapon out of reach in case I killed him", when the man walked in and took a seat.

Gert laid it on the line telling him, 'In the survey I sent you, it clearly stated that the location for the footings of our power station was not suitable. Did you not read the land survey you stupid idiot?'

The super replied that he had read it and he had indeed seen "this terrible problem", at which Gert demanded to know why the hapless supervisor hadn't told him so that changes could be made. He was utterly dumbstruck by the response:

'Sir, you told me to read it, to pick up the steel from the docks and to start the work as soon as possible. You did not tell me to call you or make changes if anything was incorrect.' The on-site manager had literally followed orders to the letter!

I also became very good friends with two great people, Christopher, a guy from Newcastle who was teaching English in Shanghai and his partner Rebecca, a Chinese girl whom he met playing pool in *Max*. I've heard they have since married and are well on their way to achieving their dream family of two girls and a boy. This vision for family planning was Rebecca's choice; Christopher was keen on just one of each. I feel some responsibility for the final decision despite the fact Rebecca had a will as strong as anyone I have ever met. One day they seemed to be having a serious debate and I was closest at hand to settle the issue.

Rebecca asked, 'David, do you think when people have children, one boy and one girl is best, or two girls and one boy?'

I have learnt from experience it is always best to side with the lady so I replied, 'Two girls and one boy, without a doubt!'

Christopher immediately jumped in, 'Typical southerner, ready to stir things up for us Geordies. You were listening to our argument!'

The reality is that my decision was based purely on the fact that I have two beautiful daughters and one handsome son. What else *could* I have said! As a thank you, Rebecca invited me to dinner at their apartment the following weekend. The directions showed that they were living in the suburbs, about halfway to Pudong airport. I had arranged to meet up for the journey with another English guy named Tommy who had also been invited. He was a builder from Liverpool who had been travelling for some time and had arrived in Shanghai about three months earlier after spending eight weeks honing his martial arts skills in a Buddhist training camp at a monastery in Thailand. Tommy was in his early thirties with plenty of testosterone flowing through his body and he told me some interesting stories about his time there including when he had arranged one evening to meet a girl from the separate ladies compound after the strict eight o'clock curfew. They found a secluded spot and were standing embraced in the act of lovemaking when suddenly their legs were whipped from beneath them by a bamboo stick. They landed heavily in an embarrassed heap and a leathery foot was placed firmly across Tommy's neck. He looked up helplessly to see an eighty-year-old monk standing over him, whose toes were now effortlessly putting pressure on a specific point near his jugular leaving him paralysed and prostrate on the ground. The girl was told to dress and return to her dormitory. Tommy's fate was not so fortunate. He was taken before the seventy-five-year-old abbot where he was told that he must need more exercise as he really should not have energy left for a tryst at that time of night. The old man then proceeded to give a masterclass in the ancient arts lasting three hours, and Tommy ended up covered in bruises with a broken toe and three broken ribs. That certainly put an end to his carnal desires for quite some time.

So, Tommy and I stocked up on beer and headed over to the home of Rebecca and Christopher for some eagerly anticipated home cooking. It was a humble apartment with a tiny fan as the only relief from the heat, humidity and effects of spicy food. Rebecca's mother had visited them the day before and had brought them a gift of live eels that were happily wriggling away in the sink, unaware of their impending plight. The food, conversation and laughter made me truly start to relax, possibly for the first time since my arrest, and I felt my stress slipping away, when suddenly my phone gave a ping and brought me crashing back to earth again. It was a WeChat text from Inspector Liu:

'You must leave Shanghai and come to Anshan tomorrow.'

It was my worst nightmare. Travelling to the far north east of China bordering North Korea was exactly what the British Embassy said we should try to avoid. I sent a text back saying it would take me a couple of days to get enough money together for the flight. I was granted the two extra days but warned that I would face immediate imprisonment if I failed to arrive by the Wednesday. I returned to my hotel and began my preparations.

Chapter 23. The dreaded trip north

Up until this point I had remained pretty strong. Once the initial shock had worn off and the first gruelling interviews were over with there had been no further interrogations and I'd convinced myself that, once the information I'd provided had been checked and verified, I'd be free to leave the country. This summons to the north of China had wiped away those hopes in a single sentence. Before embarking on this next dreaded journey, I must have spent two whole hours looking at the photo gallery on my iPad, each picture of my children causing a fresh flood of silent tears to cascade down my cheeks.

I made my way to Pudong airport to catch the one flight per day that went to Anshan. Once again, passport in hand, I pondered the pros and cons of turning left and heading to the international departures terminal instead and attempting an escape from China. It didn't take me long to dismiss this idea as I was sure the Chinese authorities would be all too aware of this temptation and would be on high alert. Reluctantly I continued straight on to the domestic terminal. Although only an internal flight, there was still quite a rigorous check-in procedure. I joined the back of the queue and shuffled towards security with my small suitcase containing one week's clothing. I passed through security without any special attention being paid to my documents that I was perhaps expecting but, as I bent down to put my papers away and retrieve my suitcase, I heard a voice calling my name. I thought I had imagined it but there it was again, even louder. I looked back at the throng of people and caught someone's eye, or rather his caught mine.

He smiled and said, 'Try to get some sleep on the plane, David. And remember, tell the truth'.

I just stared at him as the realization dawned on me that I was being followed yet again. He then raised a MacDonald's cup in a cheers motion and I suddenly realized where I had seen him before. He turned and, without looking back, disappeared into the crowd. As if I wasn't already nervous enough this set my pulse and senses into overdrive.

Once in the departure lounge, I found that I was no longer in need of the light breakfast I had intended to have, but I had a coffee despite knowing that it would likely add to my agitated state. I was sweating profusely despite the air-conditioned lounge, and my mouth felt like I had been sucking on a ball of chalk. I found a café, purchased a coffee and a bottle of sparkling water which I swiftly downed, and went and sat at an empty table directly below one of the departure boards. There were still two hours before boarding so I retrieved a book from my carry-on luggage, another Jack Reacher adventure novel. I tried reading but found myself just staring at the words, rereading the same paragraph without taking in the meaning. I was about to replace the book in my bag when I noticed a gentleman heading towards my table. He looked to be about sixty-five and, in his fedora, linen suit and stained tie, he rather resembled the spoof character, Sir Les Patterson as played by the comic actor Barry Humphries.

Money to Byrne?

He dabbed his perspiring forehead with a polka dot handkerchief, then stuffed it in the trousers of his crumpled suit and, pointing to a vacant seat, asked if it was free. He sat, placed his hat on the table and ordered a brandy from a passing waiter before I had time to reply. He had grey hair, red cheeks and broken veins on his nose. His drooping jowls emphasised a sadness in his eyes. After several minutes of silence, he emptied the last of his Cognac, rinsing it around in his teeth like a mouthwash. He then placed his hat back on his head and tucked a neatly folded copy of *The Daily Telegraph* under his arm. As he stood to leave, he made a clumsy scrape of his chair and performed a false cough to ensure he had my attention. Then he said quietly:

'Young man, we wish you the very best of luck and will do our best to keep an eye on you. But you also must help yourself. Be vigilant, stay in open areas, and be careful who you befriend. They may well be wolves in sheep's clothing.' He glanced up at the departures board, turned and walked away.

I boarded the plane, took to my seat and replayed the strange one-way conversation with the gentleman at the airport. All indications were that he was something to do with British government or the Consulate, but as he hadn't introduced himself, I couldn't be sure. I had very mixed feelings about the whole situation that had just occurred. On the one hand it was comforting to know that higher powers from home were watching my back. On the other hand, if the best they could do was a semi-retired spy, transported in time from 1940s Lisbon, I really was in trouble.

The flight lasted two and a half hours, with little to see from the windows other than mile upon mile of barren landscape defying the statistics of a 1.4 billion population. We landed at Anshan airport mid-afternoon and taxied past at least thirty fighter jets waiting on the apron. As we disembarked, I stopped briefly at the top of the steps to take in this spectacle of military might standing before me on the tarmac. I have had a fascination with all aircraft since I was a small child when my dad would take us to air shows. I felt a tap on my shoulder and turned to find a young Chinese man with a look of concern on his face.

'You must not look at military. You have big trouble.'

I proceeded to follow the other passengers, all with eyes front and seemingly oblivious to the increasing roar of the jet engines as they sparked into life. I entered the tiny

terminal and turned off the flight mode function on my
mobile phone. There was an immediate ping indicating I
had a message waiting. It was a text from Inspector Liu
with the address of the hotel where I was to head. I hailed a
taxi, showed the driver the address and hoped I had enough
cash for the ride. The initial part of the journey was spent in
mild confusion. At first there were only a few sparsely
scattered smallholdings but gradually they made way for
villages and, as the landscape became more scenic, the faint
outlines of mountains on the horizon came into view.
After about thirty minutes I could see Lego-like structures
in the distance which gradually increased in size and
number as we got closer. I guessed that this must be
Anshan city. Having spent most of my life in London there
was a strange sort of comfort to be approaching more
familiar urban surroundings. As we approached the city we
took a slip road that led to a tunnel through one of the
mountains. This was a shortcut to a district that housed
most of the region's universities as well as that of many
government ministerial headquarters. It was also where the
Shangzi Twins Hotel was located, about fifteen minutes' drive
from the city centre. While I would have felt more
comfortable had it been more central, the hotel was of a
high standard for the region and considered by locals,
including my taxi driver, to be quite luxurious. He hadn't
spoken any English but from the knowing smile on his face
when I first showed him the address, I could tell he was
impressed by the accommodation and was hoping that his
"wealthy" ride would be giving him a good tip. The hotel
cost two hundred and fifty yuan per night including
breakfast, which worked out at about thirty pounds Sterling.
This was considered top end of the market on the outskirts
but there were a couple of far more expensive hotels nearer
the centre, comparable with Western prices. Soon after the
2016 Brexit vote in Britain the conversion of the weakening
British pound meant that the cost was later to rise to nearer

£35, still incredibly cheap by British standards where an equivalent hotel in London would be upwards of £250 a night. The lobby was a vast concourse of cream marble with casual lounge seating in various alcoves, and my room was very acceptable with a king-size bed, a TV showing a few American films with Chinese subtitles, and a very decent-sized bathroom.

My eye was drawn to a note on the bedside table. It was addressed to me and was from the inspector, giving the address of his unit and assuring me that he would be in touch in the next few days to arrange an interview. I'm not sure if "unit" was a glitch in my translation app or whether it was what the police literally called their various offices. His address was, "*The Unit for Fraud and Public Protection.*" I unpacked and took a stroll around the hotel itself and the adjoining streets. The main lobby had the usual guests checking in or waiting for cabs into the city or the airport, and there was gentle piano music being played on a loop that was to become irritating over time as the tune never changed. The streets were ghostly quiet apart from a strange noise from the bordering trees. It sounded like a bunch of crazy people, hiding whilst impersonating a crow's caw. I stared up and searched the trees for signs of this strange bird, but it turned out to be a large species of cicada.

Most evenings, between perhaps six and ten o'clock there was more activity in evidence. Tables would be placed outside under an awning to the front and side of the lobby, and an adjacent neon sign lit up declaring the presence of a music bar. After a few days still waiting to be summoned, to break the boredom I decided to pop down and take a peek. It was a very modern bar situated on the ground floor which turned into a nightclub after 10pm. Hotel guests could access the venue from inside the lobby but there was also a street entrance. It served a decent range of food, had live music every night, and had prices that suited my very sparse wallet. I would mostly fill my stomach to capacity at the free breakfast buffet to save money, but the same stodge every day became monotonous; scrambled eggs with onions, various noodles, and sweet doughy balls some stuffed with mince. On occasion there would be sausages and bacon and on those days, I would stock up with a makeshift takeaway foil package and make sandwiches back in the room in the evening. I decided to try the bar and found it a welcome distraction, if not an essential one for the sake of my sanity. I would quite often visit to order some spicy lamb kebabs and a beer or two. They were quite small but at twenty pence a skewer, not a great burden on my purse. A large bottle of beer was ten Yuan, about one pound twenty a pint, so also very acceptable. Being surrounded by people who had no idea who you were or why you were there, listening to music and having fun like any other free man, was a major morale booster.

The first thing I had to get used to in this part of China was the constant staring. You could be in a bar or coffee shop, or even sitting quietly reading whilst sampling jellied pigskin for breakfast, and people would stop directly in front of your table and just stare. In fact, in the elevators, having been examined from head to toe, there seemed to be particular interest in my footwear. One day, early on during my time in Anshan I got so disturbed by this daily intrusion that I actually took my shoes off and held them aloft to afford all a better inspection. There had been plenty of attention directed towards me in Shanghai, but this north east remote region of China took it to another level. Literally the only Western face I ever set eyes on in my whole time there was the one looking back at me when I brushed my teeth in the mirror every morning.

The Chinese people, especially in the remoter regions, are

naturally very inquisitive and mean no offence by their actions. It is considered perfectly normal to take a long, close inspection of anything or anyone that seems out of the ordinary. The customary Western practice of delivering a "What the f… are you looking at?" stare, has no effect whatsoever. And a sarcastic, "Helloooooo, can I help you?" is often met by a big smile and a request to join you at your table, or even to have their photo taken with you. After a while I became immune to the attention and being treated as a walking zoo exhibit.

I was to become a regular fixture in the bar, sometimes just sipping tea and listening to music, and I looked forward to this escape from the tedium of just sitting in a hotel room. This is where I discovered more differences in the etiquette and nuances of social culture between East and West. After a few drinks, and with their inhibitions diminished, the inspections of the Anshan Chinese became more direct. People wouldn't just stop and stare. They would peer over my shoulder to see what I was looking at on my iPad or cast a glance into my bag to see what curiosities were hidden within. Of course, I would get some smiles and a "ni hau" from strangers and it was quite normal to expect people to say "hi" accompanied by "where are you from?" However, the most common icebreaker was "ni hau, ni jinnian duodale?" which translates as "hello, how old are you?" and would almost always be followed by "ni jie hun lee ma?" which means "are you married?" The same thing would be asked by both sexes and by all age groups from grandmothers to small inquisitive children, so it could not be considered a chat-up line. However, it is considered impolite to ask a woman her age so during the flirting process the men have figured a way to overcome this problem.

Using the Chinese Zodiac which operates over a 12-year

cycle, each year is depicted by one of 12 animals in order and repeated every 12 years. For instance, the year 2000 was known as the "Year of the Dragon", 2001 as the "Year of the Snake" and the following year dedicated to the "Horse". Superstition dictates that some animals will be more compatible than others so a young suitor might say, "I was born in the Year of the Rat, what about you?" This meant he was born in 1972, 1984 or 1996. The young woman might happily answer that she was born, say, in the "Year of the Ox" and from that it shouldn't be too hard for the man to establish her birth year (1973, 1985 or 1997) and therefore her age.

Before coming to Anshan, I was told that another common first question often asked is, "What you do?" I suppose this applies to anywhere in the world, but elsewhere you are rarely required to furnish this information to someone you have never met or been introduced to. For some reason everyone assumed that I was a professor from one of the local universities. Giving a nod in the affirmative would satisfy this subject matter and move away from any uncomfortable questions as to my real reason for being on an extended stay in their country.

I would often be stopped by complete strangers to have a selfie taken with them so that they could show their friends they'd met a foreigner, a great rarity in Anshan. On busier evenings in the bar I might become subject to group stares from a table of, for instance, 16 guys on a stag night. They would all cram together on one side of the table so that they could watch the Western stranger without having to turn around every two minutes. Often something surprisingly pleasant would happen that would never occur back in the UK. At first there would be the mysterious appearance of beers at my table every time I returned from the bathroom. Then I would be asked to join a group at their table, both sides fully aware that we could not communicate with each other. This became a regular occurrence and on several occasions I would discover that, on attempting to settle my bill at the end of the night, a distant table of observers would have already paid my tab, leaving a simple message: "Welcome to China!" I was warming to these people more and more and there were further examples of kindness and generosity to follow.

I had found the language very difficult to learn. Being in a region that has basically no English-speaking people, one would have thought that a rapid learning process would be inevitable. We have all been on our travels and attempted our broken French or Spanish only for the waiter or shop owner to respond in perfect English, thus forcing us down the easier lazy route of reverting to our native tongue. But this was not an option in Anshan, and it created an obvious obstacle to the learning process. How do you ask the question, "How do I say?" They can't teach you the words you need to know if they don't understand what you are asking. Then I discovered WeChat, their social media equivalent of WhatsApp or Messenger, which is equipped with a translator.

It's a pretty useful tool and it helped a great deal, though it does have its limitations. Shorter sentences with carefully chosen words tend to work much better. For instance, a sentence like, "When are you available to meet again?" has too many possibilities for wrong translation. Rather, a better way to ask this might be, "We can meet, when?"

One time I sent a message to the police inspector explaining that I wished to go for a long walk as I had been confined to the hotel and immediate area for weeks. I needed some exercise and would be out of contact should they need me. The inspector replied, and I pressed the translate button and was a little shaken.

It read: "Stay in hotel. It is dangerous you must ensure your body does not come to harm!"

By this time, I was aware that many victims of the terrible fraud were from this region, but I had not seriously considered the possibility of being attacked despite the MacDonald's incident still fresh in my mind. Acting on Inspector Liu's advice I decided not to go for that walk and just watched more Chinese TV until the bar opened again. I was telling my friend, Christopher, back in Shanghai, about the shocking message and he asked me to forward the text to him. He was married to Rebecca, a Chinese girl who said she would try and clarify the translation. I was hugely relieved when she did because the message from Inspector Liu actually said:

"Staying in the hotel is not good for you. Exercise is good for your health."

I became friends with a number of the waiters and entertainment staff at the hotel bar. Across the whole country many Chinese, including most of the bar staff, adopt English first names. This is more popular with the younger age group who consider it trendy to be named after your favourite western singer or actor. The older ones that travel to bigger cities also adopt Western names to make life easier for the likes of us. One of the female singers explained that all her friends had English names, but she had not yet found one that she liked or that was unique. She didn't want to add a fourth Britney to her group of friends and Beyoncé just didn't seem to fit her profile, so she asked if I had any suggestions. She gave me a list of her likes and dislikes relating to music and film and waited eagerly for my choice of possibilities. It was clear that she was a big Beatles fan but, being very particularly feminine, I didn't think George or Ringo would do the trick. So, I suggested Abbey, inspired by the Abbey Road Studios connection. She loved the name and it is proudly displayed on her WeChat to this day. The following evening, two more staff approached me with the same dilemma having heard of Abbey's delight with her new adopted name. Before long I had gained a considerable reputation as the "Devine Giver of Western Names" and I was inundated by strangers approaching me for my inspiration and guidance. My consumption at the bar remained modest but my humble tab was decreasing rapidly thanks to the gratitude of these newly baptised patrons.

One such person asked to join me one day accompanied by his wife and seven-year-old daughter. Once again it was a total WeChat social event. To say he was a great admirer of the UK and everything British is an understatement. His iPhone had a Union Jack cover, he had a Buckingham Palace key ring and his phone's ringtone was *Land of Hope and Glory*. It was quite surreal! He came from Inner Mongolia, had never been outside China and didn't speak a word of English. He asked me what Western name I thought would be suitable for him. He was not the biggest chap, but he was in very good physical shape and although he had a very pleasant demeanour, there was an undercurrent of toughness and authority in him. So, my suggestion was Jason Statham who typically plays a hard man in his numerous action films. He leapt from his seat, reciting Statham film titles with the biggest smile on his face. It was obvious he was a big fan. He then proceeded to the stage where he dedicated a Chinese friendship song to me declaring me as part of his extended family. We began to socialize more often, and he proved to be a kind of guardian angel during my time there. On one occasion he presented me with a double-lined leather coat as the temperatures in Northern China were by then regularly hitting minus twenty and I had only come equipped for a short summer business trip. He told me that he had lost weight and the coat was now too big for him. He would be honoured if I would accept the gift. It would not have been my personal choice of attire, but it was most welcome and a saviour in the freezing conditions. Later, when I was hanging the gift in my hotel closet, a receipt slipped from the pocket. It showed that the coat was in fact brand new and had been purchased only the day before.

Chapter 24.   The Chinese Prosecutor

One week after checking into the *Shangzi Twins Hotel*, on Wednesday, 20th July 2016 I was summoned to the reception. The grand lobby was unusually quiet, so I was particularly conscious of my trainers making an annoying squeak as I crossed the marble floor. A recently dusted crystal chandelier seemed to twinkle in time with the gentle piano music piped through concealed speakers. The comfy sofas were unoccupied and the lacquered black tables, with brightly coloured scenes of flowers and waterfalls imbedded in the surface, had not yet been tarnished by ringed coffee cup stains. Directly ahead was the buffet area where I would be eating breakfast for the foreseeable future. I had run out of cash and as the hotel did not take Visa and I had no other means of paying. I provided the hotel manager with Inspector Liu's phone number in order to help me solve the problem. The Inspector sent a junior officer along to mediate and to also give me strict instructions of what I could and couldn't do. He gave me a list of restrictions as to where and how far I would be allowed to wander in my free time. Whatever was said to the receptionist it certainly changed the way I was treated thereafter. It's possible that they thought I was an important consultant to the Chinese Police force rather than under investigation for major fraud as I was immediately given a credit line, a luxury afforded many police officials that stayed there on brief visits to the area. All hotels in China require visitors to show their passports but mine had been taken by the police some weeks earlier in order to extend my visa and was still with the immigration authorities. This was a problem but a quick call from the Inspector reassured the hotel management and, in hindsight, it was very kind of him not to divulge the real reason that I was staying in Anshan. Of course, this could have been for any number of reasons; operational secrecy surrounding the case or maybe simply for my own protection but either way, it meant that I was treated with great respect during my stay.

Five days later I was instructed to be in the hotel lobby at 8 am sharp ready to be collected by the Inspector. He arrived on time and ushered me to his private vehicle. Once again this must have looked like I was an important dignitary, having the car door held open for me and of course, no handcuffs. We travelled for about twenty minutes back through the mountain tunnel emerging on to Shengli Road, the main approach to Anshan city centre. At the end of Shengli Road was a big roundabout called, oxymoronically, Victory Square, a reference to the ousting of Japanese occupiers in the final days of World War II. The last building before the roundabout was an imposing grey structure adorned with immense Chinese flags, and along the top of the structure was a sign that read:

"Head Office of the Prosecutor for Serious Crime by Foreign Nationals"

I didn't know what to expect but feared the worst. I was guided through security and led to the fourth floor where I was told to wait in a small reception room. My mind was racing, and my increasing anxiety was not comforted by my inability to gauge the time – there was no clock on the wall and my phone and watch had been taken from me. I tried counting the seconds using my nervously bouncing knee as a type of metronome; every three jerks equating to one second with each one hundred and eighty bounces making a minute. Soon the count was in the thousands and I'd lost track, but I reckon I'd been waiting at least an hour before the door opened and a young man entered with a very disarming smile. To my surprise he introduced himself as my interpreter in perfect clipped English and my paranoia was lightened as he tried to put me at my ease. He told me not to worry, that this was a formality where the Chief Prosecutor in the country was to inform me of the procedure of such legal affairs in China.

The Inspector then returned and led us to another room which resembled a Barristers' Chamber on the Gray's Inn Road back in London. A pudgy guy in Nike trainers, jeans and a tee-shirt was waiting for us. Despite his casual attire he had at his disposal far more power of punishment than a British or European court could dispense; they still had the death sentence in China.

Prior to this meeting I had engaged the services or two law firms, one in Hong Kong and the other in Shanghai. These were affiliates of friends' offices in London and as such I was afforded "mates' rates". The advice from both, however, concluded that if this went to the Procuratorate (prosecutor) then it would almost certainly go to court where I would be tried. Should this happen, they went on to say - given the number of accusations, the video evidence of me delivering speeches around Asia, the sheer scale and size of the fraud, and the fact that Chinese citizens had taken their lives - the outlook for me would be bleak. Furthermore, the cost of them representing me in court would be at least £100,000, with the only realistic success being one of damage limitation. They were certain it would be a custodial sentence at best, informing me that ninety nine percent of cases that go to court result in a conviction on the first day of trial.

And here I was. The worst had happened. I was in front of the Procuratorate. I was going to court. The prosecutor spoke directly to me, as if I could understand everything he was saying, and communicating to me without words that I should focus on only him. Not once did he glance at the Inspector or even the interpreter who translated intermittently. If I occasionally looked at the interpreter for assistance, the prosecutor would stop until he had my direct attention again. His face remained impassive, showing neither contempt nor sympathy. He would have been an excellent poker player if that were legal in China. He told me that all serious financial crimes against Chinese citizens were reviewed by him. Those deemed less serious were delegated to another less important office in one of the provinces. But the most serious cases were handled directly by him, and his decision was that my case was the latter. He went on to say that the most serious crimes that he brings to court can result in the death penalty, but he wished to carry out more investigations as there were possible indications that I could have been deceived by others. In those circumstances, he suggested, it would be most likely that any sentence would be commuted to life imprisonment.

I have no recollection of leaving his office, of returning to the hotel, or indeed anything for the following few days. I was in a complete daze. On the Friday I received another message from the Inspector.

"You must attend our police unit at midday today."

I needed to get my head straight again, and quickly. There were only two things that kept rotating in my mind from the meeting with the prosecutor; the first, that I could be facing life in prison, the second, that there was a glimmer of hope in his proclamation that he believed I could have been deceived. Did this mean he considered me more akin to a victim or was I just hoping I could convince him that this was the case? I needed to stop the tears and prove to the authorities that the latter was true. Attending interviews with a sad pleading demeanour would do me no good whatsoever. The culprits of major crimes handled by these offices must repeatedly try this tactic, and authorities would be impervious to this approach. If anything, it might only serve to persuade them I was guilty.

The Inspector's address was printed in Chinese after the message in a business card type format. I exited the lobby and hailed a cab, showed the driver the address on my phone and watched as he shook his head in the negative and drove away. The same thing happened with the next two taxis and time was moving on. I was starting to panic as turning up late for these appointments was something I was not planning to do. Their solution to prevent this happening again would surely be to keep me locked in a cell. I rushed back into the hotel and hunted down Miss Zhou, the ever-helpful hotel manager. I hoped that the WeChat translation explaining my problem was accurate and didn't say, "My legs need bad travel fast" or some such similar mistranslation. She smiled, indicating that I should stay seated and wait for her return. Five minutes later, and with just ten minutes before the midday appointment, she returned carrying her coat. She gestured for me to follow, clearly intending to escort me to the police station, which was a great relief. But with such a short window to get there, it seemed inevitable that I was going to be late. I was extremely tense. We left the hotel, turned right and walked for about three minutes to a crossroads. We made another right turn, walked for another couple, at which point she indicated that we had arrived. The extremely close proximity of the hotel to my intended destination was obviously the reason why the cabs had declined my fare, rather than the foreboding address!

I went into the reception and, with no English speakers to assist me, I showed the officer at the desk my message from Inspector Liu. He obviously understood or likely had been expecting me. I need not have panicked about being potentially late as I was ushered to a seat where I sat patiently for 45 minutes before a young female officer arrived, indicating for me to follow her. We ascended some stairs, passed through security, and took another few flights up to the third floor. I followed her down a long corridor to the very last room on the right and entered. The windowless room contained five desks, a coffee table and a small sofa, which is where I was told to sit. All five officers were drinking Chinese tea and chain-smoking, the air was so thick it brought immediate tears to your eyes. Two female officers were opening mail order boxes and trying on shoes, scarfs and other purchases. Another officer was sitting with his shoes and socks placed on his desk as he massaged his feet. This was about as far as one could get from the scene that I thought would be awaiting me. One of the female officers introduced herself. She was to be my interpreter that day, and on a number of future occasions. She was nowhere near as proficient a translator as the young man at the prosecutor's office and, unlike him, she worked for the police and was therefore not unbiased. This was a concern which I would need to address going forward, but for now it was the only way we were going to communicate. After half an hour, during which I had my picture and fingerprints taken again and a statement of the charges I was facing read to me, the group refilled their cups, offered me a drink and a pack of cigarettes was thrust towards me. It was all very disarming, leading me to believe that perhaps it would all be ok. The Inspector, while exuding an air of authority in the room seemed to be in a very good mood, perhaps it was because nearly the weekend. He was also the only one in civilian clothes and clearly took pride in his trendy appearance. He was not a young man anymore but was in good physical condition, preferring the trim look of an athlete as opposed to that of a body builder. He wore white Lacoste trainers, white Armani jeans, a black tee-shirt depicting what looked like a

Chinese rock band, and a white, quilted puffer jacket slung over his chair.

When they had finished their third or fourth cigarettes, I was told to follow them back down the way I had come an hour earlier. I was thinking that this wasn't too bad, thinking that I would be sent on my way. As we reached the reception where I first came in, we took a left through a small security door that I had not previously noticed. Once through it looked like I had entered the changing room of a third division football team. There were small steel lockers around the walls into one of which I was told to deposit the contents of my pockets, my phone, wallet, pen and loose change. Along the wall to my left were shower-type cubicles and on the long table were strange implements lying in trays. These, and the plastic kitchen gloves, left no doubt that this area was reserved for more intrusive searches. I was filled with dread but, just as quickly, relieved again as I was led fully clothed into another room.

The walls were all covered in a green felt and there were cameras mounted in all four corners. It looked like a small studio with a green screen for adding artificial scenes to a movie. There was a raised area at the back of the room where three desks and chairs were placed, facing forwards. The cameras were all focused on the centre of the room where, to my horror, was one of the giant highchairs complete with manacles, identical to the one from my initial arrest back in Shanghai. I climbed up onto my perch and was once again secured in place by ankle braces and wrist cuffs attached to the fold down table. For the next two hours I was asked pretty much all the same questions I'd been asked three months previously.

"How much were you paid?"

"Who paid you?"

"Who collected money from the victims?"

"Do you recognise these people and what was their position?"

"Where did you meet them?"

"Do you know where they are?"

"If you didn't take the money, who did?"

It was difficult to stop myself imploring that I'd already told them everything I knew but, realising this interrogative tactic was being employed to seek out any deviation from my previous answers, I patiently repeated what I'd already said; the truth. And while I told them again everything I knew, holding nothing back, I did have a slight concern that there could have been some inconsistencies due to the thirty-six hours of sleepless fatigue during that first interview process. Back then I was in shock and those conditions can confuse the brain somewhat. Inspector Liu told the translator to inform me that I would be shown an interesting movie on a projector and I should make myself comfortable and concentrate on what I was about to see. How he expected that I would be comfortable on a rock-hard chair with my hands and ankles manacled, was ridiculous ... but maybe that was the point. A 40-year-old projector sprang into life and threw a rectangular beam of light onto the back wall. There were a few seconds of flickering as the ancient machine warmed up before the title *Euro Fx* came into focus. There were short clips of me speaking at the various events, where the locations would appear and then fade away as each scene changed; Macau,

Bangkok, Singapore, Kuala Lumpur, and so on. Then there was a scene of perhaps ten, seemingly not wealthy, individuals walking through a poor village and entering a community hall. The footage was both shaky and grainy; it looked like it had been filmed on a phone with a dusty lens, or some other outdated mobile device. The camera operator then took a seat amongst the other Chinese-looking people, arranged in a semi-circle. The camera then focused on the speaker who was standing in the middle of the group. I immediately recognised him. It was the man they called Eagle, with his impeccable suit and overly charming smile. He began giving a presentation on *Euro Fx* and my interpreter occasionally translated the script for me. Other parts of the video needed no translation. Eagle was showing pictures of his colleagues shaking hands with high-profile investors which was making a very positive impression on the group. They were oooing and ahhhing as they recognised the various Chinese celebrities and businessmen. I was confused as to why Eagle would be pitching to this poorer audience. Perhaps he had exhausted the high earners and was now milking the last dregs before shutting up shop. Of course, the success of any Ponzi scheme relies on the continual recruitment of investors at entry level in order to maintain pay outs to the upper levels. Eventually though, there are simply not enough new investors to prop up the scam and it inevitably reaches a point where the scheme collapses, with the bulk of the victims being the investors on the bottom rungs who lose their entire investment. I was still confused though. I couldn't imagine how the meagre investment these poor wretches could manage would justify Eagle's travel to this impoverished community. But when the next scene was explained to me by the Inspector, it made me feel sick to the core.

After Eagle's sales pitch, that had his audience drooling at the massive life-changing amounts of money they could make, one of the ten stood and explained that, as excited as they were, they could not afford to invest. This is when Eagle introduced a gentleman that could lend them the amounts that they needed, providing they had some sort of asset to guarantee the loan. They all jumped up, offering their corner shop or other businesses, even their homes, as collateral. They had no idea that they would never receive any profits and would never be able to repay this loan shark. The screen then changed back to a compilation of footage that had been sent to the Anshan police. It showed one of the ten investors asleep in an alley across the road from the shop that he had once owned. It showed another clip of an elderly lady self-medicating her cancer with herbs from her garden, no longer able to afford medical care. Another clip, and the worst, showed a coffin containing the body of one investor who had committed suicide by drinking bleach. My disgust at this ruthlessness, and at not realising sooner what I had been duped into representing, was impossible to contain. I broke down in tears.

We went back upstairs, and I waited for the transcript of my interview to be printed. I then had to read, sign and date each page and place my thumb print over my signature. I was then free to leave and return to the *Shangzi*. Everyone knows that there are no answers to be found at the bottom of a bottle, but I needed something to temporarily erase the terrible images that were still so fresh in my mind. I was horrified by the scale of the suffering I had witnessed and that I had been an unwitting party to such a cruel deception. And I felt so sad for the victims and so very angry at the perpetrators. If I slept that night at all, it was a fitful sleep filled with the most vivid of nightmares.

But drinking gave no real escape from the pressure, at least not for long. The following morning, I rose early, showered and then checked my email. I was hoping for any sort of good news that would lift my depression. The first message was anything but good news. It was another communication from Shanbao Li, the representative of the group of *Euro Fx* victims.

(Actual transcript)

Subject: EuroFX Trial

Hi David

I understand your current situation and the potential trial you are facing. Financial fraud leads to severe sentence in China.

I offered help in my previous emails - I hoped that you could repent and to earn credit from all your mistakes, however you ignored. I feel sorry for you, sorry for your repetitive mistakes.

You know better than anyone that you are suffering the consequence of scam designed by David Orchard and Bryan Cook. If you insist your mistake, you are eventually becoming **the scapegoat of the complete fraud. 4400 EuroFX victims in China, US, Japan, Singapore are all pointing to you as the leading criminal. But you know you are not.** *I hope you had time now to think about what I suggested previously - to confess your mistake and to provide all evidence you have to reveal Orchard &*

Cook's scam. It is your only option.

You will be sentenced in China, it's only a matter of time now. Did you ever think about the impact to your family? Your kids? It might be long departure and life humiliation to every beloved ones around you. Why not to do your best to reduce the misdeed immediately? Why to cover other's bigger crime on yourself?

I am happy to talk. I could even forgive you based on your cooperation. Again, I am here to save you from the heaviest lawful punishment ahead.

Think twice ...

Chao Ma

I was already cooperating fully with the police, but after the revelations of the previous day it was at this point that I decided to give Chao Ma as much information as I could. First though, I had to obtain permission from the Inspector. He indicated that this would be fine as they too were keeping her informed of developments. This was final confirmation to me that Shanbao was real and was indeed the elderly victim she described herself to be. I also thought it best that I give an update to my lawyers in Shanghai and find out if there was any progress being made at their end. They responded very quickly and sent the message shown below:

(Actual transcript)

My Solicitor

"Regarding the action to be taken, we would have to become familiar with the police investigation, which appears to be taken place across various police offices (which is not uncommon). The sooner we know what is going on and what the potential charges are, the bigger the chance to build a strong(er) defense or steer towards release/acquittal. We will first contact our connections at Shanghai police level, before approaching Anshan police.

Nevertheless, you may understand that your situation looks not promising given that there are many alleged victims of alleged fraud that filed complaints with PRC police, while PRC police seemingly has sought cooperation with London police to investigate this matter."

They later told me that all the investigations were now taking place solely in Anshan, being the country's centre for public protection crimes, and that their contacts in the Shanghai police would not give any insight. The only response they received from either the Anshan police or the prosecutor's office was that they would be informed of any charges to be made once the investigation was complete. This essentially meant that they would have to prepare several defences, based on a variety of potential charges, which increased the cost exponentially. It also meant that once charges were made, they would only have days to select and fine tune their representation of my case.

Chapter 25.   Shadow Banking

I needed to do more research and try to figure things out. I knew that the secrecy and restrictions in China regarding internet access would be a problem but there were things I needed to know if I was going to escape this nightmare. Were the "gang of five", seen leaving the hotel in Macau, dignitaries from China? Were they the first to invest in a foreign exchange product, testing the transaction process before the mass population were given permission? If so, why did Panda fabricate a story about a gambling win and why was the reaction to my impromptu appearance in his room met with such shock and concern? It seemed obvious to me now that the VIPs were *leaving* with the cash, not depositing it. But was this a bribe or some sort of legitimate payment? Recent news clips on TV stated that President Xi Jinping had announced a crackdown on Chinese officials taking bribes. Many of them complied with the directive or cleverly covered their tracks, but others simply fled the country … to be pursued over the coming years. How could so many of the victims have hailed from mainland China? It still seemed strange as the amounts involved and the product being offered were both illegal activities for Chinese nationals. During my research I became aware of a new phenomenon known as "shadow banking"; a system where vast amounts of Yuan were being converted, laundered and spirited out of the country, mostly to Macau and Hong Kong. Shadow banking involved so-called Wealth Management Products (WMPs) that offered much higher rates of interest to investors and it operated under the radar of the Chinese standard regulatory system.

WMPs offer higher rates because they are based on riskier bank loans which are neither held on their balance sheets nor set-aside capital against their potential defaults. Instead, the banks typically extend them via intermediaries called trust companies; firms that, while not allowed to accept deposits or formally loan out money, are allowed to manage it. These trust companies create investment products like WMPs which banks market for them in return for a commission. The trust then invests the money gathered through a WMP in a given company which, while it might be described as a "loan", is really (and legally) more like an equity investment.

Using a virtual private network (VPN), I did manage to get some more answers and my research suggested that these WMPs could invest or lend money to an entity outside of China. Was this what had happened? It would certainly explain why so many victims were from the mainland.

I also discovered a surprising amount of information on a sector known as "Gangster Grannies". These were older, seemingly respectable ladies who would solicit monies from wealthy locals right across the country without attracting any attention from the authorities. Could it have been that *Euro FX* used these ladies as Introducing Brokers?

Following President Xi's announcement of a crackdown, there were lots of stories telling of ex-Chinese officials being forcibly repatriated from neighbouring countries. As virtually every country in the Far East relies heavily on Chinese financial assistance, any request for extraditions were usually met with full approval and assistance. One evening whilst watching a Chinese news channel, broadcast in English, there was a clip of twenty or thirty scammers and exiled politicians being led from a plane onto the tarmac in Bejing. This particular flight had originated in Taiwan which China still considers to be one of its territories. Among the chained-together gang was an individual that looked suspiciously like Bear, though I couldn't be sure as it was only a fleeting glimpse. However, when the camera focussed a little longer on one of the more regal figures who was trying to maintain a dignified air despite being in handcuffs, I was sure I recognised him. And the last time I'd seen him, he was leaving the hotel in Shanghai holding a tan-coloured briefcase shortly before my own arrest. A thought came to me. If Bear was responsible for handling clients from Taiwan, could there possibly be a link between this territory and his given nametag? I googled information on Taiwan and discovered that the black bear is a national symbol. I didn't need to google Indonesia to recall that this was the region looked after by the Singaporean named Komodo. Things were falling into place. I found out that the Draco is a lizard from the Philippines, also known as a flying dragon. I was sure that Draco was the name given to one of the less senior members of the *Euro Fx* crew. Then a gargantuan penny dropped. The most senior member of the team, the one with the long fingernail, was named after the most recognised symbol of China. His name? Panda, of course!

The *Euro Fx* scammers had an in-depth understanding of Chinese culture and etiquette and used this to their full advantage. They must have known that if they convinced a few officials or other revered and respected figures to invest, then the herd would follow. If a senior member of a family or village was onto a good thing then he would be duty-bound to share this great opportunity with his friends and extended family. As is the nature of the Ponzi scheme, as more people invested, the original investors would receive great rewards, paid for directly by these new gullible investors. The tragedy was that the scammers preyed on this trusting culture, and many of the family members, too proud to say that they could not afford the investment, would borrow the money instead. This was all too familiar from the film/slide show I had been shown at the police unit. There was some limited information on the illegal loan-sharking problem in China. It told how people that got into debt suffered threats and great hardship, sometimes causing them to take their own lives. There were others who could not afford life-saving medicine having succumbed to preventable diseases as well as cancer. There is no fall-back public health service in China. These stories confirmed the police footage shown to me.

There was another group that was allegedly taken advantage of by the scammers: Many young siblings who would have traditionally taken over the family farm, sharing accommodation with their parents and grandparents, were now migrating to the cities. Here they would work hard all year round, returning home every twelve months or so with their hard-earned savings. This would be far more lucrative and beneficial to the families than eking out a living from the land. These young entrepreneurial spirits were convinced that an investment in *Euro Fx* would impress their families as they could contribute far more to the pot. However, the harsh truth was that their investments disappeared, and they were frequently overcome by despair and the loss of integrity and respect in the eyes of their loved ones. In lieu of their help on the home farmstead, these families relied on the financial contribution from their city-dwelling relations. Knowing that their families may not survive the coming year without their desperately needed contribution was often too much to bear, and the shame often drove them to suicide

Many people have heard the term "Ponzi Scheme" but few really know how that name came about. It relates to a man by the name of Carlo Pietro Giovanni Tebalo Ponzi, better known as Charles Ponzi. He was born in Italy in 1882 and emigrated to Boston in 1903. After learning English and doing some very menial jobs, he moved to Montreal, eventually becoming manager at Bank Zarossi servicing the needs of the immigrant Italian community. He rose to the position of manager, attracting a vast increase in customers capitalising on Zarossi Bank's promise of double the interest rate currently offered by other banks on new deposits. He discovered that the bank was paying this interest from the accounts of new investors and was in financial trouble. It wasn't long before the auditors discovered what was going on and the bank collapsed leaving many of its customers in penury. Ponzi, meanwhile, had already departed for the USA with a chunk of the bank's money and, more importantly, the knowledge of how it was done.

During the First World War, many Italian businesses used a postage system and network called International Reply Credit (IRC). This was a system whereby people could correspond or reply to letters without paying for postage stamps. The cost was paid by the sender as credits, encouraging a response from the counterparty. When inflation rocketed in Italy, Ponzi realised he could cash in these credits for postage stamps for a premium in the USA, and then sell them. Ponzi borrowed money and sent it to his relatives in Italy asking and told them to purchase these credits. It was working perfectly but he saw an opportunity to upscale the operation. He approached a number of friends in Boston, promising to double their investment in ninety days using this loophole. Everything was working perfectly and by March 1920 his company, *The Securities Exchange Company*, had achieved $350,000 profit in today's terms. Initial investors in the scheme were being paid handsomely and word spread. Everyone wanted a piece of the action. Turnover in the scheme increased exponentially and by July of that year, Ponzi was personally making $250,000 a day!

The Boston Post decided to investigate after receiving anonymous tip-offs about the scheme and concluded that, with the number of investors and the returns being promised, there would have to have been one hundred and sixty-million of these postal coupons in circulation. It was later verified that there were only twenty-seven thousand actual coupons traded. The stampede of greedy and gullible investors rushing to dive into the project was immense and Ponzi kept taking money, keeping the majority but still paying out very high returns to the influencers and the original investors. After *The Boston Post*'s findings were released, the whole scheme collapsed in a few days as investors demanded their money back.

This is what *Euro Fx* must have been doing. New investors' money was being used to pay cash dividends to the original investors. Once new investors began to dry up and people wanted to withdraw their money, the scheme then closed and the crooks ran off with the remaining money; basically, all the deposits less the relatively small amount that had been paid out.

There have been other infamous frauds, such as Bernard Madoffs $50 billion scam in the US, to date the largest Ponzi scheme in history. He was eventually sentenced to 150 years in prison in 2009 but his high profile and reputation meant that he had managed to continue attracting investors over the previous seventeen years, only being rumbled when a plethora of investors needed to withdraw their funds during the 2008 financial crash. Many said that the investors should have known better and deserved what they got. I think that's harsh however, because with *Euro Fx* there was a significant difference. This seemed to be the clever exploitation of people who had been kept in a financial cocoon under the communist system. With the acceptance, albeit slowly, of capitalism in

China, the people believed their new-found freedom to invest would open doors to the great riches that were evident in the West. This new breed of investor, so ruthlessly exploited, was trusting, naïve and vulnerable.

Euro Fx was so cleverly conceived, with so many collaborators across multiple borders, that even *I* believed the high returns being offered were a genuine reward for investing in a great company with its aggressive global expansion and superior technology. This was a well-organised, sophisticated and innovative bunch of crooks, and I'd been set up to take the blame.

Chapter 26. Music was a distraction

The days had turned to weeks, then months since my arrest in Shanghai. As I awoke each day, I was never sure what state of mind I'd be in. Some days I would be quite upbeat, taking solace from my theory that if they had found incriminating evidence then I would have already been summoned to court and subsequently sent to some hell hole for the rest of my life. Other days though, I would be filled with dark thoughts of never seeing loved ones again. As time went on the dark days outnumbered the bright ones by four to one. I was moody, incredibly depressed and was spending more and more time in the hotel room, finding no inspiration to go for a walk or to summon the enthusiasm to see my friends in the hotel bar. This lethargy became more acute each time my visa was extended by a further three months each time.

But music was still a distraction. It was the only thing on TV that could be enjoyed without being proficient in Mandarin. On more than one occasion I would find myself singing along, not having a clue as to what the lyrics meant. Like a parrot! The range of artists aired on these variety programmes was an eclectic mix; a traditional song would be followed by a catchy, modern tune, followed by experimental music that mixed ancient with modern instruments. It was as though I was witnessing the transformation and maturation of an industry that had previously only allowed government-approved songs.

Since Wham made the first public appearance of a Western artist in China back in 1985, it has taken some time for the music scene to gather momentum. But in the last five years or so they have witnessed the establishment of an efficient and prolific industry to fill their giant Wurlitzers or these days, Huawei or Samsung smartphones. They are churning out artists and songs at an incredible rate, just like any other Chinese industry production line. While it is a unique sound, it's also familiar in a disconcerting sort of way. There are covers and sampling of Western songs from the last hundred years along with some new home-grown productions. There is also an array of traditional Chinese songs given a fresh lease of life with modern technology and synthesisers. Somewhere behind the scenes they must have their very own version of Simon Cowell, nurturing his own stable of manufactured all-girl groups and boy bands. The music industry there has been selectively raiding Western back-catalogues from all genres, but should a Western band wish to file a lawsuit against them for breach of copyright, then good luck. It won't get very far.

Music is such a massive part of Chinese culture. Their attitude is simply, if it's a good song it should be sung often and by anyone. It is not uncommon to see three different artists have a Chart Hit with the same song at the same time. In the bar of the *Shangzi*, between sets from the live band, people would put their name down for Karaoke. More than one time I saw four locals take to the stage one after the other and give their own rendition of the very same number. Each time they would receive great applause, as if an old favourite had just been sung for the first time that night.

I enjoyed watching music channels to relax in my hotel room, partly because many songs were delivered in English and partly because those in Chinese frequently had a familiar backing track. I became intrigued watching the crowds in the audience at televised live shows. They would sit, typically uniform, devoid of any such disorder as a "mosh pit" or any individualistic expression. I had heard that a concert by Dua Lipa was raided by police who actually removed fans that were dancing instead of remaining in their seats. And, even though homosexuality is not illegal in China, others were removed for waving gay rights flags or wearing rainbow tee-shirts.

When home-grown talent was performing, audience participation was highly regimented. If the artist was a crooner, such as their own version of Michael Bublé or Barry Manilow, everyone would raise both their arms and begin a gentle sway to the music, resembling seaweed moving side to side at the command of the current. More traditional but updated songs, given a modern beat, were greeted by the entire audience clapping in time. There seemed to be an inordinate number of fans in dispute as to what the commanding rhythm of the song actually was. The final grouping, which always brought a smile to my face, were the rock fans. On entry to a concert they were provided with light sticks which were waved back and forth at the stage in perfect unison. It was as if ten thousand people were simultaneously fly-fishing with Star Wars light sabres. Head banging had not yet crossed the border between East and West and would probably have been disallowed then.

There were plenty of boy bands in evidence as well; handsome young men mostly singing songs about the girl in their dreams, and every gooey-eyed girl listening, believing whole-heartedly that the words were being directed at them, would be crying. This brought back memories of my strolls through People's Park in Shanghai on a sunny Sunday morning. The park would have clearly allocated sections for the various activities deemed suitable to be performed or enjoyed in a public space. On entering the park, the first groups you would meet would be the younger generation, preferring to stay close to the exits with easy access to the coffee shops and cafes. The guys would be doing push ups and shows of strength, pretending that this is what they would be doing regardless of the group of young girls relaxing on the grass, in turn pretending not to watch them. The girls would be giggling and sharing earpieces, listening to dreamy love songs, perhaps wondering if one of these guys could be like the vocalist in the boy band singing the lyrics.

Deeper into the park would be the much older generation, shaded from the sun, often engrossed in a most serious mind battle of Mah-jong. Closer to the centre were beautiful lily-covered koi lakes, a place of serenity and peace. No doubt this was why adjacent to the lakes was an area dedicated to the practice of Tai Chi. Originally developed in the 13th century as a form of martial arts, Tai Chi is now better known and used as a form or relaxation, to "become at one with nature". The slow fluid movements were entrancing and performed equally gracefully by all ages, from eight to eighty. Arms outstretched, slowly simultaneously moving to one side as though they were drawing back one half of an invisible set of curtains. A knee raised vertically above a pointed foot then gently placed down on imaginary rice paper that must not be torn. Like a teenager creeping back upstairs after breaking the midnight curfew.

The last section of the park, tucked away in the corner, would generally be deserted on a weekday. Sundays, however, were very different. When entering this area, I was often greeted by expectant eyes peering up from beneath umbrellas at tables adorned with pictures and poetry. There would be an empty seat at each stall where you were encouraged to sit and peruse the photos or read the correspondence. Each table contained pictures of a young lady, efficiently engaging in household chores or posing in a beautiful dress. I was welcomed with open arms at all the vacant seats but as I left the proprietor would take on a clear demeanour of disappointment. If I had been able to read the complicated calligraphy of Mandarin script, I would have understood that these people were parents from the poorer regions and were on a very specific mission; to find a husband for their daughter. A Chinese friend explained that the poetry and letters would have been written by the daughter, dictated by the parents, declaring love and loyalty to any interested party prepared and financially able to support the whole troupe, chickens and all.

Chapter 27.   I've been spotted

It was now late autumn 2016 and I was coming near to the end of another three-month period of enforced "holiday" in China. All hopes of being told I could head home, however slim, were dashed when I received another text message from the Inspector.

"I receive you in lobby of my unit at 9am to look at the visa establish."

Despite this confusing message, I was getting used to the translation nuances and understood that I was required to attend the police station the following morning to be taken to the visa office for another three-month extension. This proved to be correct and the next day all the formalities were completed. The visa office was on the far side of Anshan and took about thirty minutes by car. It was a huge building adjacent to a railway line used mainly to transport coal to neighbouring North Korea. The main hall was vast with hundreds of seats occupied by Chinese people hoping to be given permission to cross the borders for a vacation in Europe or even America. The majority of these people would leave with no visa, thus no upcoming vacation. I was led straight into one of the VIP glass-walled interview rooms. The visa officers obviously carried great power as even the Inspector seemed a little intimidated by their questions as to the reasons to grant yet another extension. The forms were duly filled out, I paid my fee and handed over my passport to be collected a few weeks later.

I was taken back to the *Shangzi* where I sat with my iPad trying to figure out how my rapidly depleting funds were going to cope with another twelve weeks. No matter which way I tried to manipulate the digits in front of me, there was no way that the money was going to stretch to my requirements. So, I logged out of internet banking and logged in to Citrip, the Chinese equivalent of Expedia or Travel Zoo. I needed to find a cheaper hotel.

I was lucky enough to find an *Ibis*, a hotel chain I recognised, that had no foreigner restrictions and was a hundred Yuan cheaper a night. I checked out of the *Shangzi* and headed to the city centre where the *Ibis* was located. Ironically, it was immediately around the corner from the prosecutor's office and, although much further from the police station, it was also much closer to the bank that facilitated the Western Union transfers. My visits to the bank, although not that frequent, were far more regular than my interviews at the police unit, so this also made sense. Virtually no establishments or hotels accepted Visa or MasterCard in this part of the world and, with my situation in their country, I was not eligible for a China Union Pay card. So, Western Union it was.

When I first arrived at the Shangzi in Anshan and discovered I had this problem, I asked the police officers if they could obtain the IBAN and Swift details for the hotel so that I could make an international transfer to solve the issue. They were unaware of what this was. After some time of making no headway I resigned myself to the tedious task of having to use Western Union to obtain my funds. I asked the officers which banks could facilitate Western Union but again was met with blank stares. I found this incredible as these people were from the head office for technology and financial crime in China. I later realised that, far from being behind the times or uninformed on the methods of moving money around, they rarely used such "antiquated" systems! More than sixty percent of the population, from the oldest pensioner to the youngest school kid, had been using mobile apps such as Wepay and Ali-pay for several years. Scanning QR codes to pay for everything from shoes to bus journeys was the norm, something that is only just taking off in the Western world of commerce.

Eventually I found a bank, the *Agricultural Bank of China* (ABC), that could handle Western Union and this establishment was a ten-minute walk from the *Ibis*, my new home for potentially the next three months. Anshan is quite a busy city, small by Chinese standards but still boasting a population in the millions and my first days were occupied exploring the city centre. The weather was still warm so window-shopping strolls each day helped pass the time. The layout of the shops took a uniform pattern: Restaurant, electrical shop, restaurant, clothes shop, restaurant, lucky cat Knick knack shop, restaurant, and so on.

It was banking day again and after double-checking my map and memorising the directions for my ten to fifteen-minute trek, I set off. As I exited the elevator and approaching the automatic glass doors leading to the street, I noticed a rather large man standing across the street who seemed to make more than casual eye contact. I watched as he finished his text message and deposited his phone in the pocket of his oversized jeans, just below the strained elasticated waist that was struggling to contain his considerable girth. I stayed in the lobby until he strolled away, disappearing into the throng of people heading to their first meal of the day. I decided this was just paranoia playing games with my head and continued on my way. The young girl at the bank was very efficient and possessed a more than passable command of the English language, so my transaction was completed with ease. As I was leaving the bank, I spotted dumpling man again, this time leaning casually against a car. There is no way this could be a coincidence; my paranoia was undoubtedly justified. I considered heading in a different direction so that I would not be followed back to my hotel, but that was a pointless plan as he already knew where I was staying. I set off at a brisk pace feeling certain that my pursuer's clogged arteries and overworked heart would not be up to the task of a close tail. I didn't need to turn around to know that I had misjudged. The heavy plodding, accompanied by his wheezing that sounded like a set of bagpipes with a hole in the wind sac, told me he was just paces behind. I decided to cut my own pace down to that of a tortoise, faking the demeanour of a man with nowhere in particular to go and all the time in the world to get there. I would speed up and then slow down and speed up again. The same result; he was still there. At the next road cross section, I decided to stop, light a cigarette, and browse in the window of a Knick knack shop for a greater time than any interest in the displays should warrant. There was a lucky cat in the display showing me a mocking grin. Its left arm rocking back and forth seemed to be taunting me with the message, "He's behind you!"

I looked in the reflection of the glass at the point where the annoying cat's arm appeared to be directing me, and there was dumpling man. I could make out a look of frustration on his face at clearly making too many fat finger errors on his text message. I could also see that his complexion had taken on a much brighter appearance, half sunburn and half impending coronary. Whilst he was distracted, I slipped into a side street and sprinted for a full five minutes. I then kept up a brisk pace until I was safely back in my hotel room. I was certain that unless he spotted an SUV taxi with the back seats removed there was no way he could fit into a normal cab and beat me back to the *Ibis*.

For the next few days I confined myself to barracks, only popping out for a quick bite to eat, exercising far greater vigilance when I did so. Everything seemed calmer in my mind. After all, if the big man intended me any harm, he had had plenty of opportunity. The following day it was a beautiful morning and I decided to have a meander through the myriad streets and alleys to get some fresh air and exercise. Although Anshan is historically an industrial hub, the mountain winds rushing across the peaks from inner Mongolia meant that most days were clear, unlike Beijing which had already seen three red weeks so far in 2016. This is when the air is approaching fifty times the limit deemed safe for inhalation by humans. When this happens, factories must close, children cannot go to school, and the car rotation system comes into play. This is an odd and even number system whereby only even-number plated cars can be used on the first day, odd-number plated cars the following. Cars without the correct numbered plate for the day must be parked up, their owners forced to take public or share private transport. When there are big ceremonies planned in Beijing, such as those attended by international dignitaries, it is common for factories and other facilities to be closed for a month beforehand to ensure blue skies on the big occasion.

One day, when passing through one particular alleyway, I heard a shout from an upstairs window followed by a shattering crash, just behind my last footfall. A large food bowl, full of Chinese hotpot, had slipped from the upstairs window of a restaurant and missed landing on my head by inches. I looked up to see heads and arms hanging out of the window with a look of great concern on their faces. I called back to them that I was fine and not to worry, fully aware that it was highly unlikely that they could understand what I was saying. I gave a pleasant wave and proceeded on a casual, indirect route back to the hotel. But there was something playing on my subconscious that just would not go away and it gradually dawned on me that the faces from the window had actually looked decidedly angry rather than concerned. Could the falling clay pot have been dropped deliberately? I was starting to think this was a distinct possibility. On returning to my room I saw that the LED light from my phone's display telling me that I had a message waiting. It was the longest and most clearly worded message I had received from the Inspector to date and confirmed my worst fears:

"Mr Byrne, Anshan is a bustling city and you have been seen by angry victims. Are you ok? We placed you in the *Shangzi Hotel* because it is not a busy area, it is close to the police unit and good for your safety. We are trying to help you."

I sat on the bed knowing I would need to move hotels yet again. The *Shanzi* was the safest but also the most expensive. Everything went black for the second time since arriving in China. I opened my eyes and the ceiling gradually came into focus. As my senses returned, the hard drive in my brain started to process a billion pieces of information.

This was a genuine loss of consciousness due to extreme stress and nothing like the event back in the McDonald's in Shanghai. Back then I had felt normal and hadn't sensed a blackout coming on, but this time I headed for the bed knowing that I felt dizzy. When I awoke on this occasion there was no violent headache or disorientation. Being drugged had been a shocking experience, but it had been carefully planned as a warning. This incident with the falling pot could have been fatal. They were unlikely to be part of a vigilante group, but with emotions running that high I could not take the chance of bumping into them again. It was all becoming too much and, for the first time in my life, I briefly wished that I had not woken up. Then my thoughts again flashed to images of my children and I summoned the courage needed to pull myself together.

I packed my bags and headed back to the *Shangzi* wondering how I was going to afford the stay. I had enough money left for perhaps two or three weeks. Then the first bit of good fortune for a long time came to my rescue. The CEO of a financial brokerage back in London had emailed me. I had provided market commentary and technical analysis for him in the past and he asked if I would be interested in doing some more of the same for his new company. He was unaware of my plight but having told him, and although he was shocked by my revelations, he had no reservations about leaving the offer on the table. Having known me for many years he had no doubt that I was not a fraudster. I accepted the commission and was immensely grateful for this financial boost that, although a modest sum, went a long way to easing the financial burden. Fortunately, the cost of living in north east China was very cheap and I now had enough to survive from week to week until my nightmare was over. It also gave my morale a boost as well as giving me something to do a few times a week that relieved the boredom. I felt the positive effect almost immediately: A renewed sense of purpose and the feeling that there were still people out there that trusted me. It was like an elixir. I was able to draw on the determination and reserves of inner strength I needed to fight on.

Chapter 28. A surreal night out

It amazed me how one small piece of good fortune had raised my spirits immeasurably, especially after a couple of traumatic days. I was back in a safer environment, close to good friends, and a stone's throw from the police unit. There was no doubt that the Inspector had my safety and best interests at heart. I allowed myself to believe that perhaps his investigation was indicating my innocence, leading to a kinder attitude towards me.

One day I was contacted by one of the performers at the *Shangzi* informing me that this would be her last night working there. She would be starting in a new club that weekend and asked if I would be her guest. Once I had cleared it with the Inspector, I agreed to accompany her. She said it was a famous venue on the far outskirts of Anshan city and I arranged to meet her in my hotel reception at 7pm when she would drive us to her first performance. I dressed conservatively not knowing what dress code would be acceptable in an Anshan nightclub, and headed from my room fifteen minutes early. As I exited the elevator, I could see that she was already waiting. Karen, her chosen English name, was in her mid-thirties but with a 1970's Western fashion style. Her clothes were quite garish and only partly concealed by a short fake mink jacket. She sported a permed hairdo with Elton John style glasses, but minus the glitter. After a half hour drive, we turned into a back street full of bars and restaurants. It was the first time I had seen a street anything like this in the north of China. She parked her car and we entered a doorway to be greeted by two burly bouncers. Other than us, the two black-tied gentlemen and a security camera, all that occupied the four by four metre reception was a single elevator. I wondered how big the venue upstairs would be or how long the vast queue that we had bypassed, as performer and guest, would take to filter into the club. The lift ascended two floors and, as the doors opened, I was amazed at the size of the place. It could have hosted four basketball games simultaneously. It was extremely trendy with retro décor consisting of old Chopper bicycles hanging from the walls and gramophones and ancient TVs strategically placed. We were led to a small table right in front of the stage where the interest in the only Westerner made me feel like the first act of the evening for the four hundred Chinese patrons. Most guests looked to be between eighteen and thirty, all except the occupants of a table immediately to our right around which sat four military personnel and two police officers. At 7.45pm the lights dimmed, and a projector kicked into life showing footage of the communist party, the Great March and President Xi along with Chairman Mao. Everyone in the place stood for this fifteen-minute tribute. During this time, having ordered me a beer, Karen had gone backstage to change for her first performance. Then, after an intro from the MC, twelve of the artists including Karen marched on stage in army uniforms. This was not at all what I had been expecting! There were another fifteen minutes of them singing communist songs while marking time with perfect precision. As this part of the show concluded, the police and military officers stood, saluted, and left the establishment. From that point onwards the whole mood changed. A saxophonist in a sparkling suit leapt into action playing amazing jazz whilst hopping from table-top to table-top to the cheers of the crowd. Next up was an even bigger shock; a transvestite entertainer from Bangkok took to the stage belting out a Cher medley. After my host performed her set of modern ballads she returned to our table and some typically Western basket nibbles appeared. We were having quite a fun evening and Karen explained that as long as the club promoted a strong and powerful communist China at the start of each show, they were then free to choose the rest of the content. As another beer appeared at our table the waitress handed me a note. It said, "I hope you have enjoyed your evening. Make sure you leave before eleven thirty and are back in your room by midnight or you will go to jail. Inspector Liu". I made my excuses and took a taxi home immediately as I no longer felt relaxed or able to enjoy the evening.

The next day Karen texted to ask if everything was okay and could she buy me dinner. I felt bad about leaving early the previous day so agreed on the condition that it was an early meal and close to my hotel. I entered the restaurant to see her sitting at a table with her ten-year-old son. That was a surprise as his existence had not been mentioned before. He spoke perfect English which negated the use of WeChat for our conversations. Not only was I not expecting this, neither was I expecting the offer that her son delivered on her behalf at the end of the evening. He said that his mother would like to marry me and would pay me $50,000 if I would agree. He said she wanted him to live with me and study in England, but she would not come with him if that is what I preferred. She had obviously got the wrong end of the stick, or more likely I had. It was, to me, the strangest offer; entrusting your child to someone you barely knew. In the short time we had become friends nothing had happened to suggest that we shared anything more than a mutual love of music. The other thing that surprised me was that the youth in China had been reaching levels of education that, in most cases, surpassed that achieved by UK students. Even so, it seemed that the priority for much of the population was to leave China by any means. I kindly declined the offer which she took to mean that the cash prize was not enough. She went on to explain, via her son, that her ex-husband was very rich but not a nice man, and she asked what an acceptable price would be? I took the kindest escape route available to me by stating that I was already engaged to be married the following year. I said that

I hoped we could remain friends but, unsurprisingly, didn't hear from her again.

Chapter 29. Whiling away the days

It was now late summer, and I was becoming very familiar with this part of China, or Anshan at least. I knew my way around and took frequent walks in the intense heat which now regularly hit thirty-five degrees Celsius. The police seemed to be more relaxed about keeping tabs on my movements and I took full advantage to escape the boredom of hotel confinement. Sometimes it was a twenty-minute stroll to the Carrefour supermarket where I could stock up on some Western staples. I even bought a slow cooker for my room where I would be able to cook stews in the coming months, which I was told would be extremely cold. Other times I would take longer walks through the woods, up to mountain trails where I first saw evidence of Japanese occupation. High on the mountainside, overlooking Anshan city, were concrete structures that once housed the powerful guns of the controlling Japanese army forces. Unlike defensive positions, where guns are trained away from a city, these were pointing inwards, towards the city as a warning against any attempted uprising. The vista was amazing, affording spectacular views over Saddle Mountain to the east after which Anshan is named, and south over the city centre and to the west, where tall residential skyscrapers rose from the ground like giant man-made stalagmites.

Anshan and the whole north east of China still retains a heavy influence of Japanese culture. Back in 1931 following a dispute called the Mukden incident, divisions of the Japanese army made the decision to advance along the Manchuria railway line, to begin an occupation of Northern China. This decision was taken independently of central government approval by a Japanese General called Shigeru Honju. But as city after city was easily taken, the Japanese government eventually backed the plan, sending in more troops and forming a puppet government to rule the area. This remained relatively localised for some time, in terms of territory, with the full-blown conflict, known as the second Sino-Japanese war, beginning in 1937 and ending at the conclusion of WWII. Anshan was one of the first cities to be taken and was quickly industrialised for the extraction of iron ore and minerals.

Many legacies of the occupation remain to this day and the Anshan region is still China's largest steel producing area. Just on the outskirts of the city, in *219 Park*, is the "Yo Fu Yuan", or the "Jade Buddha Palace". It houses an enormous Buddha carved from a single piece of jade excavated from one of the local mineral mines. It stands almost eight meters high, seven meters wide and four meters in depth, weighing in at an enormous two hundred and sixty tonnes. I found *219 Park* to be the most interesting legacy. A beautiful recreational area enjoyed by thousands of people every day, some without knowing its history. The park is called *219* to commemorate the Japanese expulsion from the region on the 19th of February 1945, or 1945.2.19 as it is written in China, and was landscaped and built with the bare hands and primitive tools of Chinese female slaves of the occupation.

I enjoyed many strolls through the park with its beautiful lakes, gardens and amusement area. The old-fashioned funfair, complete with thrill rides and novelty stalls, was a great release. I didn't use the Ferris wheel or drive the bumper cars but found the children's excitement and laughter a welcome distraction. However, on occasion I could not bring myself to hear parents and families having fun, fearing I would never manage to participate in these moments again with my own children. There was one other area of the park that evoked sad memories. Close to the main entrance was a zoo which had been recently refurbished and was again open for visitors. Entry cost ten Yuan and once inside there was no choice but to follow the trail through all the exhibits to the exit on the opposite side. If this had not been the case, I would have turned around immediately. The first exhibit was a monkey cage that, being so overcrowded, almost made me cry. Behind this enclosure were cages no bigger than cat baskets containing primate offspring that, unbelievably, would soon be introduced to the main cage. Farther on was the big cat enclosure where five sad lions competed for some ground space on which to lay their weary bodies. Worst of all was a concrete enclosure that housed two black bears; no bigger that a London tube station lavatory with much the same smell. The crowds of people gathered around the bars would cheer whenever the bears would engage in a frustrated wrestle, sometimes poking and goading the animals with long sticks to encourage them out of any lethargy.

To this day, tensions and emotions remain very high over the occupation mainly because of Japan's refusal to apologise, in some cases choosing to totally deny the many atrocities suffered by the Chinese people. One such example came to the fore on the 80th anniversary of the Nanjing massacre. As the occupation expanded further south, the Japanese marched into this historic former capital and proceeded to abuse, murder and rape over 300,000 people during a six-week period. A Japanese hotel chain, the APA Group, had recently placed history books in all its hotel rooms claiming that the event never took place and was a total fabrication. The company was immediately placed on a banned business list by the government, barring them from working with airlines and travel agents in China. No Chinese citizen was allowed to use this hotel chain again.

The more closely recognisable relative of the Japanese Karaoke club is called a KTV in China. These are found in every city across the country and are far more expensive than the local bars or clubs. They all follow the same format and are called the same thing, but there are KTVs and there are KTVs. They are opulently decorated and consist of varying sized rooms, depending on your number of guests, and offer self-contained private facilities for groups. The family-oriented ones will offer a food and drinks menu and even provide a companion, should one of your group be in-between girlfriends and feeling a bit out-of-sorts. They also provide attractive singers, trained to create the desired atmosphere for the mood of the evening you have planned. Their professionalism has Geisha undertones, clearly another leftover of the occupation. This is all very clean and above board though; not frowned upon at all. Young children and teenagers can often be seen accompanying their parents for an evening of singing and dancing on a special occasion. Then of course, there are the more expensive KTVs, frequented by businessmen or groups of wealthy lads on a stag or birthday party. The format is the same, but the menu is considerably extended, particularly the "female companion" section. In addition, there is often a "take away" menu where prices start in the hundreds and swiftly move into four figures. There is no food or drink available on *this* menu!

Chapter 30. The duck neck shop

Things had been quiet for a while now, but when I looked out of my hotel room on the twentieth floor, my eyes were always drawn to the west where the roof and car park of inspector Liu's offices were located. I felt safer being there in the proximity of the police than I had in the centre of the city, but it was still a constant reminder of my powerlessness and the daily uncertainty. I felt terribly homesick.

Over the next few months I had to attend several further interrogations at the police station. Whenever I was summoned, I would endure a restless night and completely lose my appetite. Once the interviews were over I would, therefore, be absolutely famished. Halfway between the police station and the hotel was a shop that sold nibbles. Its speciality was duck necks, although there were many other titbits on offer, like chicken feet, sautéed sea horse and crispy insects such as crickets.

I had tried the duck necks before a few times, and while quite tasty they tended to be more work than enjoyment. You usually ordered two or three because they were very scraggy, a bit like gnawing the remnants off the bone of a Sunday leg of lamb or rib of beef. There wasn't much meat. The shop owner's name was Mr Tang, a happy soul evidenced by the ever-present smile across his face. We got to know each other fairly well, or as well as you can via WeChat. One time I ordered some duck and asked:

'How big is the bill?'

The joke didn't translate, and I had to explain. Once Mr Tang got it he roared with laughter, and so the banter began. The next time he saw me approaching he was clearly excited.

'Mr David! Mr David. I have something you have lost.' He looked down at my feet and continued, 'But you have not lost one'.

It was a hot day and I was wearing shorts, with my bushy legs leading down to my hairy feet stuffed into a pair of Birkenstock sandals. Most Chinese people are devoid of such an abundance of bodily hair, often staring at my arms and on occasion giving the curly protrusions a tug. He reached into a cool box and brought out a bright pink hairy pig's trotter.

'I thought this belonged to you!' he said, pointing at my feet then back at the trotter. It was clearly intended as a riotous joke and he meant no offence. It was now my turn to get my own back so I ordered just a single duck neck.

He frowned and said, 'Only one duck neck, you not very hungry today?'

I said, 'Yes, I am hungry and would only like one duck neck please. But could you leave it attached to the big part please, the part that you normally chop off and throw away!'

This brought on an immediate fit of hysterical laughter and he proceeded to summon his family from the back of the shop to relay the joke to them. He went on to explain that some of the ducks were chopped up for other nibbles but the majority he sent to his restaurant around the corner. He handed me a leaflet and said I would be treated very well as his special guest and that I should visit. The information was obviously all in Chinese but there was a clearly defined map giving directions. When I got back to my hotel, I was curious as to the restaurant's name, feeling certain it would be called "The Headless Duck". I had an app on my iPad that would translate any writing by just uploading a picture of the text, so I took a snap of the leaflet and waited for the results. The restaurant's name was in fact "The Happy Duck" though I couldn't imagine any ducks destined for the restaurant would feel that way! And the picture on the leaflet was a painted scene of a beautiful pond, with a solitary duck paddling away in the middle, clearly happy to be too far out of reach for Mr Tang's cleaver.

Over time our conversation inevitably drifted to what I was doing in China? I used the "teaching financials at the university" ruse again and I also explained that I wrote analysis of the currency markets for a company in London. He asked if I could show him an example of my reports showing the US Dollar vs the Yuan. It seemed like a strange request for a fast food duck shop owner to make. He also asked if I was well paid by both my employers. I told him that it was a modest income but the cost of living in China was relatively cheap. Regardless, I obliged and managed to get the commentary translated to Chinese. He asked if he could invest and if I could trade the markets for him. I told him that I did not trade my own, or anyone else's money anymore and respectfully declined.

Mr Tang also helped me solve a painful foot problem that had been troublesome for some time and was getting worse. Many years before, on my way home from work, I saw my daughters playing ball on a field by my house. They were excited to see me and eager for me to join them. I had just purchased new shoes and wanted to change out of my suit, but their pleading eyes demanded my immediate attention. So, I removed my jacket and shoes and promised them a quick ten minutes. Whilst leaping to catch a throw, I landed on a patch of fallen branches containing rose thorns. After screaming and muffling some expletives I hobbled home to remove the offending thorns. The next morning my feet looked like a pin cushion and as I tried to walk the pain indicated that I had not found all of the sharp invaders. I spent the next two hours trying to extract the remaining thorns, but I must have missed one. Over time a callus developed and proceeded to give me much grief. I had been to the chiropodist on several occasions, but the problem always came back to cause me pain.

One of the most important escapes from boredom was my regular walks but my foot problem was becoming more troublesome. Although I told myself that these were pleasant random rambles, the truth is that they were pre-planned as my route and timings needed to be filed with the police beforehand. It seemed that even this brief escape from house arrest at the hotel would be taken away from me as my foot flared up again causing considerable pain. Mr Tang had noticed my limp and told me about a shop located in a small doorway, and that I was to look for pictures of painful foot conditions. I decided I would go along and give traditional Chinese medicine a try. I saw a sign on the wall displaying a WiFi code, then dropped my gaze to the masked Chinese nurse perched on a stool and said simply, "WeChat?" I visited her on eight occasions, each time having circular slices taken from the bottom of my foot followed by an application of what I can only assume to be a powdered acid. The few hours that followed each visit were excruciatingly painful but eventually, after my last treatment of acid powder, I found that I could walk comfortably. I was cured. On my way to another appointment at the police station I decided to buy Mr Tang a small good luck Chinese trinket by way of thanks. I approached his shop and saw a completely different man behind the counter. I asked if Mr Tang were available and was told, 'I am Mr Tang'. I was a little confused but decided that perhaps they were brothers or maybe cousins. I thought it best to pop by on my way back or on another day.

When I reached the police station and was led to the small interview room, I was shocked to see an addition to the usual officers there. A fully uniformed Mr Tang, complete with badge and stripes on his sleeve. It turned out that after stealthy surveillance of my habits, the police had commandeered the shop on days that they knew I would visit and had been trying to glean information as to my finances. They obviously knew that I was doing no teaching at the university and that I was just protecting myself from potential animosity amongst the locals. After scrutinising my bank statements, they said that I could continue producing reports for my London client even though I did not have a work permit. It was of no great concern to them; they were more interested to see if I would have accepted illegal investment from a Chinese national. I decided to keep the good luck trinket myself as I obviously needed it more than Mr Tang ... or whoever he was.

Chapter 31. Winter is here

As November 2016 approached, Anshan took on a very different feel. The trees were bare and devoid of any wildlife. The birds had already migrated south, and the eerie mating shrieks of the Stinkbugs were a distant memory. The temperature was dropping daily and the katabatic winds rushing down from the mountains, to flow through the streets, chilled the bones.

The first snow of the winter occurred overnight, and I awoke to a white blanket as far as the eye could see. I quickly showered and got dressed in several layers of clothing that I felt sure would keep me well-insulated. After so many lonely months in exile, any event was a welcome escape from my Groundhog Day existence. I left the hotel with the intention of going for a brisk thirty-minute walk. As the bracing wind hit my face it was clear that my limited wardrobe would be no match for the assault on my body. After just ten minutes, as I passed the frozen surface of an adjacent water inlet, I did an about-turn and headed back to the hotel. Within minutes the freshly fallen snow would be turned to treacherous ice making short journeys like a scene from Disney's Bambi, trying to walk on unsteady legs. By the time I returned to my room I was overcome by pins and needles as my skin recovered from the brief but painful exposure. My phone's weather app registered the temperature as minus twenty-five, without the windchill.

A few days later, with no sign of a let up in the weather, I decided to dip into my depleted financial resources and make a trip to the Carrefour supermarket. The journey took almost an hour by taxi, with cars slipping and sliding the whole way. The tunnel, a shortcut through the mountains, was closed causing a five-mile tailback on the arterial route to the city centre. My taxi stopped several times to pick up other passengers, the driver's prerogative and not that of the original passenger. I had no problem with this given the conditions and found it a very considerate practice. I would also benefit from this kindness to one's fellow man over the coming Arctic-like months.

The superstore was massive and sold reasonably priced clothes. The winter collection had arrived. I had no choice but to invest in some appropriate clothing or else I would be confined to my room for months. The last time that I ventured out I had used layers, but they were still layers of summer clothing and proved woefully inadequate against the fierce conditions, even with the donated coat. I used this same excursion to visit the bank and pick up another Western Union transfer. After purchasing new clothes, buying some food and settling my tab at the *Shangzi*, I needed to once again find cheaper accommodation. I contacted my interpreter who offered to assist me in finding something suitable. He emailed me a small selection, one of which caught my eye; the *Sihai Grand Hotel* on Shengli Road west. The website showed photos of a buzzing establishment with a gym and swimming pool in the basement. I couldn't believe my luck to find such a venue at half the current rate I was paying. It was also just ten minutes' walk from the bank and fifteen from the superstore. It was also just far enough from the city centre that I felt comfortable I would not be spotted again by irate victims.

I spent that last evening at the *Shangzi* in the hotel music bar, saying goodbye to all the wonderful staff that had become good friends. I was joined by Jason Wang and his wife, the kind policeman that had given me the now much needed leather coat. That evening was a particularly busy one with a whole section reserved for a party of forty or so. There was a huge buffet along the centre of the room which all were encouraged to delve into. It turns out that this was a once-a-month occurrence, all paid for by a group of entrepreneurs from a neighbouring city called Dalian. This city is on the coast about two hundred and seventy kilometres east of Anshan, still in Liaoning province but just a short hop to North Korea. Apart from being the most affluent part of the north east, it is also a major naval base. China's first domestically built aircraft carrier was nearing completion, the only other craft in this class being a ship purchased from the Ukraine and refurbished in 2012. Staff told me that this wealthy group of philanthropists held meetings once a week in different cities. Their aim was basically to do good for the less fortunate and this altruism was a very new concept in China. In the not too distant past, adhering to communist ideals, wealth was distributed evenly. Now however, success accompanied by philanthropy was encouraged.

As the evening progressed and the celebrations escalated, the usual curiosity got the better of several members of their party. As was becoming the norm they would ask to join my table and insist on buying me a beer. Again, I was asked what I was doing in China? I gave the usual answer about my supposed university teaching post and this seemed to satisfy them until I visited the bathroom an hour later. After washing my hands, I left the facility to see a gentleman waiting for me. He asked, in very clear English, whether he could have a word with me. He told me that several of the group had recognised me and were upset to see me relaxing and tapping my foot to the music. He said that they, along with many family members from Dalian, had been scammed by *Euro Fx*. He was not threatening in any way, but I still felt it appropriate that I should return to my room and finish packing for my next hotel the following morning.

Chapter 32. The Sihai "not so" Grand Hotel

As I arrived at the *Sihai Grand*, I recognised the entrance and the lobby from the website photo album. The pictures must have been taken some years ago as the furnishings and decoration were now looking very tired. I checked in and was taken to my room but immediately felt an inclination to get back in the taxi. It was a tiny box, located in the centre of the building with no natural light or windows to the outside world. The internet didn't work and nor did the air-conditioning. It was truly dreadful. I called Jason Wang, my police friend, who spoke to the hotel management. He must have used all his influence as a law enforcement officer as well as explaining that I could be a long-term customer, because I was swiftly moved to a small suite overlooking the indoor pool on one side, with floor to ceiling windows on the other. I tried the Wi-Fi which also worked fine and decided to Skype my children. As their faces filled the screen and their voices streamed through the iPad's speaker, my spirits lifted considerably. I was concerned though that the small screen reflecting my face was showing a decidedly bigger mass with a double chin. My side profile in the mirror was also changing to one I was not accustomed to. Don't get me wrong, it has been many years since I could boast a flat tummy, but this image was that of a 1970's darts player. I must have put on at least twenty pounds. I joined the gym that evening and promised myself to swim every day.

As with the lobby, the reception, and the bedrooms, the pool area must once have been quite a spectacle but was now in need of some TLC. I decided to get started on some exercise straight away and headed down for a swim. There was a reduced charge for hotel guests to use the facilities, which included the provision of some plastic flip flops and a locker key. I got changed, rinsed in the shower, and dived straight in the deep end. I couldn't believe that virtually everyone was spitting into the overflow gutters after each lap of the pool. One of the lifeguards started blowing his whistle and shouting in his own tongue. I was sure it must have been to one of the hoikers who'd missed the gulley but to my surprise I realised his attention was directed at me. Apparently, it was deemed unsanitary behaviour to go swimming without a rubber swim cap, though if you were wearing one it was quite okay to spit until your saliva glands ran dry. I went to the pool reception to purchase my own cap and returned to the pool. I waved to the guard showing him that I was now suitably kitted out. He indicated that it was now fine for me to enter the water and returned to smoking his cigarette in his poolside chair.

The next day I took a tour of the gym. This was a brand-new facility with all the latest modern equipment; a private franchise that rented the space from the hotel. The grand opening was not for a few weeks as the final furnishings were still being fitted but his delay suited me fine as I was waiting for more funds to arrive. I was given an invitation to the grand opening where super-fit male and female models would be demonstrating the equipment, and efficient sales staff would be giving details of the types of membership available. When I attended the event, as usual there were goody bags being handed out. And as usual there were throngs of people with no intention of joining lining up for their freebies. There were even eighty-year-old pensioners in wheelchairs queuing for some gifts.

Things were ticking along smoothly for the next few weeks but as Christmas approached, I was beginning to feel a depression set in once again. My passport was back with the visa office which meant that I could not collect my Western Union payments. This was the third extension of my temporary visa and as each expiry date drew closer, I hoped that their investigations were nearly concluded, only to be disappointed yet again. I eventually received a message to say that my passport was ready for collection but on this occasion the Inspector said that I could make my own way to collect my documents and he emailed me a letter of authority; a small sign that there was some sort of trust developing. It was difficult not to cling on to the hope that their investigations and subsequent discoveries were supporting my innocence. I had no cash left; the visa office was a two hour walk in good conditions and it was minus twenty degrees outside. I had no choice, so I wrapped up and set off on my quest on foot. After half an hour I had only covered a fraction of the distance that could be managed during the summer months. I pushed on regardless, ignoring the shooting pains entering my toes and up my calves. My soaked Chinese training shoes were no protection for my aching feet and their five pounds price tag all but guaranteed virtually no water proofing. I cut through *219 Park* and found I could take a shortcut across its dissecting lakes which were now frozen solid. There were people ice skating as well as others riding bikes and playing games on the icy tundra. I eventually arrived at my destination some three hours later, feeling like I had achieved something that Scott of the Antarctic would have been proud of. I collected my passport but knew I still had another marathon walk ahead of me as, without my documents, I had been unable to go to the bank. The queues at the bank could sometimes be quite lengthy so asking a taxi to take me there and wait while I got money out to pay was not an option. I grabbed a coffee and sat in the warmth of the cafe for at least an hour before embarking on another two-hour journey back to the Agricultural bank then onto the hotel.

Chapter 33. A loofah for Christmas

The run-up to Christmas 2016 was really depressing. Not so much because they don't celebrate it in China - they save *their* festivities for their New Year - but more because the recent renewal of my visa, meant I would be having a lonely yuletide, thousands of miles away from my family. It was around this time that I became aware of a leak; a flow of information to others before me. I had received an email from Chao Ma saying, "You have another chance to reveal the truth next week." There was also a WeChat message from Engen Tham at Thomson Reuters asking if my next interview with the police on Monday was in the morning or the afternoon. Until that moment I'd been completely unaware that I was due to be interviewed again, but sure enough on Monday morning I got a message from the Inspector to attend their offices.

I had first seen Engen as I left the bathroom at the first police station in Shanghai after my initial arrest. I met her again in Shanghai where I had agreed to meet and answer some questions. Reuters picked up the tab for brunch which was a welcome touch. She asked me many questions: Who had paid me? Who had paid the staff? And who had offered me the position of consultant CEO in the first place? It was at this same meeting that I was told the first details of victims that had taken their own lives as well as the plight of many thousands that were now in debt to loan sharks. Shortly after that brunch I received an email from Orchard's lawyers which denied any involvement in *Euro Fx* and threatened to increase my woes with a lawsuit.

There is no doubt that *Euro Forex Investment Limited* and *Euro Fx* were linked. And using these two names was intentional as *Euro Forex Investment Ltd* was, more often than not, inadvertently abbreviated to *Euro Fx*. This is exactly what happened when a UK based journalist, Carolyn Cohn, Interviewed David Orchard. She questioned him about my statements to her colleague, Engen Tham; that he was the paymaster and the person who had offered me the position. She had, however, quoted *Euro Fx* and not the London subsidiary. When referring to Mr Orchard whilst in China, I was very clear that my statements about him related to *Euro Forex Investment Limited* in London. This mistake by the journalists meant he was able to deny my allegations.

I received a letter from a law firm representing WGP and David Orchard. It stated that all my comments made to Engen Tham were entirely false and at no time was he my boss or involved with Euro Fx. The news firm had misquoted me, to a point. But, It is crazy to say that he had no knowledge of a link between the two companies, even though the statements that I made regarding Orchard only referred to *Euro Forex Investment Limited*, the UK subsidiary.

I stated was that he was the paymaster of the staff including myself, and that he paid for the offices and the daily running costs. He was also the duly authorised person that offered me the position on behalf of the client as shown on my contract. I had, and still have, irrefutable evidence that this was the case including bank statements showing his company paying my salary for my one-year tenure. If there was no link between *Euro Forex Investment Limited* and *Euro Fx*, why were there so many visits organised for the latter's clients to visit the London offices? One of the emails that, on my friend's sound advice, I cc'd to my personal email account, had details of how Orchard and one of his advisors had edited one of the proposed speeches I was to make in South East Asia for *Euro Fx*. In that interview with Orchard (excerpt below), Thomson Reuters reported that he could not remember the name of the company that he recommended me to. How can someone engage you in a position, pay your salary for a whole year and not remember who they were?

'Orchard told Reuters in June that he knew Byrne from previous business dealings and had bumped into him in the City of London in summer 2012 when Byrne was out of work.

"We put his name forward as someone who had forex expertise who could help" by managing a London office, Orchard said, but could not remember whom he recommended Byrne to.'

(Source) Thomson Reuters 12*th* August 2016

This was a real surprise as I couldn't figure out why they would deny carrying out the duties that they did on behalf of their client. It was clearly an attempt to distance themselves from all but initial, basic involvement in this operation (for which I held proof to the contrary). The implication of his statement was that I was the person in control. I was livid and sorely tempted to give Orchard a call and demand an explanation, but this would have been a bad idea as the authorities in China had forbade me to make contact with any of the people that they were investigating. Every one of my phone calls and emails was being intercepted and monitored, transcribed and translated, so I would have immediately been in hot water if I had made the call.

I needed cheering up but couldn't concentrate on anything that would snap me out of my bad mood. That is until I received a message from one of the staff at my first Anshan hotel, the *Shangzi*. Although Christmas is not such a big thing for the Chinese, it does mark the beginning of the exodus of people returning to their rural villages across

China in preparation for the New Year. The *Shangzi* bar was having a party before closing for a couple of weeks and I was invited. Taxis were very inexpensive and did not double their rates over holiday periods. I decided that it would be nice to attend the event the following evening. I hoped it would lift my spirits. The next afternoon I laid out some of my newer, warmer clothes on the bed and went into the bathroom. One of the better features of the *Sihai* was the shower which, although a bit antiquated, managed to maintain a steady powerful flow of piping hot water and did much to ease the ever-present tension knots in my neck and back. I exited the cubicle and began my usual drying ritual; head and hair first, followed by chest legs and feet. I grabbed a second towel, swinging it over my shoulder, gripping opposing corners with each hand, and assuming a ballerina-type pose began the back and forth shuffle with the rhythm of two lumberjacks sawing a log. My back began to sting a bit and I initially thought that perhaps I had turned the temperature in the shower too high. But this felt more and more like severe sunburn. I decided that any patches of skin that had avoided the brush of the white cotton towel could simply drip dry as I applied hair gel and took a shave. I threw the towel into the laundry basket and was shocked to see multiple red stripes decorating the normally plain white cloth. I turned my back to the mirror to see corresponding candy stripes across my skin. On closer inspection the towel seemed to be sparkling and as I lifted it from the basket, I heard the sound of tiny jingles of glass dropping onto the tiled floor.

The towels were neatly folded on a rack and I couldn't imagine how glass could have found its way inside one of them unless it had been a deliberate act. The maids had always been very kind, and their eyes betrayed no signs of hidden animosity towards me, so I couldn't imagine that one of them had been the culprit. Equally unlikely, but not impossible, was that someone had obtained or cloned my room card. Then I remembered leaving the "Do Not Disturb" sign on my door the previous evening. When this happens, the maids leave the fresh towels on a stand directly outside your door. This must have been when the item was doctored. Someone must have slipped the glass into one of the lower towels in the pile because I had suffered no injury after bathing that morning. This made sense as the added weight would have helped the crushed shards to embed themselves in the fabric. This was a reminder that I was still being watched and could still be found, no matter how many times I changed address. Although this was no deadly assault, the outcome could have been far worse had I used that towel to dry my eyes first.

I was determined not to allow this latest episode to turn me into a paranoid recluse and I decided to continue with my night out which turned out to be a very pleasant evening despite the discomfort of my deeply scratched, lacerated back.

Chapter 34.   Chinese New Year

During January I received a number of requests for further information from the investigators but was told I could respond by email or, in some instances, print off documentation, sign it, and hand deliver it to the police unit. I was also informed that as the police would be concentrating on public order during the holiday period, I would not be required to attend any interviews until well into the middle of February. The Chinese New Year celebrations began properly at 5am on January 27th, 2017, their New Year's Eve and the first day of the "Year of the Rooster". I was well aware that the Chinese had invented fireworks but hadn't expected them to begin exploding at that ungodly hour. Nor was I prepared for the Chinese enthusiasm for setting them off: I was still being woken at the same time every morning for the next two weeks!

It is said that fireworks were discovered by accident some two thousand years ago. At that time, various cooking ingredients and preservatives including saltpetre and charcoal were commonly stored separately in bamboo tubes to keep dry. When one careless cook mixed up the tubes, the rumour goes, an explosive mixture was accidentally created and a rogue spark in the kitchen ignited it, leading to the invention. It was not until about a thousand years ago that the firecracker was invented by a man named Li Tian during the Song Dynasty. The firecrackers, about a metre long, resemble a fat snake not dissimilar to a door draught excluder. They are extremely loud and are believed to scare away evil spirits.

The Chinese are far more superstitious than anything I have witnessed in Western culture, and there is a far greater belief in the meaning behind traditions passed down through the centuries. One great example is the pre-New

Year visit to the barber shop or hairdressers. Everyone wants to look their best during holiday periods, when family gatherings inevitably include appraisal of how well and tidy you are looking. This ritual takes on a far greater significance in China though. The barbers and hairdressers get extremely busy. The Chinese believe that by having their hair cut before New Year they are cutting away any bad luck that befell them in the previous year. Conversely, the first three days of the New Year are a no-no for the scissors as it is believed this will cut away the good luck promised in the months ahead.

The roads and public transport systems were packed to capacity, to a degree that I had never witnessed before. The news channels like to feed on this situation to deliver ground-breaking announcements about China smashing new records or being number one in the world at something. Every day there would be an announcement like: "There were more train journeys today in China than any other country in the world", or "There were more lucky money dumplings consumed on New Year's Day in China than anywhere else in the world". Being a nation of 1.4 billion people and it being their biggest holiday seemed to be of no consideration in the excitable reporting of these record-breaking achievements.

There was one news flash that did catch my attention though. One young man, who had left his home to seek work in Beijing, had been saving all his earnings to take back home to his family over New Year. He had worked for eleven months without a day off and, because his family were so dependent on him, he decided to cycle his way home and not spend his hard-earned cash on a train ticket. He worked as a foot massage therapist at one of the big hotels but only earned money from commission and tips. Because of the New Year exodus, most hotels in China operate at only forty or fifty percent capacity and clients would be few. So, by taking the month off he would not be missing out too much and would have plenty of time to pedal the 2000 km journey home. After ten days in the saddle he stopped off for a bite to eat and check directions. New Year was fast approaching, and he didn't recognise the names of the towns he was passing through. It was then that he discovered to his horror that he had been cycling north instead of south and would never make it home in time, being now twice the original distance from his intended destination. He was in despair because he feared he might also therefore lose his job. This story had a happy ending though. Some local police eating in the café felt sorry for him and had a whip round to buy him a train ticket and not only did he made it home in time for New Year but he also kept his job. This was a heart-warming story, demonstrating a friendly spirit so often missing in this modern self-centred world.

One thing that really became apparent to me, especially in the north, was the striking difference between embracing advancement on the one hand and clinging to the past on the other. Even New Year celebrations have not escaped the advancement in technology. It is a well-known fact that the Chinese have a tradition of giving their children, nieces and nephews red envelopes for New Year containing money. In 2016 there were as many virtual envelopes given away as physical ones. Social network sites such as WeChat had created an App which allowed you to give a virtual envelope containing cash that is loaded from your e-wallet. You would upload a picture from your phone, place a virtual envelope containing cash inside, then provide some hints or clues. When your nephew or cousin was close to the item, they would get an alert. If they thought they had found the correct object concealing their gift, they would take a photo and the app would let them know if they were indeed correct and how much money they had received. It could be hidden anywhere, from a cookie jar in their parent's kitchen to the fountain in the town square.

The date of this celebration varies each as it is based on the lunar cycle and not a set date. On New Year's Day I decided to go for a stroll and catch one of the many firework displays. These are mainly impromptu random bursts of firecrackers, not at all organised, and most would not wait for nightfall before shattering the usual sounds of daily life. It's more about the noise to scare away demons than it is to create a pretty spectacle. As I walked out of the hotel, I saw kitchen staff preparing a long table similar to a decorator's bench for pasting wallpaper. There were baskets of fruit and vegetables being emptied of their contents and arranged on the cloth-covered table. It reminded me of the Bonnygate Primary School assembly hall in my junior years, just prior to Harvest Festival. Every year the children were encouraged to bring in whatever food their households could afford to spare. Once enough was amassed it was then boxed up by the pupils and delivered to local pensioners. It brought back happy memories of more simple times, as well as a feelgood factor not as prevalent these days in London. After a short stroll during which I stocked up on some food and a couple of treats, I came across an amazing sight. One of the tables was decorated with beautiful flowers and artistically arranged fruit and vegetables. But sprawled along the centre of the twelve-foot table was an entire freshly slaughtered pig. There was no sign of a mortal wound, and steam was still rising from the corpse as rigor mortis set in. I couldn't imagine how the poor beast had met its demise but only hoped that it had occurred before the fresh leeks were stuffed up its nostrils, the onions placed in its mouth, and the radishes tucked in its ears. This turned out to be an offering to the heavens and was not intended for consumption, and by the time it was disposed of some two weeks later the skin had mostly turned black.

During the New Year celebrations, I had to surrender my passport yet again. This time however, there was a far greater meaning associated with the regular extension to my visa. I had been told that the maximum time that I could be held by the police without charge was one year. This latest visa stamp would take me to within a week or so of that deadline and I was clinging to the hope that this might be the last one before my release. I was also thinking that after nine months of interrogation the police would have at least confirmed a court date … if there was going to be one. My thoughts were that maybe they had concluded that there were no charges to be made, and that there was no conclusive evidence of any misdemeanour on my part. I was trying to control my emotions. If they still had nothing, then why prolong the situation for a further period? Or maybe they just intended to keep digging until the final day to reassure the victims that they had conducted as thorough an investigation as possible. This was not a situation where the result would sit somewhere in the middle ground. I would either be going home or facing many years in jail, or worse and knowing this reality was at times almost impossible to bear.

Chapter 35.   Another extension

It was now February 2017 and I was approaching the end of my tenth month in China. We were two days into yet another holiday, the Spring Festival that basically rolls straight on from New Year. This in turn was immediately followed by the Lantern Festival, by which time most people had returned to work. The streets were adorned with elaborately decorated paper lanterns with candles providing the illumination. Some were immense in size and were fashioned on dragons or other mythical beasts. The date reminded me that I would miss my son's birthday which turned my mood sour again.

It was uncanny how the weather suddenly turned warmer during the Spring festival, almost as if the Chinese understood the forces commanded by Mother Nature far better than us. For the first time since November the snow had melted, and I could once again see the Dalmatian-like spots of saliva decorating the pavements. When I was a youngster, I received the solid advice to avoid handling yellow snow with much amusement. In China I would advise avoiding touching *any* snow ... at any time.

Even after all this time I was still finding the language incredibly difficult to pick up, let alone master. And quite frankly, I didn't see the point. If I were released, I had no intention of returning and if not, I had potentially a decade or two of incarceration and I could learn it then. But I had discovered that people from bigger cities such as Shanghai would not understand this local Anshan dialect anyway. Shanghainese contains many abbreviated words, as well as new ones to describe things or situations only seen in this modern metropolis. This linguistic divide is less severe in other major cities farther north such as Beijing, where traditional Mandarin is still adhered to. I was accumulating some knowledge though of the more common superstitions that are uniform throughout China, Hong Kong and even Taiwan, in particular those relating to numbers. For instance, the number eight is regarded as very lucky. People pay many thousands across Asia for a car number plate registration that contains this special numeral. The number eight is considered lucky because "fa cai" means to come into money and is shortened to "fa", which in Chinese sounds like "ba", the number eight. Conversely, the number four is deemed to be the unluckiest number. In Mandarin the number four is pronounced "siiirrr", slightly stretched out and tailing downwards in tone as the word ends. The word for death sounds very similar, except that it is pronounced very short and curt with an opening emphasis: "Srr".

Here's the irony though. There are two lotteries in China, both state run, with huge jackpot prizes. If your numbers came in and they contained the lucky number eight, it is likely you would share the jackpot with hundreds, if not thousands, of people. If however, your numbers roll in but contained the unlucky number four, you stand a very good chance of being the only recipient of the total prize! One time, whilst scanning through the television channels, I was fascinated by the presentation to one particular lottery winner. The winners are required to receive their cheques on live television. Many recipients do not wish to be recognised and turn up on stage in varying levels of disguise in order to avoid a deluge of begging letters. It is not mandatory to show one's face so it is very common for people to appear on TV wearing a panda mask, a Mickey Mouse outfit or even dressed as Spider Man. On this occasion the jackpot winner appeared wearing a pantomime horse's head. He must have owned a pair of very distinctive shoes though because he also insisted on wearing black plastic bags to cover his feet to further protect his anonymity. I'm sure that once he sold his tiny farmhouse, moved to a swish Shanghai penthouse and bought a brand-new car, his friends and relatives would have more than a slight suspicion about his good fortune. Even if he did buy a new pair of less recognisable shoes!

Another superstition or tradition that I learned more about is that of *Feng Shui*. I could take up chapters about this subject alone but basically, it's all about balance. If a room has a dark side, then it should have a bright side. The bright side should be where any work is be done and the dark side is for rest. But here's where superstition kicks in again. The Chinese would never place a bed where their feet point at the door because in their tradition, when people die, they are always carried out of the room feet first. Thus, placing a bed in this position would be akin to inviting death.

For me, the jury was out as to if clinging on to old traditions was a good or a bad thing. By doing so there was a clear national identity and sense of pride. But it also promoted a naivety and willingness to accept antiquated laws and prejudices. Along with national pride, there is also an unashamed persecution of minorities and an unbalanced attitude towards male and female rights.

Chapter 36. The tension builds

It was now the middle of March 2017 and things had been eerily quiet for some time. I was wondering why the hell they had insisted on another extension if they had no more questions for me. I was increasingly believing my theory that that were purely waiting for one year to expire before sending me on my way.

Then I received the dreaded text message. I was summoned to see Inspector Liu and was told to bring my laptop and iPad. I had not seen my computer since my initial arrest in Shanghai and I was confused as to why Anshan police did not already have this in their possession. I was hoping they would send a car for me, as the extended holidays during January and February meant that I still had not been able to collect my passport and, as a result, had not been able to do any banking. Had I still been at the *Shangzi*, a short walk from the police station, it would not have been a problem, but I was now at the *Sihai* which was a reasonable taxi ride away but a very long walk, perhaps two hours. It's difficult to describe how having no passport and funds exponentially increases tension and has the opposite effect on preparation and confidence, especially at such a crucial point in the investigation. I searched every pocket for change, looked behind every cushion and delved into every crevice and compartment of my bags and suitcases to find some elusive coin. I had eventually gathered enough cash to get me two thirds of the way there, but the last portion of the journey and my return to the hotel would have to be completed on foot. This was not a big issue. I had plenty of time before the interview, the weather was already touching twenty Celsius on the thermometer, and a long walk would probably do me some good anyway.

On arrival at the police station the procedure was much the

same. I announced my arrival at the unit and was eventually escorted upstairs to the Inspector's office. Once there, little had changed. Everyone was smoking, the girls were inspecting their online clothes purchases and Inspector Lui was sporting his latest trendy spring outfit. Rai, the police interpreter was there. Although I now felt like I knew him quite well, it was only at our last meeting that he had told me his name. It was pronounced "Ray" but I didn't know if he had adopted an English name or just spelt it incorrectly. Rai told me I needed to forward any emails that related to *Euro Fx*, the Singaporeans, the Cooks and the Orchards. I knew that my data would contain the very last private emails to friends, days before my resignation, stating that due to the continued lack of requested information from the Orchards, Julie and the Singaporeans, I felt I could no longer continue in the position. They had all agreed that this was the right thing to do.

I did all of this from my iPad which seemed to satisfy them, but when they asked why I hadn't brought my laptop I explained that this was taken from my bag at the police station in Shanghai. The room burst into animated discussion. Inspector Liu was throwing out instructions in Mandarin, the two female officers immediately picked up their phones, rapidly punching the buttons, and the other chubby officer gave me his best "We do not believe you" stare. They clearly thought I was lying and had my laptop stashed in my room. I gathered that the ladies were calling the two police stations in Shanghai and, when their conversations ended, I was roughly taken to an isolation room and instructed to hand over my room key. Someone had taken my laptop from my case last April and I had always thought it was the police. Now I was thinking it must have been an opportunist, a corrupt officer perhaps, or maybe even one of the victims that had been loitering around the location of my arrest.

I had to go through the undignified ritual of the highchair in the interrogation room yet again, being asked all the same questions as before. At the end of this I was given a list of things that I had to produce for them, within seven days. The most difficult of these demands was providing a complete set of bank statements for the entire period my employment, from when Orchard started paying me all the way to the current date. Screenshots from internet banking would not suffice. I needed stamped, verified statements, not photographs or photocopies. This was going to be a problem.

I was permitted to leave the unit and found the journey home to be a slow but surprisingly pleasant three hours walk. The exercise and fresh air were most welcome. The temperature was also conducive to enjoying a long walk and it gave me plenty of time to figure out how I could retrieve original bank statements. I was getting more optimistic as I knew that these documents would be evidence of who paid me and didn't show extravagant amounts on deposit. I started to think and became frustrated as to why they had not requested this crucial information earlier. I also became annoyed at myself for missing an opportunity to provide a massive piece of vindicating evidence, not thinking to collate this information earlier. In the interview with Thomson Reuters months before, David Orchard stated that he had recommended me to a client but could not remember who that client was. I knew back then that these bank statements would shoot that excuse to pieces as they showed clearly his company had been the paymaster throughout my engagement to *Euro Forex Investment Ltd*. My pace quickened as I discovered a new sense of purpose. The streets were fairly deserted save for the sporadic street market along the way selling fruit, vegetables, clothes and snacks. There were butchers' stalls that were now getting the attention of the newly hatched flies, and the fish stalls were also quite sad affairs. Although the fish could be transported from coastal areas such as Dalian in quite a short time, the milky glazed eyes of the catch and their pungent waft indicated they had not arrived today. Perhaps not even yesterday.

Once past each market the streets would again take on a ghost town appearance. Every so often there would be a gathering of old folk sitting together on a street corner; their daily ritual. They might be chatting about the old days or reading a letter from one of their children who had moved to Beijing or Shanghai for a better life. The now cool rusty metal bins containing the ash from the winter fires that had kept them warm, would still be the focal point.

I got back to my room and could immediately tell that it had been thoroughly searched. It hadn't been ransacked like you'd expect from a rushed burglary, it was just that things were not where they should have been. My favourite aftershave was on the second shelf not the first. My socks were in the correct section of the drawer, but blacks and coloureds were mixed together and were not arranged dark to light, from right to left, as I habitually stored them - a simple habit of mine as opposed to an obsessive-compulsive disorder. They had obviously been searching for the missing laptop, believing that I still possessed it and there was information I was trying to conceal.

I no longer banked with Lloyds, but I had the contact details of my old bank manager and asked for her assistance. Because of data protection and fraud, the statements for the whole period I was employed and those to the current date had to be sent to my home address. I asked a neighbour from home to retrieve the documents and scan them for me. This I knew could be another stumbling block as scans would not be seen as originals as requested. But this was the best I could do along with providing a cover letter from my manager along with her details should they need official confirmation that these were genuine and not doctored. I was sure this would be another step forward as it clearly showed who had paid me, and the amounts corresponded precisely with those agreed on my employment contract that was already in the possession of the Chinese authorities.

Chapter 37. One-year approaches

It was now the middle of April 2017 and, although I had only had my passport back a few weeks, because of holiday delays it was coming close to visa expiration once more. More importantly it was fast approaching my one year's detention in China. I had been told time and again by the British Consulate, Inspector Liu, the interpreter and even Reuters that one year was the limit where I would either be charged or told to leave for home.

Every day that passed was torture. I had made the mistake of giving this information to my children and family members and as such was getting regular messages saying how they couldn't wait to see me. None of them seeming to understand that this one-year deadline could actually have a very different outcome to the one they were expecting. One day before the year was up, April 23rd, I got a message from the inspector stating that he was coming to see me in my room at the hotel. He had never visited me before. There was no more I could give or tell them. I felt certain that this could only be good news and I could barely contain my excitement. I paced the room until he arrived, avoiding the temptation to pre-empt the news and begin packing.

The inspector knocked on my door and I rushed to let him in. He was accompanied by two other officers and the interpreter. He told me to gather my iPad and phone and accompany him to their vehicle. He said that I was being taken to a high security facility for further investigation. It hit me like a hammer. Did they mean a prison or some sort of torture chamber?

I managed to calm down as my brain processed the request for my electronic equipment. I was confident that I had told the absolute truth, and nothing would be proved to the contrary. If anything, with the technology they had at their disposal they may have discovered something important that I had missed or inadvertently deleted. It again baffled me as to why they had left it so long to undertake this part of the process and I tried to convince myself that this was one final check before they might let me go. Rai told me not to worry and confirmed that we were not going to a prison, just a high-tech facility where my equipment could be examined to ensure no files or other information had been missed. I gathered my things, and my room was thoroughly searched again in case whilst alone in the room I had retrieved my laptop from some secret hidey hole. We got in the car and proceeded towards Anshan city centre. Just before the Shengli road we took a diversion across an overpass. At this point a blindfold was placed over my eyes so that I would not remember any further part of the journey. I had gone through a whole range of emotions in under an hour: Anticipation, excitement, confusion, disappointment, and now fear.

After about an hour the car pulled to a halt, the blindfold was removed, and the rear passenger door was opened. I was instructed to follow the officers. It looked like a massive industrial site and every building had aerials and satellite dishes directed to the heavens. There was also a very high military presence with armed guards at the entrance to every building. My escorts produced their identification and documents stating the reason for our attendance at the facility and we were allowed into the building. We were immediately faced by another two army personnel guarding an elevator who conducted the same inspection procedure as before, followed by a brisk search. The first guard placed an odd-looking key into a small receptacle and the lift doors opened. Then the second man entered the lift and punched a code into a small keypad and pressed the button that would take us up to the fourth floor. There were twenty-one buttons in all: Zero, where we now were, ten higher floors marked with Chinese inscriptions and ten floors below us. It was these basement floors that intrigued me. There was no inscription beside any of them, just a small flag. Most of them were familiar, but those that caught my eye were relating to the bottom five; Germany, France, Great Britain, Japan and finally the United States. It seemed obvious that some sort of clandestine activities was conducted on these levels which explained the blindfold and extra security around these buildings.

We exited the lift and in front of me was a huge room about one-hundred-foot long and half as wide. At the far end was a glass fronted office with huge portraits of President Xi and Chairman Mao. The left wall was floor to ceiling with computers, printers and servers. The main floor contained rows of computer geeks busily tapping away, each wearing airline pilot style headphones. All of the huge windows to our right were painted over with scenes of Tiananmen Square, or of beautiful countryside and waterfalls. There was no natural light and these murals seemed like an attempt to brighten the now windowless space with reminders of the great country they were serving and to create a feeling of patriotism. I was led to the glass room, told to sit and power up my equipment. Once they had been turned on my devices were plugged into a small box with multiple leads protruding from holes in its casing. I sat in awe as I watched my security codes jumping across their screens followed by passwords to my files and email. This was all happening without any human interaction that I could see. Half an hour later a tech worker entered the room and stated that they had everything downloaded and the search bots were scanning the drives. I was not concerned; I had revealed everything to them and was convinced I had concealed nothing. I was angry though. I kept wondering why they had not done this nine months earlier when I first arrived in Anshan. Eventually I was led back to the car, my eyes were covered again, and we set off, I guessed, back the way we had come? Or, were we going to another "facility"? I was playing games in my head, trying to count the distance between every left or right turn, wondering if I would be able to work out the location later using a map and my mental notes of the journey. I was listening for running water or train sounds just like you see in a thriller or spy movie. My blindfold was removed as we went back across the overpass but, instead of turning left towards my hotel, we turned right and arrived outside the visa office. I was told that my passport was being extended for *another* three months. I could not believe my ears and I silently sank into a deep, dark depression. This would take me past the year cut-off and could only mean one thing: I was going to be charged and sent to court.

Chapter 38. The end is nigh, one way or the other!

At the visa office the procedure was the same as on previous occasions; the same desk, same forms and the same indifference from the officers. Once back in my room I made a video call to my children and then I called my elderly parents. My mum and dad had just about got the hang of a mobile phone under tuition from my sisters, so a WhatsApp basic voice call was the limit of their expertise. Consequently, I had not seen their faces in over a year. I delivered the bad news about another extension but tried to lighten everyone's mood by insisting that no news was good news. I even tried to convince myself that this was one last ditch attempt by the authorities to find some incriminating evidence. The police had always been cordial to me since I left Shanghai and I couldn't believe they would fabricate anything. But it did cross my mind. After all the suffering endured by the victims the police were duty bound to explore every possible avenue in order to get some sort of result that would satisfy them

When I'd finished the call, I checked my inbox and amongst the spam I immediately saw two senders that jumped out at me. The first message was from Engen Tham at Thomson Reuters. She asked if I had any comment now that I knew the case would be going to court? I asked how she knew this, and she said that everyone involved, including the victims, had been informed. I fell silent. How could they all know this and yet not a word had been said to me? She then asked if I would agree to be interviewed by a man named Benjamin Sveen from ABC News, Australia. I declined this request as the authorities had warned me on no account was I to talk specifics about the case to anyone. I figured that, should the worst happen, I might perhaps need press exposure at a later date, so my actual response was, "Not at this time".

I was also surprised to hear that ABC were preparing to fly a film crew over to China had I agreed. Within seconds of sending my reply to Tham my cell phone buzzed; she probably had Sveen on the phone as she typed. Sure enough, it was him. I reiterated my reasons for why any interview would have to be deferred to a later date and reminded him that, in all probability, our conversation was being recorded and transcribed. He then told me that they were making a documentary about one of their nationals, Bryan Cook! By now I had figured that he was somewhere high up the ladder at *Euro Fx* but it was still a bad idea for me to make any comment. It was during this conversation that I was made aware of Cooks involvement with another scheme, *Power Eight*, subsequent to my resignation. I had only recently discovered that Cook had been a key figure in yet another scam, *Virgin Gold Mining Corporation* early in 2012. I found out about this when scouring social media in my hotel room and was shocked to see pictures of him on stage with Chinese investors as well as the Orchards. I agreed to stay in touch with ABC and contact them should I have a change of mind.

I hung up and opened the second email. It was from Chao Ma who also confirmed that the victims were aware I would be going to trial, but it gave no indication of the source. Since obtaining permission from the inspector to answer any of Chao Ma's questions we had, more or less, been working side by side towards a common goal via email. Perhaps information that I had would be the missing parts of the puzzle for the victims to find their stolen money. Reciprocally, during this process, she might be able to fill in some gaps for me that would prove my innocence beyond doubt. The upsetting thing for me was that she still felt that I was somehow protecting the bad guys and that I had more to give. She even said that if I speak up now, she would be prepared to speak on my behalf for a lighter sentence. This was so disheartening; I had told them everything I could.

I had told the truth and had provided evidence of the paymasters and delivered my bank statements. I was representing myself and was not using ill-gotten gains to engage the best, most expensive law firm available. I hibernated in my room for the next few days waiting to be informed of my court date, wondering if it would be here in Anshan or, more terrifyingly, Beijing.

On the 3rd of May 2017, eight days before my 53rd birthday, I received a message to say that I would be picked up the following morning to hear the prosecutor's decision. This was it: The most important day of my life and a potentially devastating one for my family. It seemed ominous that in recent years, every time my birthday was approaching I would get some bad news. That period in 2014 was when I received the first email from the victims and the envelope had been shoved under my apartment door. The same happened again in 2015 when the scam became official and social media was plastered with news that *Euro Fx* was a fraud with there was to be no takeover by the fictitious *FX Cap*. And it was only two weeks before my birthday in 2016 that I was arrested at the resort outside Shanghai. The days when I used to look forward to this anniversary seemed a distant memory.

I was watching an English-speaking TV news channel and discovered that Leicester City had won the English Premiership football league at odds of 5000-1. I couldn't help thinking that if *that* could happen then maybe I had a chance but with ninety-nine percent of cases that go to court in China ending in punishment, I figured my odds were much worse. My nerves were on edge and I struggled to take my mind away from the situation, even for a moment. I flicked to another channel to see Mark Selby beat Ding Junhui of China in the Snooker World Championship. Selby was also from Leicester. I'm not overly superstitious but the saying that things happen in threes did find its way into my mind. In truth, I was just grasping at straws for any sign that could help keep my hopes alive and my sanity intact.

The following morning, I received a message from Inspector Liu saying he would be picking me up in the lobby at midday. I ran to the bathroom and, not having had or been able to face breakfast, spent the next ten minutes dry retching. It was too early to make a last call to my children as it would have been approaching midnight back in England, so I sat on the edge of the bed and allowed a weird sort of calm acceptance to wash over me. I sat in that same spot for the next three hours until it was time to meet the Inspector.

I made my way down to the lobby, taking in the surroundings for the last time. A swimming lesson was in progress and I looked on with a wistful sadness at the parents urging their children to kick hard for the edge as they grasped the float aids with white knuckles. The lobby was packed with a new coachload of visitors checking in for a convention whilst another pack were jostling to check out at the one desk allocated for this (less important) service. I saw the official police car arrive which was another cause for concern as I had previously been escorted in private or unmarked vehicles. The Inspector was in the driver's seat where he remained while a fully uniformed policeman exited the car and greeted me. My eyes searched his face for any hint of what was to come, good or bad, but he was impassive. We sat in silence for the whole journey. We pulled up at the Prosecutor's building on Shengli Road and the vehicle squeezed into a small space between hordes of pedestrians waiting to cross. The sun was chasing the mercury up the vial once again and the summer stalls and street sellers were out in force. The shorts and tee-shirts were in stark contrast to my one and only suit that I was probably wearing for the penultimate time before the trial.

These official buildings of the Prosecutor are hardly known for their cheery ambience but, as I passed through security, the mood on this day seemed particularly sombre. We headed to the fourth floor again and I was led into the same small office I had attended only once before. The two seats behind the scratched and weathered colonial type bureau were high backed but just as tired as everything else in the room. The two spare seats were of a hard-wooden construction, bigger and sturdier, but not unlike oversized primary school furniture. I was offered a seat and then I was left alone with my thoughts. An hour must have passed when the door opened to reveal a secretary holding a cup of recently boiled water which she placed on the desk for me. She turned and left. I continued to watch the clock. Another forty-five minutes or so passed before the door handle creaked again. In walked the prosecutor with a colleague that I assumed to be his assistant, Inspector Liu and Rai, the interpreter. I was told to stand as the two legal officials took their seats behind the desks. Inspector Liu sat in one wooden chair and Rai sat in the one that I had just vacated. Rai said that I was to stand perfectly still in front of the prosecutor and look at no one else in the room as he delivered his findings. Rai said I was to ignore him completely and just focus on the prosecutor as the adjudication was translated, sentence by sentence. The double use of this word sent chills of woe down my spine. Once he began everything started to fog over and the voices became muffled. I could still make out the first few pronouncements though:

"Our investigation has found that you were a senior and important member of a company that intentionally engaged in international fraud".

"We have concluded that Chinese nationals were the main target of this fraud for which you were instrumental in their decision to invest."

The prosecutor paused until he was satisfied that I had digested the seriousness of his words. At this point I knew it was the worst outcome and I drifted off to a place somewhere in the depths of my memories. Days out with my children, Christmas with my parents, birthdays. At one point I could have sworn I heard their voices and laughter in happier times.

There were more words being spoken but they were just muffled noises going through my head. It was as if my brain's defence mechanism was blocking out the bad news surely to come.

… and then there was total silence. I was only brought back to the present by a smiling Rai.

"You are free to go home", he repeated.

I just stared at Rai for what seemed like an age, my brain not being able to process this information before I asked him to repeat the last part.

Rai said, "You have made many mistakes and your actions are responsible for great hardship to a great many of our citizens. But we do not believe that you did this knowingly and as such we will be closing our investigation and you are free to leave China".

I thought that I was going to cry but the shock had shut down all my brain's functions and emotions. Rai's offered handshake was left suspended in front of me as I just stared at his extended digits. As we left the office the prosecutor asked if we could stay in contact via WeChat. I assumed this was for further assistance should they manage to apprehend any of the real perpetrators in the future, rather than a sociable drink at a KTV club! We left the building to be greeted by the "chubby officer", the female police interpreter and a photographer. They each took turns to have their photo taken with me and Rai insisted on recording a video of me proclaiming my joy. He later sold this to a news channel in China and it also appeared on an ABC news feature. I regret allowing this to happen as it undoubtedly sent the wrong message to the many victims that would surely have seen the footage. The vehicle I had arrived in was quite small and, with all the additional people, I figured there was no space for me, so I shook their hands and thanked them for treating me so well. Whilst I had enough money for a taxi, I felt I needed to savour the walk home to the hotel and, perhaps for the first time, really appreciate what I was seeing. But the Inspector called me back to the car and insisted on driving me. I thought maybe there must have been a second car parked nearby but this was not the case. The chubby officer opened the boot of the car and took out a collapsible pushbike which he assembled before proceeding to pedal back to the police station. It is true that they had always treated me with respect, but the process of interviews and being searched had not made me feel that way. And now here I was; being treated like a long-lost friend with everyone bending over backwards to help me.

I arrived back at the hotel and immediately started the many calls to family and friends, and later that afternoon I was picked up for one last time by the Inspector. We had to visit the bail office and then go to the Bank of China to retrieve my ten thousand Yuan bond. It was the most money I had had on my person for a whole year and I felt like a millionaire. It took a couple of days for the release papers to be completed and when the documentation arrived, I immediately booked a flight to Shanghai leaving in the morning, before searching for the onward connection to London. Unlike years ago, when a last-minute flight could be secured for a fraction of the normal cost, these days the opposite is the case. If I wanted to leave urgently, I would have to pay a significant premium. I eventually booked a flight for about five hundred pounds one way from Pudong to Heathrow, leaving on Tuesday the 10th. Even though I was eager to get home, the slight delay was not a problem as the inspector had told me that I was free to stay or travel around China until my visa expired in two months' time. As if! I just wanted to go home.

Whoopee!! I was no longer a suspected criminal nor a "person of interest" to the authorities. I settled the hotel bill, packed my bags and arranged to meet my friend, Jason (Statham) Wang, for one last time. We decided to go back to the *Shangzi* bar that evening where there were many other friends that I wished to say goodbye to. It was a strange evening of mixed emotions. I was obviously in a tremendously good mood but there was an undertone of sadness at leaving these new friends that had done much to make the whole experience bearable. I resisted the temptation to get completely inebriated as the one and only flight to Shanghai was early in the morning. Back at the hotel I checked my emails one more time before placing my iPad, charger, adaptor and any other cables into the front of my small carry-on case. There were two messages; the first, from Chao Ma stating that I must be happy at the result but should understand that I had, in her opinion, been very lucky. She urged me to stay in contact and try to assist in any way that I could, including agreeing to an interview with ABC News. The second, timestamped just thirty minutes after that first message, was from Engen at Reuters. She too congratulated me and asked if I would be prepared to meet Chao Ma when I arrived in Shanghai. She offered to interpret. I just wanted to say goodbye to my friends in Shanghai and go home but I felt a real sense of responsibility to meet this head of the victims' movement. I replied that I would have to consider this request, taking into account my own personal safety. Talking with an elderly lady was not a concern of course, it was more the worry that other, more able and less amenable victims, might become aware of the potential meeting.

Chapter 39. Back to Shanghai

The taxi arrived with plenty of time to make the flight; light traffic at that time of day meaning the journey would only take about half an hour. We drove through the city of Anshan passing so many now familiar landmarks. It was difficult to refrain from recommending shortcuts to my driver having walked every street and avenue many times. We took the last exit off the roundabout at Victory Square and I turned and gazed back at the city one last time, and at the giant flags on the Prosecutor's building as it faded into the distance. As we drove along through a now barren landscape, I closed my eyes and allowed the moment to sink in, my mind replaying so many events at fast-forward speed. I was jolted out of my daydream by the sound of four F-60 Shen Fei Stealth Bombers screaming by, followed by four J-10B fighter jets. The roar was deafening as they could only have been one hundred feet above us and confirmed we were getting close to the airport. After I'd paid the taxi and retrieved my bags from the boot, and with an hour to spare, I took a stroll outside to watch the military spectacle. There didn't seem to be any objections to this when you were outside the barriers, unlike when I was descending the aircraft stairs upon arrival in Anshan nine months previously. As the military jets were roaring into the sky, I found myself reminiscing about the first air show that I had attended with my father and my young son. It was at Biggin Hill, a small airport in Kent that had played a major role during the Battle of Britain in the autumn of 1940. These days it is mainly used by the rich and business executives, flying their private Lear jets to this convenient and quiet airstrip close to London. I remember my dad and me shedding a tear as three generations of the Byrne family walked hand in hand. I couldn't wait to do this again; something that only a few days ago had seemed an impossible prospect. This memory brought tears to my eyes once again. There were no Lear jets here though, just an awesome collection of heavily armed fighters ready to defend the skies of China.

I boarded the plane and took to my seat for the three-hour journey back to Shanghai, one I had feared I would never be taking. My thoughts turned to how I would surprise my friends at the *Max* bar that evening. I had not booked a hotel but was sure there would be no problem booking into my previous accommodation close to the square and People's Park. I could afford a much nicer hotel now that I had the bond back and was not budgeting for an indefinite length of stay. But this hotel was not too bad, and I had a feeling that by retracing my journey I could somehow find some closure to the experience. For most of the flight I was preoccupied with the decision of whether or not to meet with Chao Ma. She had been very gracious for the most part, but there was a clear undertone in her correspondence with me that she felt I was lucky to be going home and that I should instead be receiving some sort of punishment. I'm sure there were many others who felt outraged at my release. It needed careful consideration given the drugging incident many months before in MacDonald's, the glassed towel in the hotel and the falling plant pot, as well as me being followed on numerous occasions. I knew that my concerns were justified. After all, these things had all happened when the victims believed I was soon to be punished. Would they now try to take matters into their own hands before my departure? There would no doubt be some that did not believe the authorities had reached the right verdict. But after weighing everything up, by the end of the flight I had decided that I would meet with Chao Ma and would email Engen later and ask her to make the arrangements for the following evening.

I landed at Pudong at midday on the Saturday after some

delays to our departure from Anshan. I decided that, now relatively flush with cash, I would take the Maglev into Shanghai. I also felt a need to do everything as speedily as possible, hoping that this would expedite the end of this nightmare. Of course, regardless of whether I ran everywhere, took the Maglev or hired a motorbike, it would not change the time of my flight home. The eight-minute journey to Longyang Road, as opposed to an hour or so using the underground, gave me less time to worry about things but I still had a nagging fear that something would go wrong that would delay my departure. Although the Maglev was very impressive in terms of performance, surprisingly the seating and décor of the carriages was extremely basic and uncomfortable. The seats were as hard as concrete and the cladding of the carriages was very poor. But, for eight minutes, who cared! I arrived at Longyang Road and followed the signs to the taxi rank. To my dismay, the queue was enormous; what I had gained on the swing I had lost on the roundabout.

A young man approached me and offered a slightly upmarket service and, in my eagerness to check in to my hotel, I allowed my street smarts to desert me. Unofficial taxis that are not in a designated rank, in any city, are often a rip off. I was shown to a Mercedes and my case was put in the trunk, but the driver seemed not to understand my request for a quote before we set off. I knew that there would ultimately be a disagreement, but I was too tired to get out of the vehicle. Our starting point back to the city was a few miles south of the Bund and the Shanghai Tower but I still estimated that the cost would not exceed fifty Yuan, even in this luxurious car. But when I arrived at my destination the driver, now speaking perfect English, asked for four hundred. I delivered a few expletives in Mandarin, threw seventy-five Yuan on the front passenger seat and exited the car to retrieve my bags from the trunk. I was met by four menacing colleagues who had obviously arranged to meet the driver at this destination. I pulled my phone from my pocket and dialled Inspector Liu's number, making sure they saw who I was calling. They all jumped in the vehicle and sped off, tyres screeching.

I had arranged a meeting with Engen and Chao Ma on Sunday evening and made my way to one of the outside bars in the square, close to *Max*. I'd chosen the location because it was always full of tourists and was adjacent to a police parking rank for the many officers ensuring the safety of visitors to the city. Pickpockets and street hawks tended to avoid the vicinity of this drinking hole, and the police presence made me feel considerably safer. I found a table for three and ordered a beer. About ten minutes later Engen arrived and said she would join me once she had found Chao Ma. Although the bar was predominantly open air it had many cubby holes with a curtained effect which gave it the feel of an Arabian tent. I decided to move to one of these more secluded tables and waited. A few minutes later I saw Engen re-enter the establishment with confusion on her face, evidently believing I had changed my mind and left. I stood and gave a wave, trying to get her attention without attracting the interest of the many other guests. She saw me signalling and headed to my table followed by a gentle-looking Chinese lady, obviously in her sixties. Chao Ma was smartly dressed in a typical friendly grandmother type attire. There was nothing obvious to suggest that she could afford to forget about her lost investment. She had simply been convinced that she would be increasing her nest egg for later years. Engen was around thirty, quite petite and wearing modern Western clothes. I ordered tea for the three of us but changed my mind for another beer as I felt a bit nervous and defensive. The meeting was very civil and polite with no raised voices or finger pointing. The series of questions put to me were well thought out and measured and I did my best to answer them as fully and honestly as I could, leaving nothing out. I freely admitted that I had made some mistakes. Chao Ma said that she appreciated my candidness in relation to how I thought I could have possibly done things differently. Of course, hindsight is a wonderful thing. She smiled and asked why I did not touch the snack provided on the internal flight and suggested that I should take less sugar in my tea. I realised that I'd clearly been followed all the way from Anshan and that someone had even been on the same plane! She told me that many victims wanted to have me rearrested and had considered approaching an alternative jurisdiction where some of the other victims hailed from. This was a very unlikely scenario because if a huge city like Shanghai had passed control to the head office for fraud in North East China, other requests would probably have been rejected. She said that by my agreeing to meet, she had placed me under her protection, and I would not have to worry about being harmed once home ... provided I continued to cooperate. The meeting ended with her reiterating her request for my ongoing cooperation and my agreeing to do the interview with ABC News, Australia. The news team had already flown to Shanghai in anticipation of a scoop. I agreed to stay in contact but told her I would only do an interview once back home in England. Reporters sometimes have a way of misrepresenting or being selective about which parts they choose to publish, and I couldn't be sure that they would report the facts objectively. I was concerned that any article published in an insensitive manner, or one creating question marks due to distortion of facts, would be upsetting for victims and possibly delay my departure. Once our discussion came to an end, we parted company and I headed to *Max*. It was time to say my final goodbyes.

Although my friend Christopher and his fiancé, Rebecca,

knew that I was coming to the bar, I had intended to surprise all my other friends. As I walked through the doors, there they all were; sitting at the bar in a line, each one of my friends holding a card displaying one letter in bold red print. When sitting in the correct order it spelt out, "We will all miss you Dave". As well as Chris and Rebecca, there was Bill, the American photographer, Gert, the South African construction manager, John Mallins, the Howard Johnson manager from Yorkshire, Michael Yang, and all his bar staff. I was completely choked. A good night was had by all at this last mass gathering before I left for home. It's difficult now to imagine feeling sad at leaving China but these were my friends and deep down I knew it was highly unlikely I would ever see these wonderful people again.

Chapter 40. Time to leave

I had hardly slept on my last night in Shanghai. I still had a feeling that I was not truly safe and wouldn't be on my way until the wheels left the tarmac. The previous day I had received my final communique from Inspector Liu. He wished to know the flight number, the time I was setting off, and my planned route to the airport. There were several obvious reasons why he needed to know this. Firstly, my leaving the country would allow him to officially close the case against me. Secondly, my name would probably still flag up at security and he would need to notify Pudong airport police to give me clearance. And lastly, and most worryingly, there was still a strong possibility of protests, or worse. After all, a year previously after my initial arrest, a posse had been sent to Pudong. I took the elevator down to the hotel reception and settled my bill. There was a police car sitting outside. This was not unusual as the narrow thoroughfare outside the hotel was a popular stop-and-check hangout for the authorities, scrutinising the licences of the many young scooter riders, or checking the contents of an overladen truck. I hailed a taxi and told him to take me to the Maglev Station. As we pulled away the blue flashing lights on the police car sprang into action, though without the siren, and it followed us all the way to my destination. Once there I paid the taxi and retrieved my travel bag. Two officers exited the back of the police car and walked over to me. I turned towards them, heart thumping, and waited for them to speak. They said nothing and just stood there, so I extended the handle on my wheeled suitcase and set off to the ticket office. The officers quietly followed me and stood silently a few yards away as I bought my ticket. They sat opposite me on the train, again without saying a word, bar one quick communication into their radio. I would only have to endure another eight minutes of being constantly watched and followed, but in truth I was comforted by the security now that I knew it was for my benefit. We soon glided to a silent halt at Pudong and the doors opened with a satisfying swish. Immediately outside my carriage were another six officers, heavily armed and clearly awaiting my arrival. I began to wonder if they had intelligence that suggested that I could be in danger. I was escorted to the check in desk and allocated my boarding pass. One of the officers who had been part of the escort from the hotel signed some papers and then I was taken to a small security room. I was instructed to open my bag and a full search of my belongings was carried out. I had a thick folder with transcripts of all my interviews. These were confiscated. My phone and iPad were also taken but were, thankfully, returned a few minutes later. The photo galleries of each had been erased but that was okay as I had already emailed most of them to myself and saved them in the Cloud. I was then ushered through passport control and handed over to another sextet of officers, also heavily armed, who lined up either side of me and took me to yet another bland room where I was detained until it was time to board. It was only then that the police engaged me in conversation, smiling and assuring me that all of this was for my protection, and wishing me a safe flight home.

Once in my aircraft seat, and as we thundered down the runway, the feeling of relief was indescribable. As the seatbelt sign was turned off, I ordered a large scotch and soda and turned on the in-flight entertainment system. I was looking forward to watching one of the latest English-speaking movies but that could wait. Instead, my attention was totally focussed on the moving map on the screen and I promised myself another large scotch when we passed out of Chinese airspace.

Money to Byrne?

The food trolley made its way down the aisle and it was the one and only time ever that the smell of airline food had actually made my mouth water. I went for a straight English menu, ignoring the Asian delicacies also available on British Airways flights to and from China. After I'd eaten, I fell into a deep, restful sleep, only being roused by the beep of the "fasten seatbelt" alarm as we began our descent into London Heathrow. I pressed my face hard against the cabin window trying to pick out the familiar landmarks that I hadn't seen for so long. The river Thames could be seen just below the right wing, with Canary Wharf and the old City hugging its banks. I could just make out the Tower of London and Tower Bridge. A few minutes later I could see the steel arch that rises majestically over Wembley Stadium.

Then we joined the stack of aircraft awaiting their turn to bank into the final approach to the runway.

Once inside the terminal I switched on my phone and my ears were assaulted by what seemed like a thousand message alerts. I responded to my children, sisters and parents; the others would be replied to later. As I headed towards passport control, I wondered if I would be questioned or whether there would be any special attention paid to me going through customs. Or worse, would there be reporters waiting at the other side of Arrivals? But everything went smoothly. I was just another anonymous traveller arriving in London. I still had my Transport for London timetable in the front of my bag and I wondered if the information was still correct. The timetable was a gift from a friend known as TFL Tom and was a joke birthday card from him back in 2015. The fact that the schedule had not changed was strangely reassuring. I decided to take the Heathrow Express into Paddington, then the tube to Liverpool Street station. From there it was a short walk back to my apartment above my friend's pub in Shoreditch.

Chapter 41. Back Home

I walked into my local bar on the very edge of the City. The establishment remained essentially unchanged since pre-Victorian times, when Gin Palaces and slums were its closest neighbours. Back then Jack the Ripper had prowled the streets nearby and East End villains were hidden in every shadowy corner. Now modern luxury dwellings had replaced many of the old shops and houses, and other pubs have been transformed into trendy cocktail bars and restaurants. I had been renting a room there ever since *Euro FX* and the crooks' actions had ensured I was virtually unemployable in the only industry I had ever known. My pal, the owner, had kept my room clean, dusted and vacant, like a shrine to a long-lost friend. Word of my return had spread quickly, and all were present. The same familiar faces were serving behind the counter. Two friends who had done so much running around for me were perched on their usual seats. The couple who had been scanning my mail and sending copies to me were also in their usual spot. A guy who still lives in the room adjacent to mine was busily feeding the jukebox. Even the two resident Labradors, tails wagging, seemed to be smiling a welcome grin. The celebrations had been cleverly prepared. A Chinese buffet was wheeled into the bar, the last food I ever wanted to taste again! Every song from the jukebox carried the same theme; "I want to break free" by Queen and "Freedom" by George Michael were the first two songs and as incarceration and China-themed songs began to dry up the guys had to be more creative. My mind could not work out the connection to the latest lyrics being blurted out. That is until Glasgow Mark informed me that his choice was a song by China Crisis. Another two friends each gave me a gift. I should not have been surprised to see a pair of fortune cookies in their hands. If my emotions were not already running at an all-time high, they went off the scale when my daughters entered the bar. After ten minutes of cuddles and tears I had to walk outside to regain some level of composure.

After a wonderful and emotional evening and having seen my daughters to their taxi, I retired to the solitude of my room. As I entered, I had a strange feeling seeing all my belongings exactly as I had left them. Nothing had changed apart from a slight coating of dust in places and the odd evidence of one friend or another crashing there overnight, having been stranded due to train strikes or some other necessity. I plonked my case on the bed, kicked off my shoes and just sat for what seemed like an age. Then, in the corner of my eye I spotted an envelope that had been slid under my door. I picked it up and tore open the top to find a single piece of paper which slipped out and fluttered to the floor, avoiding my clumsy attempts to catch it. I picked it up and could not believe my eyes. There was a message that read….

David, 欢迎回家，我们很快会见面。

I could only understand my name but, the Chinese writing left no doubt whom it was from … or so I thought. I immediately took a picture of the note and sent it to Rebecca in Shanghai. She replied within half an hour with the translation:

"Welcome home David. We will see you soon."

Of course, I was initially convinced that this message had been delivered by the victims. It was quite upsetting. I had agreed to meet Chao Ma and had already made arrangements with ABC news to do an interview. What more could I have done? The note was from their film crew which was en route from Australia even as I read it. I was also angry though. I was not forced to meet with Chao Ma in Shanghai before returning home but had taken the difficult decision to do so without any prompting. They must have been informed that I had agreed to the interview and I felt that this note was unnecessary. After all, I had endured a twelve-and-a-half-month intense and thorough investigation. Most of all, I was concerned that they had once again trespassed and invaded my personal space. I thought that we now had a line of communication in place where we would work together to track the culprits. This all still felt like a threat, just like back at my old apartment. My initial inclination was to call everything off, offer no further assistance and no interviews. But I had made a promise and I would keep to my word.

I picked up the piece of paper once again, and again reread the message. There was something odd about the note that I just couldn't place. I noticed what looked to be a coffee stain in the centre of the notepaper. Then I realised it was something on the reverse side trying to demand my attention. I flipped it over to see a crudely drawn eagle with wings spread sitting on a globe of the world. This was not a note from the film crew, nor was it a warning from the victims. This was almost certainly from the Singaporeans.

I could have reported this to the police but what could they have done? I'd had enough of questions and police stations to last a lifetime so decided to take no action. The organisers of the scam were far too clever and meticulous to have left any trace of evidence anyway. Eventually this note only served to increase my resolve to help the poor victims that had lost so much.

Arrangements were made with the film crew from ABC for the following Monday, the 15th May and I met them at the front entrance of Fenchurch Street Station in the heart of the City. This was where I had met Orchard back in the summer of 2012, and it was on this very same escalator that they decided to shoot the first footage. The team was very courteous, professional, and they carried an immense amount of kit. I had to repeatedly descend the moving staircase to get the scene right, ignoring the cameras, pretending to be on my way to a meeting. It must have taken thirty attempts before they were satisfied. We had to wait for a suitable space between regular commuters, hoping that they would ignore the cameras in order to capture a natural working day scene. I had sat in front of large audiences and television cameras on many occasions but I found it surprisingly difficult to pretend to be going about my normal business; my eyes would keep being drawn to the cameraman, exactly the opposite of what they required, or I would trip slightly delivering an expletive under my breath that would take no expert to lipread. Once this was done there was further footage that they needed with recognizable London landmarks as the backdrop. Strolling, briefcase in hand past the Gherkin building, or having a coffee whilst reading *The Times* newspaper with Tower Bridge and the river boats in the distance. During the filming of this particular scene, two police officers approached to ask what was happening and to ascertain if the crew had permission. This took some time, so when filming finally resumed I had already finished my hot coffee and had to pretend to drink. One of the officers began to laugh at my ham attempts to fake it and called out to ask if I would like a refill. When the outdoor footage was completed all the equipment was packed into two cars and I was taken to the Hilton Hotel in Edgeware Road. Here they had hired a room and arranged some seating to create an informal interview setting. After about an hour of moving and adjusting lighting and umbrella-style foil reflectors, the filming started again. It began very gently with questions about *Euro Fx* and my arrest in China. It went quickly on to an inquisition and the previously friendly film crew now became much harder and accusatory. I felt as though I was on trial. I was asked if I felt personally responsible for those who had taken their lives, or for the ones that were ill but couldn't afford medical care. They were, in my opinion, stupid questions. *Of course* I felt terrible and wished that I had seen through the deception earlier, but *I* was tricked too. By the time I decided to resign I now had no doubt that the victims' money had already been spirited away. I answered everything openly and honestly, saying as much as I knew about whom I thought was ultimately responsible. When the interview was over, I refused the offer of a lift back to the city. I was angry. This had been a complete media sting, having been originally told that their main questioning was to be about Bryan Cook as part of their investigation into his chequered business past. Of course, I was not naive enough to think that I would not face some difficult pot shots from reporters, but not to that extent. A few weeks later I received an email from Benjamin Sveen, the main editor for this exposé for ABC News Australia. He said that, having read the transcripts a number of times, he was astonished at how honest and brave I had been in the interview. This made me feel a lot better about the whole experience. However, when the program was screened it made me look totally complicit in the scam, not someone who had been duped. But regardless of how I felt, or how it had made me look, I had met my obligation to Chao Ma that I had made at our meeting in Shanghai.

During my time in China I had done lots of online research into Cook. There was a lot of information on social media and scam sites about *Virgin Gold Mining Corporation* (VGMC). This was another alleged Cook scam based in Dubai and also described as a fraud that had specifically targeted Asian investors. There was also mention of a group of Singaporeans that were involved in sales or procuring investment. This felt all too familiar and, had this information been in the public domain back in 2012, I'm certain that I would not have taken the position at *Euro Fx*. Although the product was different - gold instead of foreign exchange currency - and the amounts involved, though substantial were not as large, the similarities were there for all to see. Cook and other familiar names were mentioned in the complaints. Investors had been promised one ounce of gold per month for every $10,000 invested. With the price of gold at that time being around $1200 per ounce, the returns equated to approximately 12% per month or 144% per year. This was another classic Ponzi scheme where new investors' money is used to pay interest to the initial investors. These people had realised a significant area to maximise the scam. Many Chinese investors were happy to see their accounts accruing the interest but did not withdraw the funds as they intended to build up an offshore pot of wealth as they could not legally bring the money back to China. This meant that investment and interest were all held in named accounts at VGMC. Once the investment started to slow down the company was closed, and thousands of investors were faced with the realisation that they would not be getting their money back. On the face of it this looked to be a dry run for the even bigger scam that was *Euro Fx*. The systematic process of theft, particularly targeting the vulnerable Chinese, was now perfected and could be employed to even greater effect. When I watched the footage of the ABC expose on Cook, I was amazed to see that, immediately after the closure of *Euro Fx*, a new scheme had been put in place, *Power 8*. This was another product that would particularly tweak the interest of investors from Asia. They are fanatical about football, so *Power 8* used initial investment to secure sponsorship deals with Fulham FC, Everton FC and RDC Espanyol. Everton even saw their stadium renamed "*The*

Power 8 Stadium" for a short time. Cook's name appeared on the cheques paid to these clubs but in the interview with ABC he denied this, even though they were waving copies of the documentation in front of his nose. This last scam was closed very quickly but it is astounding that these guys had the gall to execute three scams back to back; *VGMC* (2010-2012), *Euro Fx* (2012-2014) and then *Power 8* (2013-2015). Whilst playing a major part in all three, Cook even had time to spend a year in a German jail for market manipulation.

Epilogue

Now that I was back home, I could for the first time reflect clearly on the whole situation. During the months immediately after my resignation I had not been aware of the full gravity of what had happened nor the degree of suffering. Then, when back in China, and as more revelations emerged, I was numb; my future life looked horrific and dealing with my own nightmare in this foreign land was all-consuming. The outcome could have been so different had I not taken advice to begin copying myself in on the final emails during my tenure. And if my salary had been paid from a *Euro Fx* account and not the Orchard's, the consequences would have been unimaginable, and I almost certainly would not be writing this.

It must have taken amazing courage for Chao Ma and the victims to reach out to me. I'm grateful that they did. Their suffering was, and continues to be, too deep, too absolute and too varied in nature for me to fully comprehend. I was the person that they saw on stage and believed in and while I too was deceived, this is something that will weigh on my conscience forever. I promised myself then that I would do whatever I could to find justice for them.

In August of 2017 I was contacted by the Crown's Official Receiver and summoned to an interview at their offices, a stone's throw from the Houses of Parliament. As I ascended the escalator at Westminster station and emerged from the underground labyrinth of London's subway network, the sun was high above the majestic St Stephen's Tower that houses the great bell called Big Ben. Its enormous gothic shadow seemed to be pointing in the direction I needed to follow. Spookily, this matched the directions shown by Google Maps on my smartphone. I entered the Receiver's building and was shown to a small interview room. There was no giant baby's highchair with wrist and leg cuffs, nor was there a panel of scary interrogators carrying weaponry. The room contained just a small desk, two chairs, a tape recorder and a serious looking government official. Since my return I had endured many a sleepless night and more than a few nightmares, but for the first time I suffered a wide-awake flashback which quickly developed into a full-on panic attack. My hands turned to ice, my forehead was dripping with sweat and spots started appearing in front of my eyes. I felt like I was about to pass out. The lady investigator looked concerned and left the room, returning with a glass of water. I took a sip and squeezed my eyes shut, trying to shake away the spots from my vision but when I opened them again this middle-aged Caucasian lady had taken on an Asian appearance complete with almond-shaped eyes, and the stapler on the table had morphed into a weapon. I ran from the office and sat in reception for about ten minutes. It was proposed that we postpone the interview, but after another fifteen minutes I had managed to compose myself; I just wanted this over with.

There followed another three hours of recounting and relaying the exact same questions and answers that the authorities in China had put to me. I was asked yet again for proof of who employed me and who paid my salary, along with all correspondence I still had relating to *Euro Forex Investment Ltd*. I gave the investigator all the documentation I had, including copies of the original bank statements that friends had scanned and sent to me in China, and I handed over the chronological file of emails and the threads of correspondence that the authorities there had taken most interest in.

Another couple of months passed before I was summoned to the offices of *Grant Thornton* close to Finsbury Square.

They were acting in conjunction with the Official Receiver as joint liquidators of my old company. *Euro Forex Investment Limited* had in fact already been wound up but, after complaints to our authorities from a single Chinese investor, had been re-opened and placed back into administration. The objective was to discover if there were any recoverable assets of the company. I was interviewed for many hours on several occasions and again was asked for all supporting documentation. I was in much better shape by now and was able to assist without any dramas even though I was once again under the microscope and clearly suspected of being part of the scam. In my mind, the idea that I would travel to China and risk the possibility of life imprisonment, or worse, just as a cover for being complicit in the fraud was ludicrous. I stressed this repeatedly.

I was asked to explain to them the difference between *Euro Fx* and *Euro Forex Investment Limited*. I relayed to them exactly as it had been described to me; I had been told that *Euro Fx* was a successful private Asian investment company with wealthy investors that now wished to expand globally into a regulated environment. To do this they had set up a subsidiary in London (*Euro Forex Investment Limited*) and wished me to be CEO of *that* entity. *Grant Thornton* then asked, if that was the case why was I introduced on stage across Asia as the CEO of *Euro Fx*? I told them that when I had flagged this to the Singaporeans, they had said that once the London entity was regulated all client monies would be transferred, and the name "*Euro Fx*" would cease. Furthermore, the Singaporeans had assured me that introducing me as the head of both companies would be a comfort to both staff and investors. I was also referred to the ABC TV interview and shown footage of Bryan Cook who, despite his alleged wealth, was depicted as a man in inexpensive clothing standing by a modestly priced vehicle;

the insinuation clearly being that I too could be playing the poor man whilst in reality sitting on a pile of cash.

By this time, a number of arrests had been made in China including some previously high-ranking officials, but (at time of writing) none of the key players from Asia had been caught. I did hear that one of the Singaporeans was kidnapped from his house by angry victims before being released again a day or so later. Bryan Cook was believed to be back living in Australia, under investigation by the authorities there and in many other countries, not just for *Euro Fx* but also the *Virgin Gold Mining Corporation* and *Power 8* debacles. And those are just the ones I know about ... perhaps others are still to be uncovered or even another underway right now.

However, I still felt unable to construct a clear picture of what had happened from the hundreds of jigsaw pieces of information I had. That is until I was contacted by Shanbao in October 2019 who asked me if I would be prepared to meet with the daughter of a Chinese friend who was visiting London. I had no hesitation agreeing to this and contacted her immediately and a few days later I headed to the café area of the hotel at the arranged time and was greeted by a well-dressed and highly intelligent young lady. She was in London for work commitments but had promised her mother (who had personally lost around $3 million to the scammers) that she would make some time for a one-on-one discussion with me.

We spent several hours revisiting the events of 2012-2013. I told her about my discoveries since then and about the subsequent interviews with the Official Receiver and *Grant Thornton*. There was little I could tell her regarding their investigations as I was not privy to this information, but I could tell her that as far as I knew they had not as yet recovered any monies. She confirmed that "shadow banking" was the method investors had used to plough money into *Euro Fx*. She explained that there were a number of Chinese citizens that owned businesses that could legally send monies offshore through bank accounts in China to others held at more recognisable institutions, mostly in Hong Kong. They were encouraged by the Singaporeans to allow friends and family to use their facilities to join the *Euro Fx* investment scheme. This turned out to be a fatal mistake because, while making these offshore payments was totally legal in China, allowing friends to invest through their vehicle was definitely not. She told me that not only had these individuals lost all their money and that of their friends, but the authorities had now arrested these unfortunate people, handing out prison sentences of up to eight years. In some cases, it was a family business and both parents had been jailed, leaving young children to be raised by other family members. In an article published in 2014, *The New York Times* estimated this unregulated practice accounted for an astonishing 40% of China's GDP. And yet, even though legal, the only ones being punished are the victims and those that just wished to help their friends.

Shortly after this meeting Grant Thornton told *Finance Magnates*, a financial news service, that they were looking for further funding and that without it they would be unable to continue their investigation. Our meeting in the café cleared up the reasons for cessation of this funding: Anyone sending money to assist in the recovery of their lost assets were basically admitting that they had used these banking facilities in a manner that was not the intended purpose. This would be an embarrassment to the Chinese authorities who wanted to hush up the scandal and silence any news that might stymie their ascendancy to the second largest economy in the world. With this clamp-down on anyone declaring lost investment there would be no paper trail, and therefore no cross-border co-operation to trace the monies. What was becoming ever clearer was that the ruthless fraudsters must have known this would happen; they had taken full advantage of the situation.

For the first time I felt that I had the whole picture, but I had never felt more frustrated at not being able to do anything about it. The perpetrators had used every conceivable trick and loophole in the book and a system of smoke and mirrors regarding the setup of the companies: *Euro Fx, Asia, Euro Forex Investment Limited, London,* and *Euro Forex (EFIL), New Zealand*. They had engaged my services as a City of London executive with an unblemished record and had instructed me to regulate two of the subsidiaries, without me knowing that funds would never be sent across. They had solicited monies from naïve investors using a method that would see their own authorities clamp down on those being defrauded. Worst of all, this was not the first time. They had already done it before on a smaller scale with *Virgin Gold Mining Corporation* which was undoubtedly just a practice run for the bigger fraud to come that was *Euro Fx*. And it is claimed that these very same people were behind the subsequent third scam, *Power Eight*. One wonders how much money these people need or whether they do it just for the thrill.

The End

Footnote

Yes, my name has been tarnished and many doors are now closed to me in the world of finance, but I will recover. There are thousands of people from China and South East Asia, however, who will not be able to. To some this experience was a financially costly lesson but no more, as they had enough wealth to weather their losses. While they have been able to lick their wounds and move on, it doesn't make it any less wrong. At the other end of the scale, less fortunate investors lost their life savings with some now owing huge escalating sums to debt collectors that they will probably never be able to repay. Families have irretrievably broken apart, blaming each other for making the investment recommendation or for acting on it. And some people have even taken their own lives.

I am still in contact with Chao Ma and her lawyer in Shanghai. I will continue to assist them in their quest for retribution and compensation in any way I can, but it seems that all the victims can do now is wait for these gangsters to trip up.

In the meantime, I believe the right thing to do is publish this book and hope that, in its own small way, it acts as a warning to those tempted to invest in such schemes and helps to prevent further suffering of the innocent at the hands of these cruel, callous and pitiless criminals.

Contributions

Author: David Byrne

www.davidbyrneinsights.com

Editor: Mole Vessey

www.mole@moreorlesseverything.co.uk

Illustrations: Mark Osborne

mjozzy73@gmail.com

Money to Byrne?

Printed in Great Britain
by Amazon